CW01651769

ESTD 1957

John Moores Painting Prize 2016

National Museums Liverpool

Walker Art Gallery

In partnership with

JOHN MOORES LIVERPOOL EXHIBITION TRUST

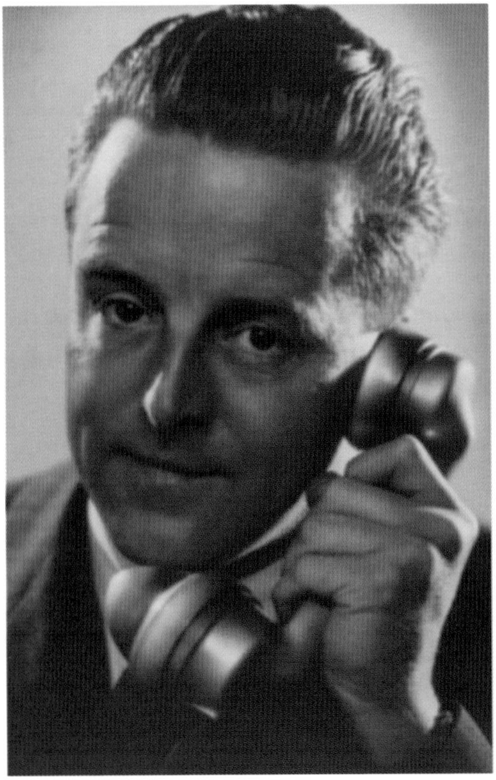

John Moores, 1933. Photograph in the collection of the Walker Art Gallery.

In 1957 John Moores (1896-1993) sponsored a competition for contemporary artists at Liverpool's Walker Art Gallery, with the intention of showcasing the best of new British painting.

The exhibition's main aims, stated in the first catalogue, were:

'To give Merseyside the chance to see an exhibition of painting and sculpture embracing the best and most vital work being done today throughout the country' and 'to encourage contemporary artists, particularly the young and progressive.'

The *John Moores Painting Prize* has since been held almost every two years. It has become one of the most familiar events in the British art world and now forms an important part of the Liverpool Biennial, the UK's Biennial of Contemporary Art.

This year brings the 29th exhibition since 1957, the *John Moores Painting Prize 2016*, and celebrates the fourth *John Moores Painting Prize China* in Shanghai.

Contents

Cover image: Michael Simpson, *Squint (19)* (detail)

Foreword

The *John Moores Painting Prize* is fast approaching its 60th anniversary, yet it remains as fresh and exciting as when it began in 1957. It continues to hold a very significant place in the Walker Art Gallery's exhibition calendar and that of the UK art world. In an ever challenging political and financial landscape for the visual arts, the Prize has an important role: it uncovers new talent, supports young artists on their journey through the contemporary art world, and celebrates established artists. It is a privilege to showcase the best of British painting at the Walker and to establish new relationships with some of today's most exciting painters.

As always, the *John Moores Painting Prize* acts as a catalyst for energetic debate around the subject of painting in Britain today. The number of entries from artists of all ages, more than 2,500 this year, defies any notion that painting is on the wane. In parallel, increasing levels of discussion via social media highlight all the more publicly the widely held respect for the show and its exceptional profile.

Since its inception, the Prize has played a significant role in encouraging young artistic talent. At a time when applications to study art and design at GCSE are falling, we are even more conscious of this important aspect of the show's character. An exhibition which allows our younger student visitors to see a broad spectrum of high quality contemporary paintings, in a free public gallery, offers an inspiring insight into the art world.

The ideas, subjects and techniques of works offer great variety, as do the training and careers of the exhibiting artists. The Prize provides a perfect platform to show the world at large how much this diverse creativity is nurtured and valued.

Our jury this year were the artists Gillian Carnegie, Ding Yi, Ansel Krut and Phoebe Unwin and the writer and freelance curator Reverend Dr Richard Davey. They reviewed all the entries with enthusiasm and careful consideration. We are extremely grateful to them for their generous involvement and commitment.

We also extend our heartfelt thanks to all the members of the John Moores Liverpool Exhibition Trust and their Artistic Director, Bev Bytheway, for their ongoing support.

Our deep gratitude also goes to our supporters – Weightmans, Liverpool John Moores University, and our official hotel partner The Richmond. We also give our thanks to Rathbones who generously continue to fund the ever-popular Visitors' Choice Award. Through our partners' help and foresight, this project continues to provide a wonderful arena for the artists.

In March 2016, the *John Moores Painting Prize China* was held for the fourth time in Shanghai, at Minsheng Art Museum. The jurors were artists Gerard Hemsworth, Liu Wei, Yang Ji Cang, former UK *John Moores* first prizewinner Sarah Pickstone, and Tim Marlow, Director of Artistic Programmes at the Royal Academy and juror in the 2014 UK prize.

We are greatly honoured to display at the Walker the dynamic prizewinning paintings from this exhibition. Our thanks go to Lewis Biggs and Wang DaWei, Dean of the College of Fine Arts, Shanghai University, for their contributions to this catalogue. We also thank Lingmin, Director of Overseas Arts Projects at Shanghai University, and Susu Hua, Director of ArtBang, for their smooth running of the Chinese project.

We would finally like to mention Sir Peter Moores' considerable contribution to the showcasing of contemporary art in Liverpool. A generous art patron like his father, with strong ties to the city, the 'Peter Moores Projects' exhibitions were held at the Walker from 1971 to 1986. Peter remained a strong supporter of the arts until his death earlier this year. He will be remembered with affection and respect by all those who knew him.

There are 54 works in the *John Moores Painting Prize 2016*. First-time exhibitors join returning ones to create a broad-ranging, powerful exhibition. Our special thanks go to the exhibiting artists and to all those who entered the Prize. Please continue to share your paintings with us and allow us, in turn, to share them with others. Your work is definitely something to be celebrated.

Joanna Vazquez
John Moores Liverpool Exhibition Trust

Sandra Penketh
Director of Art Galleries,
National Museums Liverpool

The jury

Gillian Carnegie
Artist

Richard Davey
Writer, freelance curator

Ansel Krut
Artist

Phoebe Unwin
Artist

Ding Yi
Artist

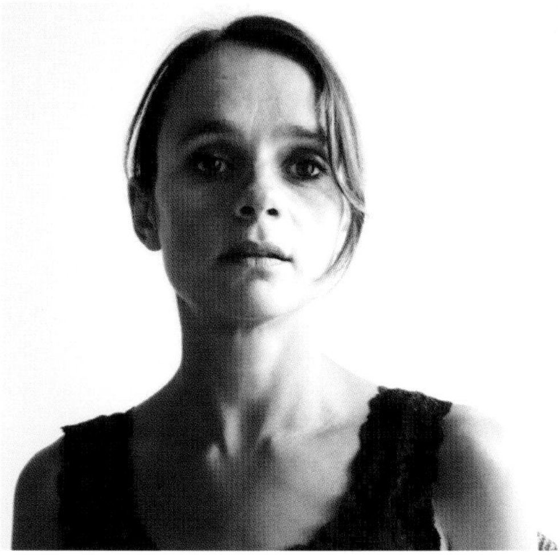

Gillian Carnegie

British artist Gillian Carnegie was born in Suffolk and studied at Camberwell School of Art and the Royal College of Art, London. Shortlisted for the Turner Prize in 2005, her work has been presented at numerous solo exhibitions in London, New York and Cologne. Carnegie's paintings have also featured extensively in group exhibitions held across Europe and the USA.

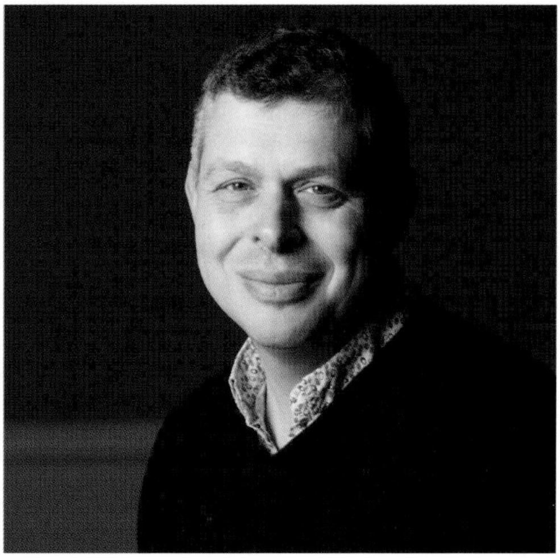

Richard Davey

Richard Davey is an internationally published author and freelance curator. A member of the International Association of Art Critics, he has written and contributed towards numerous titles commissioned by the Royal Academy of Arts, including the exhibition catalogue for its Anselm Kiefer show in 2014 and the 2015 Summer Exhibition catalogue. Davey was ordained as a priest in 1994 and holds the position of Co-ordinating Chaplain at Nottingham Trent University.

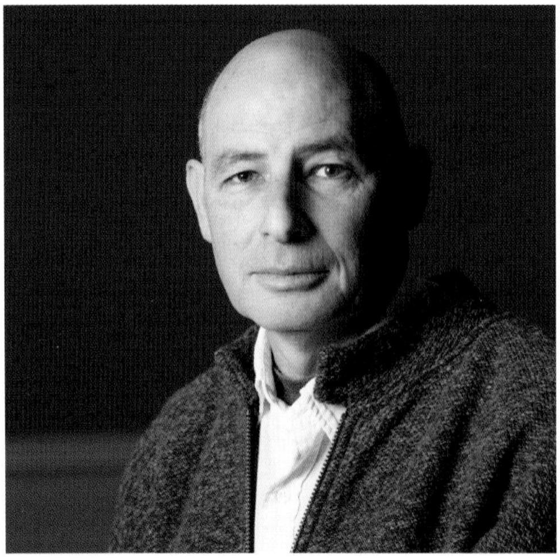

Ansel Krut

Born in Cape Town, South Africa, Ansel Krut studied at the University of the Witwatersrand, Johannesburg and the Royal College of Art, London. He was awarded the Abbey Major Scholarship in Painting to attend the British School at Rome in 1986/7. Recent solo exhibitions of Krut's paintings have been held at Jerwood Gallery, Hastings; Stuart Shave/Modern Art, London; Marlborough Chelsea, New York and KAdE Kunsthal, The Netherlands.

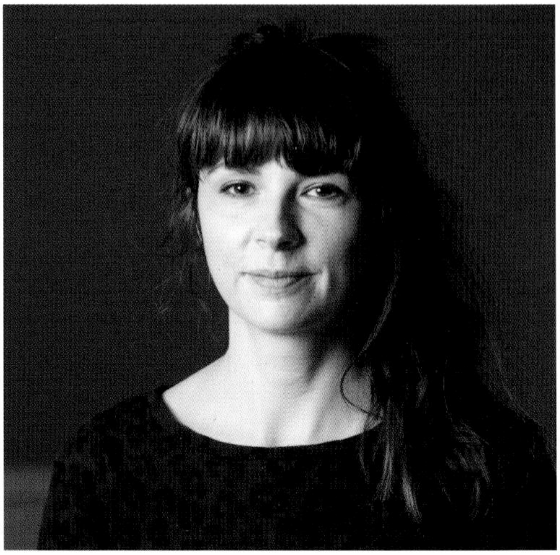

Phoebe Unwin

Phoebe Unwin was born in Cambridge and lives and works in London. She studied at Newcastle University and Slade School of Fine Art. In 2011 she won a Philip Leverhulme Prize and in 2005 she was shortlisted for the Max Mara Art Prize for Women: 6th Edition (2015-17) in association with the Whitechapel Gallery, London. Her work is in major public collections across the UK, Europe and the USA, and has featured in numerous exhibitions. Since 2010, she has held a lecturing position at the Slade.

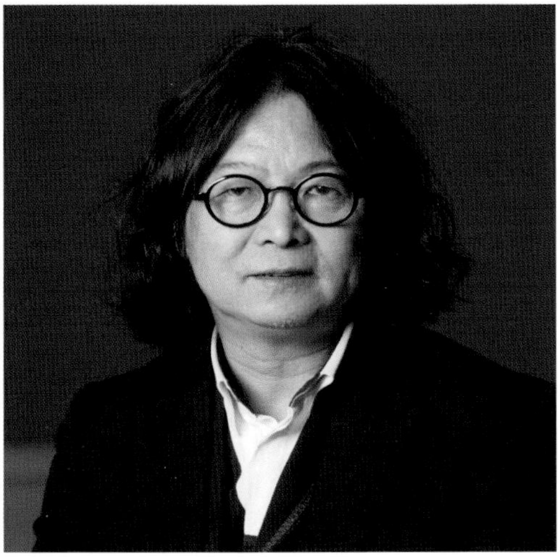

Ding Yi

Ding Yi was born and currently resides in Shanghai. He studied at Shanghai Arts and Crafts Institute and Shanghai University. His practice encompasses painting, sculpture, spatial installation and architecture. Ding Yi has exhibited extensively at various institutions and galleries across Asia, Europe and the USA.

A Diverse Selection

by Richard Davey

Five paintings rest against a white wall, clustered closely together so that they can be seen in a single glance. Beyond their obvious material connection as paintings they appear to have little in common. One is a geometric abstract, three are figurative, and one hovers in a poetic space between figuration and abstraction. Around them are 49 other paintings, some small, some large, some representational, some abstract, each bringing their own distinctive timbre to the cacophony of visual noise that fills a large gallery in Liverpool's World Museum.

These 54 works have survived two rounds of judging and the competing voices of more than 2,500 entries to become the selectors' final choice – and the five prizewinners – of the *John Moores Painting Prize 2016*. These are the paintings that have consistently teased the eye and demanded our attention. They have intrigued, mystified, and sometimes split opinion, but ultimately they have stayed in our memory and held our gaze, transcending our individual concerns to prove painting's continued relevance as a universal visual language.

Ten years after making his gloomy proclamation that 'painting is dead', the 19th-century French artist Paul Delaroche still had enough faith in the medium to

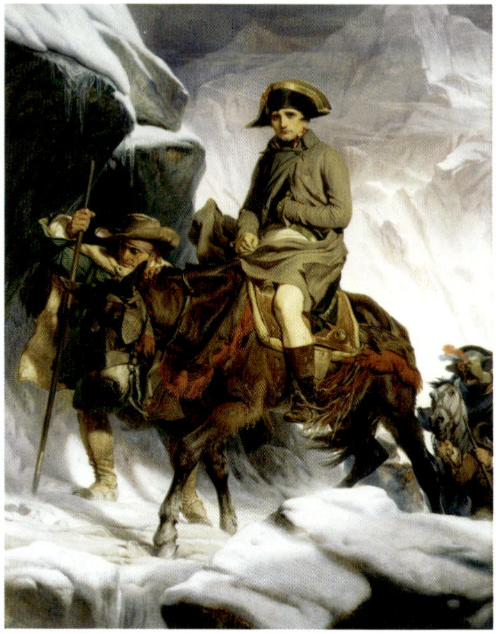

Napoleon Crossing the Alps, painted by Paul Delaroche in 1850. Oil on canvas.

paint the epic canvas *Napoleon Crossing the Alps* (1850), now hanging in the Walker Art Gallery. Painting didn't die with the advent of photography, but it did change. Modern artists responded to the challenge of the Daguerrotype and Modernist thought by self-critically questioning their medium, looking for its unique qualities, recognising the limits of its two-dimensional flat surface and giving new attention to the nature of the painted mark.

As a result, the act of painting is no longer seen as subservient to the subject but has become a subject in its own right. Painters now investigate the nature of pictorial space and the expressive possibilities of colour. They manipulate line and explore qualities of mark making. They utilise the uncertainties of perception to play optical games. Drips and dribbles are celebrated for their honesty to the materials, and childlike forms for their emphasis on artistic integrity, their joyful exuberance a celebration of innocent vision. Paint is no longer a transparent window through which we see an illusion of the world but an opaque veil through which the world is discovered and reality revealed.

As the *John Moores Painting Prize* has shown since 1957, photography liberated painting. Among the submission and selection in 2016 there was a vibrant sense that it can be anything it wants to be. There were paintings that emphasised their nature as solid objects alongside those that sought to be transparent windows on the world. There were paintings that imitated nature and others that constructed new, imaginary worlds. Some made reference to classical myths, others to contemporary culture. Where some looked to the world outside for inspiration, others focused on purely artistic debates. They explored materials and questioned pictorial conventions. They were painted on paper, card, canvas, concrete, plastic sheet and foil, and in oil, watercolour, acrylic, ink, spray-paint and Plasticine. Some were tightly controlled compositions, others vibrantly expressive. Some were made with bold, painterly gestures, others hid the artist's hand. Some shouted and screamed, others stood back, quietly imprinting themselves upon our retinas. Some were made according to strict rules and systems, others were made as an impassioned and direct response to the world.

There were large works, filling walls with waterfalls of colour, and tiny, jewel-like objects that intrigued and lured the eye in. Some engulfed us in luminous colours, several unsettled us with sickly, pastel hues, whilst others seduced us with the subtlety of their apparently drab, muddy tones. Sometimes they drew us into complex visual spaces, trapping us in cubist structures that manipulated the gaze. Sometimes they permitted us to step into convincingly realistic worlds, and sometimes they forced us back out into our own space – their flat surfaces offering no entry into a space within. They beguiled with memories and teased with unintended associations. They filled our imagination, danced through our minds, and invited us to respond.

The rich diversity of the submitted works transcended geographic and cultural boundaries, transgressed the new art orthodoxies and asked us to consider the nature of painting. They spoke to our daily experience as embodied beings, through explicitly material objects made by artists who listen to music, go for walks, read books and papers, think about philosophy and science, watch TV and go to films. People who visit galleries, go shopping and trawl car boot sales, who eat and drink, go out with friends and family, run, swim, talk and laugh, feel the sun on their face, the wind in their hair and the rain on their skin.

In his essay '*The Painter of Modern Life*', the 19th-century French poet Charles Baudelaire described the modern painter as a *flaneur*. He argued that universal beauty wasn't to be found in the classical models of the past, but in the everyday and the here and now. Rather than visiting galleries and museums the modern artist wandered the streets, looking for those moments of universal beauty which exist in the ordinary world. Instead of starting with a universal ideal, they began with the individual and the particular.

The artists selected for *John Moores 2016* are emphatically 'modern artists', highlighting the need to look from multiple perspectives in order to glimpse the whole. They show us, through a veil of paint, the reality of living in the world, exposing that which we may never have consciously considered. They translate their daily experience into colour, form, texture and pattern. They seek to understand by making a mark, using paint to hold the unknown and contain the unseen, exploring the nature of space and the significance of play, and finding poetry in the commonplace.

Space

The critic Clement Greenberg argued in his 1961 essay '*Modernist Painting*' that modernism was the search for a discipline's distinctiveness in order to establish its area of competence. The question for the modern painter was what set painting apart from other media – what made a painting a painting? Realism and imitation were shared with photography, and colour and three-dimensionality with sculpture. For Greenberg, and for modern artists, the uniqueness of painting was in the flatness of its support, and therefore in the problem of representing reality within two dimensions. By the time Greenberg wrote his essay, artists had been wrestling with the problem of pictorial space for almost a century. They had flattened it and fractured it. They had used colour relationships to suggest it, and played optical games to construct it. They had even tried to ignore it. But the problem cannot be ignored. As soon as a line is made it opens up a spatial relationship. The moment more than one colour is used, depth is implied. But for the artists of the *John Moores 2016*, the representation of space is not a problem, it is an opportunity – a tool to either disrupt or reinforce their narratives, a source of play and a subject in itself.

At first glance Mandy Payne's *No Ball Games Here* seems unconcerned by modernism's rejection of illusionary realism. Despite the very contemporary nature of its materials and subject matter, Payne's naturalistic painting of the Park Hill flats in Sheffield has a distinctly classical feel, similar to the Walker's *Landscape with the Ashes of Phocion* (1648) by Nicolas Poussin. Both use zigzagging diagonals to lead us into the landscape. In Poussin's case, he takes our gaze from the foreground figures to a classical temple and rocky crag. Payne leads us along a shadowy passageway, further into the crumbling estate. But then, just when she has taken us into these urban depths, Payne stops us dead in our tracks, confronting us with a grid of red, yellow, black and white rectangles reminiscent of a Piet Mondrian painting. Suddenly, this three-dimensional urban landscape demands to be read as a flat abstract painting. The illusion has been shattered as reticent depths are brought to the surface and flattened out.

Prizewinner Gabriella Boyd's *Birthyard*, in contrast, appears at first glance to celebrate painting's essential two-dimensionality. The high view point tilts the composition towards the surface. The red babies lying next to their pink mothers are left un-modelled, painted with bold blocks of bright colour. Yet these flatly painted figures lie on dark green beds, with black edges angled towards a common vanishing point. Below the women's bent legs and under the furthest bed are dark shadows, whilst the glass on the table has an elliptical mouth. Together these compositional elements turn this ambiguous setting into a three-dimensional space, one we could walk into and around, our gaze drawn through it by repeated triangles and along the *repoussoir* pathways of bold, diagonal lines.

But Boyd doesn't just offer us a shifting amalgamation of two and three-dimensional space. Beneath the bent knees of each truncated adult body she has placed a white triangle, steering us into entirely new realms. Here are two snow-capped mountains contained between calf and thigh, or two colourless voids to absorb our gaze like Correggio's clouds. They take us from this enigmatic interior into a vast landscape, and from the physical realm into immaterial space.

Ben Cove's *Freeloader* celebrates space without the distraction of landscape or scenery. As architectural as it is painterly, *Freeloader* hovers on the boundary between abstraction and figuration. Using nothing more than sudden tonal shifts to suggest shadows, form triangles and draw diagonal lines, Cove has created a vivid *trompe l'oeil* frame to hold a shallow three-dimensional space. Two abstract entities, resembling Brancusi's simplified birds, are its occupants. Perched on the frame, facing each other, these flat, painted silhouettes are laid onto a grey background. Whilst their heads are suggested by a transparent pink and their bodies by an area of textured blue, they are also constructed from smaller segments, whose darker and more opaque colours create subtle tonal shadows – creases and folds, which evoke contoured bodies as well as flat surfaces. Both sculptural and painterly, two and three-dimensional, Cove's 'birds' oscillate between background and surface, pulling our gaze in and pushing it out – two partially solid forms within an almost solid space.

Selma Parlour's *One, The Side-ness of In-Out*, another prizewinner, also shows us space without the distraction of illusion. But where Cove's starting point was architectural, hers is painterly, each element of the work designed to highlight the flatness and materiality of painting and the individual elements of its construction. Parlour begins with colour, her use of thin, transparent glazes allowing the woven surface of the canvas to remain visible, whilst giving the work an inner translucent glow. The division of the canvas horizontally creates an horizon line to suggest distance and space. This sense of depth is reinforced by the shadowy smudge that shades each of her lines. Along the top and right hand edges a broad blue frame holds the space in and flattens it out, creating the impression of a painting within a painting. But the frame is incomplete, and the two diagonal lines that terminate each side converge towards a vanishing point, turning the frame into a proscenium arch and the painting into a stage.

The actors on this stage, or the subjects of this painting, are two four-sided shapes: a trapezium, whose converging sides draw the eye in, and a quadrilateral, which seems to fold over towards the viewer. The trapezium appears flat, the quadrilateral freestanding and solid. They reinforce the sense of three-dimensional space, but they also disrupt it. The blue frame suggests we are looking at the space head on, yet the trapezium only reads as a painting on a wall if we imagine ourselves looking down on it from above. The quadrilateral doesn't really work from either of these positions. Parlour's pictorial space is impossible. It breaks all the rules and confounds all expectations, demanding to be read from multiple perspectives rather than a single viewpoint.

The 88 panels of Bella Easton's *Passageways* also break apart the unity of the picture surface, confronting us, like a cubist painting, with multiple facets of a single whole. What initially seems to be a work of mirror symmetry, inviting us to choose which stairs to ascend, which door to go through, and which hallway to navigate, becomes less certain when we draw closer to the picture surface and examine the individual panels. Each is a unique abstract painting, a shifting colour field in which the physical elements of the building's solid structure have disintegrated. Here is an endless hall of mirrors, where recognisable forms are shattered into countless pieces, and solid reality has become formless space.

The tiny individual objects, abstract forms and shards of painted light that cover Donal Moloney's *Cave Floor* are so densely packed that any feeling of three-dimensional space has been completely eliminated. He starts with found objects and his own little sculptures. He photographs, scans, prints, cuts and pastes, selects and positions them until he has built up a complex design, which he then paints. The work's complexity is compelling. It invites us to explore its myriad facets and to be dazzled by the fractured light that disrupts its solidity. Yet it simultaneously defies our scrutiny, confronting us with a chaotic surface across which individual elements are lost within the anonymous whole. Like staring at the stars, this small painting shows us the sublime, something too vast for our minds to contemplate.

Towards the top of Michael Simpson's *Squint (19)* is a small rectangle, its bottom half a deep black, the upper a pale yellow. It could represent a simple abstract painting hung on a wall. But the black has an intensity that hints at a void rather than solidity. It teases with the promise of something beyond. In medieval churches a squint, or hagioscope, was an opening through a wall which allowed people in the transepts or outside the church to see the priest elevating the bread and wine at the moment of consecration. Like an icon, it granted a view of sacred space.

Beneath the squint, Simpson has placed a short stepladder, ready, in theory, to offer access and a way of seeing. On the left the structure's subtle diagonals, shadows and yellow highlights suggest a rounded form in a rounded space. But to the right, a long black vertical line, like a Barnett Newman zip, acts to flatten everything out. Instead of three-dimensional substance we see a two-dimensional flat profile. With this, the invitation to climb up and look through the squint is negated. Simpson leaves us on the outside, withholding our ability to peer into this divine realm.

What we see in Simpson's deceptively simple painting – the winner of this year's first prize – is the history of western art. Here is the sacred, intangible space of religious art, the rounded space of illusionist representation, and the increasingly flattened space of the modern. On the edges of the canvas, however, Simpson suggests another form of space. In smears of pink and purple paint we discover the different colours that lie hidden beneath this work's surface. For like every canvas, this is a palimpsest, a sedimentary accumulation of marks and colours. It is a fossilised domain recording both the individual brush marks that make up each layer of paint and the moment of temporal space necessary to separate one stroke from the next.

Play

Modern painting can at times seem over serious, weighed down by its history and an obligation to justify itself, couched in visual languages that can exclude all except those in the know. But in these 54 works there is a palpable sense of playfulness that seeks to shake off – or at least to shake up – these responsibilities. They taunt our eyes and our expectations, they surprise and shock, they re-appropriate and make possible several interpretations. Provocatively, they coax us to play their game, reeling us in and demanding our participation.

We have already contemplated the spatial exuberance used by some of the artists to animate their paintings, whether shifting between dimensions towards multiple ways of seeing the work, or using the rules of perception to play optical games that tease the eye. Others, however, rely on contrasting languages to create a sense of multi-dimensional play. In Emma Talbot's *You come to me in a dream*, a cartoon-like combination of the visual and verbal, the abstract and the figurative, captures the vivid blur and alien familiarity of our dreams. Disconnected objects merge into impossible combinations that make perfect sense. Duncan Swann's *I choose the child*, likewise, warps reality. His use of floating numbers and unexpected shapes generates an eerie, unnatural feel in this large monochrome painting.

Laurence Owen's *Ritual to the Westfield* begins with a visual pun: four large ceramic pins quote the large-headed tacks once used to secure canvas to stretcher in old oil paintings. But here the canvas lies flat on the wall and the pins are visible not hidden. This reference to historic paintings is central to Owen's intentions. He is fascinated by the collapsed time of our postmodern world, where diverse works of art can be accessed at a mouse-click. Using simplified visual quotations sampled from different genres and periods of art history he flattens time into a riot of colour and shape, playfully combining references to landscape, abstraction and three-dimensional realistic space into a shopping mall of artistic associations to tempt the viewer.

Julie Cockburn and Mary Wood offer a very different type of playfulness. Their works *The Playground* and *Series 15 Cerulean 2* celebrate the joy and feeling of spontaneous, carefree release that comes when manipulating materials, not knowing where they will go and what they will do. Cockburn's *The Playground* is just that, a place to play in contrast to the intricate delicacy and craft of collage and embroidery she employs in her other artworks. Instead of paint, coloured pieces of Plasticine were kneaded, sliced and applied to the cover of an old art book before being scraped off again. She then cut the cover in half and reassembled it to form a perfect rhomboid, with the centre now the outside edge. The result was unplanned and magical, an abstract landscape alive with flecks of vivid, iridescent colour. There is no great meaning, no underpinning theory, just a visualisation of joy.

Wood's engagement with her materials is even more direct. She paints with her fingers. When painting is so often given over to concept and based on abstract theories, Wood reminds us that painting is essentially nothing more than 'pushing coloured dirt around'. Using her fingers she feels the substance of the pigment and its tactile sensuality, gaining bodily knowledge as she manipulates this fluid substance across a material surface. She learns about colour from her 'gut' and her skin, and from what feels right, in the moment. It is instinctual, tactile and primitive, a reminder of painting's origins on prehistoric cave walls.

The visceral and emotional response demanded by a painting can perturb, alienate and fascinate the viewer. It can also bring wonder and joy, creating lightness and lyricism that makes our eyes dance and our emotions soar. Whilst these opposing feelings are often kept separate, they are sometimes, deliberately, brought together, as in Benjamin Jamie's prizewinning *Dissolver*. His use of sinuous organic forms, reminiscent of Art Nouveau and painted in decorative pastel tones, challenges the aesthetic conventions of today. They have a saccharine appearance far removed from the intellectual seriousness or playful irony that exemplifies most contemporary art. But this pink paint has a physicality that leaves a scab on the canvas. Surrounded by its complementary green, it thrusts out at the viewer in a way that cannot be ignored. It pulls us into this abstracted thicket, trapping us in its sinuous, sinewy forms. Our eyes caress the delicate curves and whorls before us, they weave in and out of this airy woodland, and plunge into the background mist, where pale circles and loops invite us to dance. Our minds may be repelled by the sickly sweetness, but as our bodies respond to the siren call of these lyrical forms, we find that Jamie has elevated the maligned to the marvellous.

Seeing poetry in the world

Unlike the other prizewinning paintings, Talar Aghbashian's *Untitled* doesn't take us into abstract or imaginary worlds, but shows us the world around us. Whilst not painted from life, or reality, her broken, sculpted hand, monumental and massive within its simplified, ruined landscape, is a cipher for all those other toppled statues and overthrown dictators that fill our newspapers or television screens. Roughly modelled, with a single, delicately observed fingernail offering just enough to give a sense of realism, it remains ambiguous, a truncated hand that could be from anywhere and belong to anyone. The broad black border around the image betrays the work's origins, the blown up photographs Aghbashian projects onto her canvases as reference points and guidelines, turning the work into a declaration of fact and an apparent statement of truthfulness. But this is a painting and therefore poetic. It can show more than facts, it can show possibilities. The individual brush marks that give the hand its substance also dissolve it, uniting it with its rock strewn background and returning it to the dust of the rock from which it was carved, a stark reminder that this is the way of all empires and all life.

Steph Goodger's *Les Non-réclamés (The Unclaimed)* also shows us the fragility of human life and the consequences of violence. Based on two contemporary photographs showing the bodies of those killed in the 1871 Paris Commune uprising, Goodger's powerful diptych transcends the specificity of the photograph, blurring faces and abstracting forms so that this morbid scene could also be an image of contemporary migrants drowned in the Mediterranean or the dead of the Syrian civil war. But paint doesn't just make this scene universal, it transforms it. Each brush mark feels like a gesture of compassion, a gentle caress that holds each of the bodies, blurring them, dissolving them, and releasing them from the boundaries of the physical into universal hope.

The poetic power of paint permits us to see the world differently. It can transform derelict flats into an abstract painting, and a muddy Suffolk pig field into a visual meditation on the transience of life. We might drive past the empty landscape of John Stark's *Beasts of England II* without noticing it. Yet there is a compelling stillness in this almost photographic painting that forces us to stop and look. Lingering before it we become aware of the limpid winter light, and the way it gently dissolves the distant wooded horizon. We trace with our mind's eye the delicate spider's web of branches piercing the sky, and we glimpse the colour relationship between the turquoise green roofs of the pig arks and the green grass of the narrow headlands connecting the natural with the man-made.

Richard Kenton Webb's *The Landscape as Discourse* also halts us in our tracks, teasing us with a surreal image of Tasmanian scenery confined improbably within a museum case. He gives us a God's eye view, showing it from above and below, from the outside and the inside. He invites us to roam through this nocturnal land, scaling its contours and diving into its lake, becoming miners and mountaineers, geologists and geographers. But this is more than a painting of a landscape, it is the landscape itself, for Webb's rich pigments are ground from the very rocks they portray. Here, in this reimagined setting, made from its re-formed matter, Webb turns the world into a treasure – a precious, beautiful object held up for all to see.

And here, then, is the world we live in, the life we live, offered from a different point of view: manipulated, enhanced, reduced and distilled so that we might experience it more clearly. We are challenged to become *flaneurs*, to enter the world we know, but may never have seen. The prizewinners Aghbashian, Boyd, Jamie, Parlour and Simpson, and their fellow artists in the *John Moores Painting Prize 2016*, expose fresh perspectives and new points of view, not as they actually are, but through the prism of paint. In so doing they show us our reality and far more. We are confronted with the sublime, the beautiful, and the ugly. They take us from the microscopic out to the macroscopic, to transcend and transform the sometimes narrow horizons of our individual perspectives. Life is here, death is here, despair is here, joy is here, hope is here. On these simple flat supports, contained within these grains of suspended pigment, we can find the whole world.

First prizewinner
Michael Simpson

Prizewinners
Talar Aghbashian
Gabriella Boyd
Benjamin Jamie
Selma Parlour

Michael Simpson

Squint (19)

2015
Oil on canvas
228.5 x 130 cm

Squint painting; a continuing series.

Biography

Born in Dorset in 1940, Michael Simpson is based in Wiltshire. He attended Bournemouth College of Art 1958-60 and the Royal College of Art London 1960-3. Exhibitions include *Tightrope Walk: Painted Images After Abstraction* White Cube Bermondsey 2015, *The Painting Show* (British Council touring) CAC Vilnius 2016. Solos include *Recent Paintings* Serpentine Gallery London 1985, *Bench Paintings 1992-1995* Arnolfini Gallery Bristol & Oriel 31 Newtown 1996, *Bench Paintings, Recent Work 2005-2006* David Risley Gallery London 2007, *The Leper Squint Paintings* David Risley Gallery Copenhagen 2013, *Study #6. Michael Simpson* DRAF London 2014, *Flat Surface Painting* Spike Island Bristol 2016. In *John Moores Painting Prize* 1989, 1991 (prizewinner), 1993, 2010.

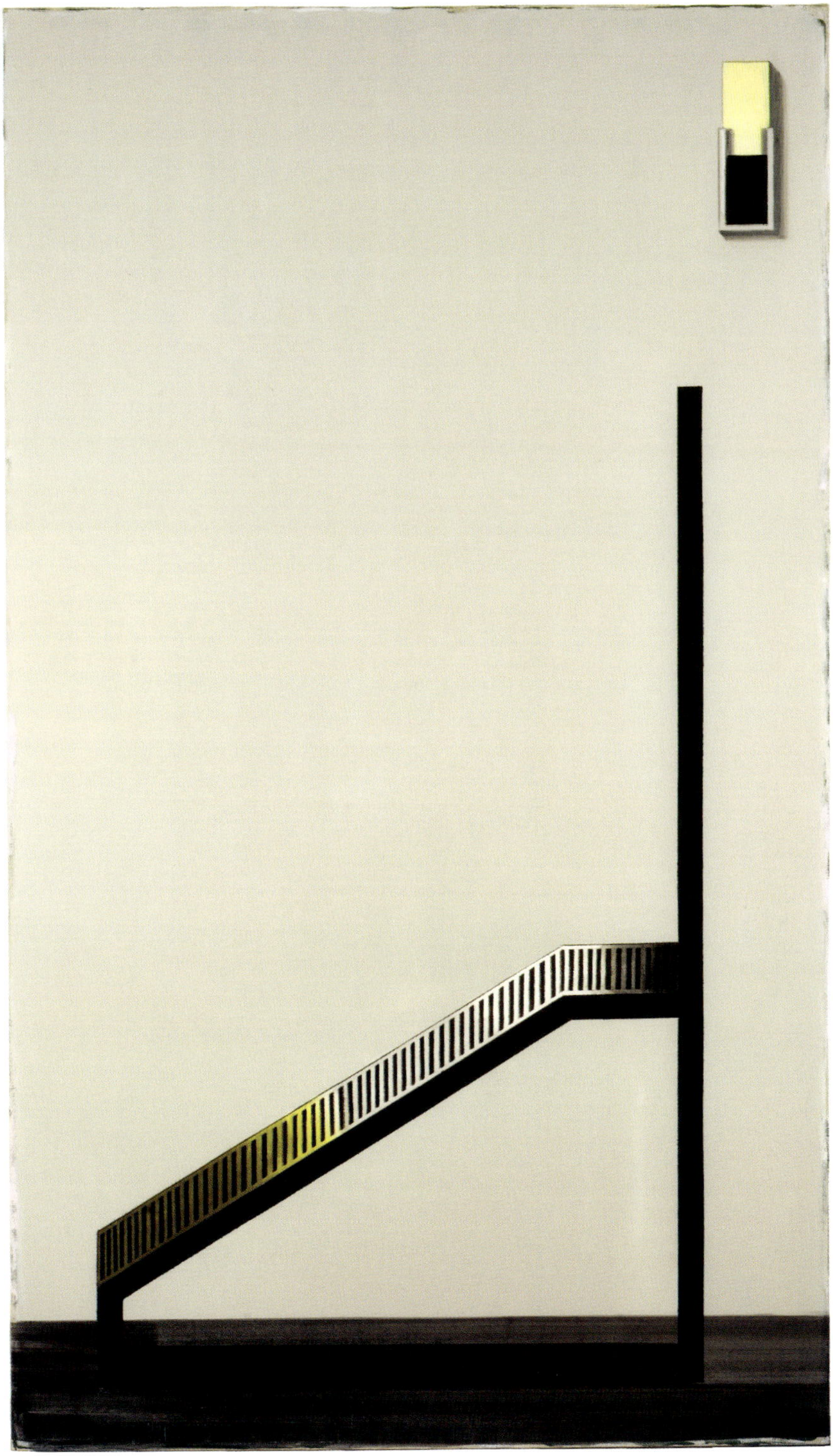

Michael Simpson | First prizewinner

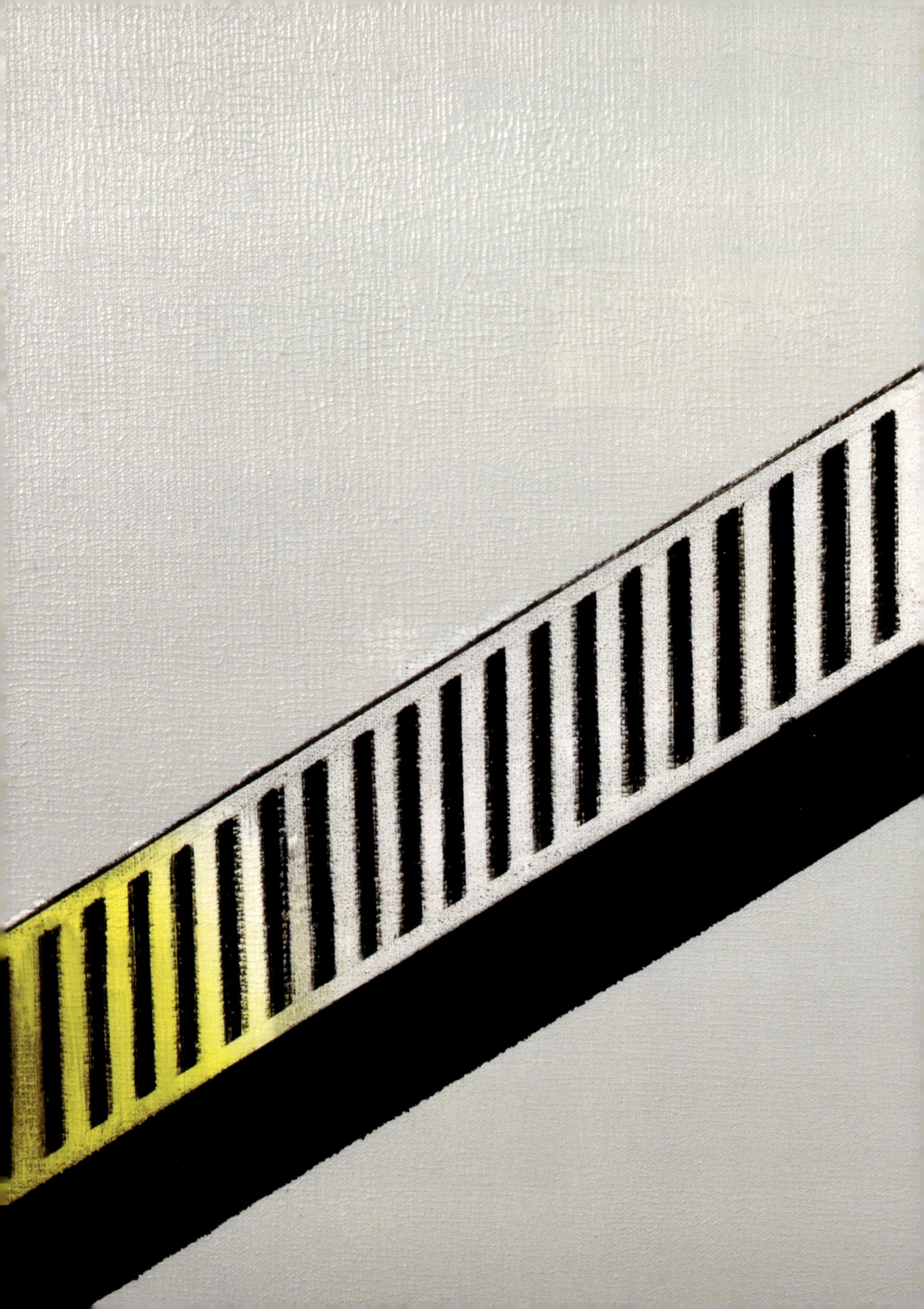

Talar Aghbashian

Untitled

2015
Oil on canvas
75 x 60 cm

A persistent memory of a disproportionate, ill-sculpted arm of a statue of an assassinated politician, a memory of the toppling down of another statue seen on news footage, and scenes of destruction of historical monuments, converged into an emblem of a hand, as if from another world. Painting landscapes came to me after I first visited the ancient city of Palmyra six years ago. It has revealed itself in different interrelated themes ever since.

I use photo print outs, and project them onto my already heavily built up or thoroughly sanded down canvases. As I work, a painting's alchemical make up, and the substance and process, is reflected in sync with my ideas and experiences. It forms in layers: some remain transparent, others dense; some blur, expand and shrink, get wiped, ever evolve and coexist.

The paintings are eerie, and haunted by a sense of unease. It is important that they are not exaggerated and that they look convincing. Left ambiguous, they are open to interpretation. They respond to our times, in which reality is continuously manufactured in our everyday, throughout the news and media.

Biography

Born in Beirut in 1981, Talar Aghbashian attended the Lebanese University of Fine Arts 1999-2003, St Martins School of Art London 2007-08, Birkbeck University London 2009-10. Received AGBU grant 2007, Benlian Trust grant 2008. Exhibitions include *Salon D'Automne* Musée Nicolas Sursock Beirut 2007, *This Constant Cracking of the Surface* Bargehouse London 2008, *Spiritual Promises from Lost Prophets* Cordy House London 2008, *The Minuco Art Show '09* Coningsby Gallery London 2009, *Treasured Objects* Brunei Gallery SOAS London 2010, *Odds Against Tomorrow* Bearspace London 2012, *The Discerning Eye* Mall Galleries 2012 London. Recent solos *Blind Finds* The Running Horse Beirut 2013, *Site/Sight* Carbon 12 Dubai 2015.

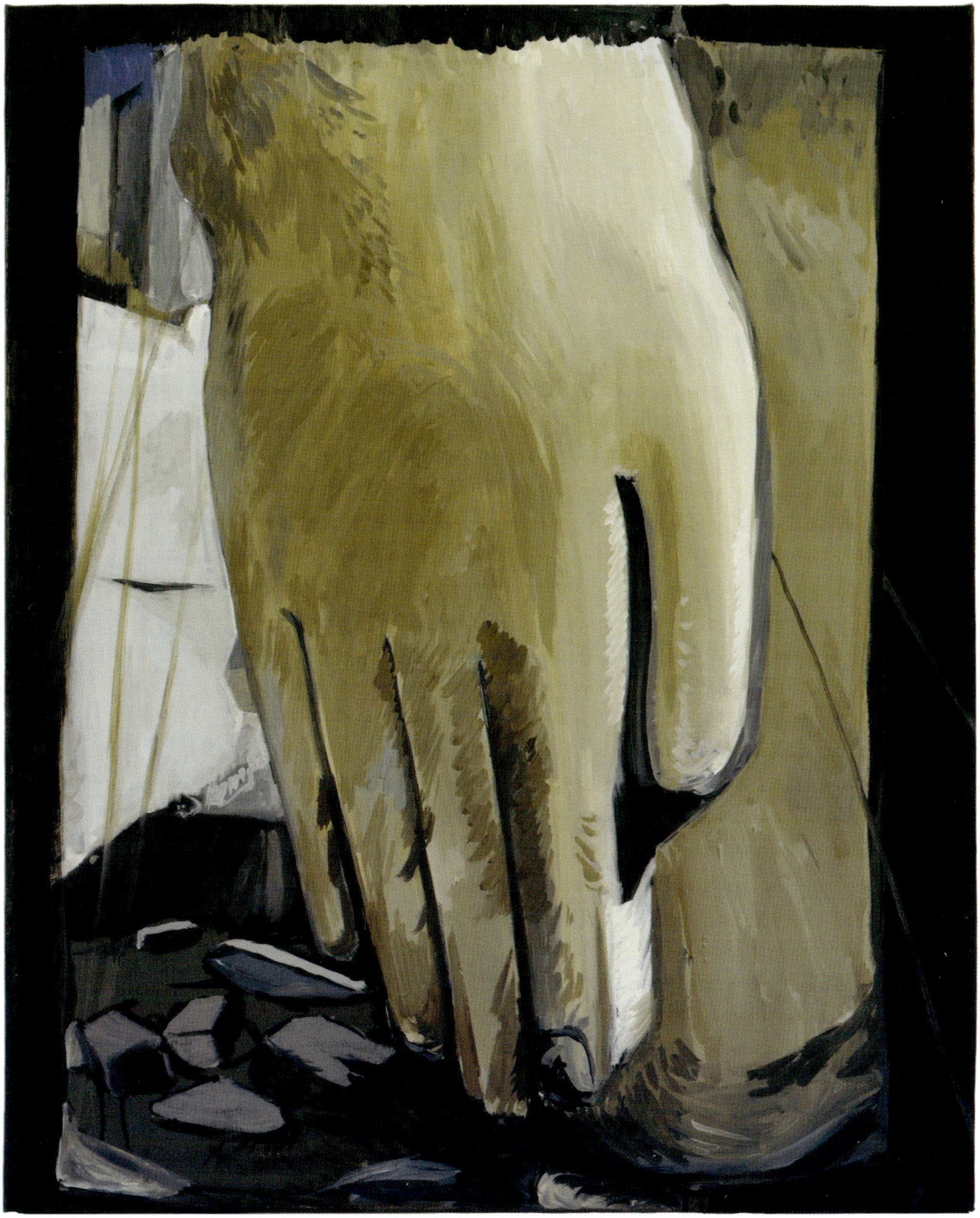

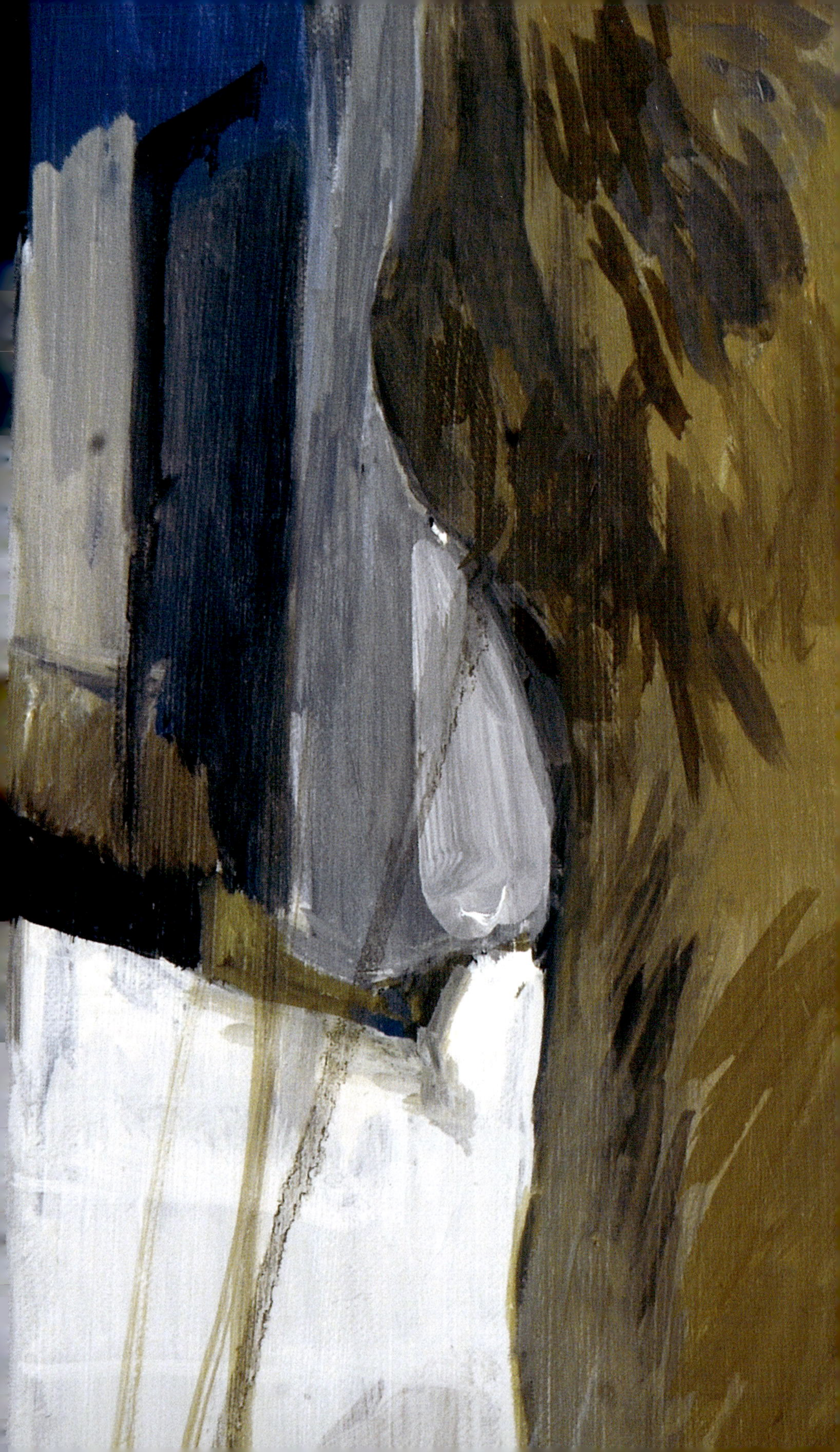

Gabriella Boyd

Birthyard

2015
Oil on canvas
167.8 x 152.4 cm

My works, which consist mainly of oil paintings on canvas, revolve around the merging of private and public spaces. I build up paintings of imagined locations in stages, often allowing purely formal considerations of colour and line to determine their direction. It is through this process that figures emerge. Psychological states become theatrically realised as characters' inner and outer realities blur and shift.

Working from photographs, drawings and recalled social observations, I try to depict fleeting interactions or moments of failed intimacy.

Biography

Born in 1988 in Glasgow, Gabriella Boyd studied at Glasgow School of Art 2007-11 (Chairman's Medal 2011) and is at the Royal Academy Schools London 2014-2017. Exhibitions include *Saatchi New Sensations* (special commendation) Victoria House London 2011, *Catlin Art Prize 2012* Londonewcastle Project Space London, *Beijing International Art Biennale* Beijing 2012, *The Yellow Wallpaper* Cob Gallery London 2012, *Go Figure* Cob Gallery 2014, *Whispers* Ronchini Gallery London 2015, *Premiums: Interim Projects* Royal Academy London 2016, *Gabriella Boyd & Marco Giordano* (Glasgow International) House for an Art Lover Glasgow 2016. Solo *Strong Necks* High House Gallery Oxford 2013. Illustrated Freud's '*Interpreting Dreams*' Folio Society 2015.

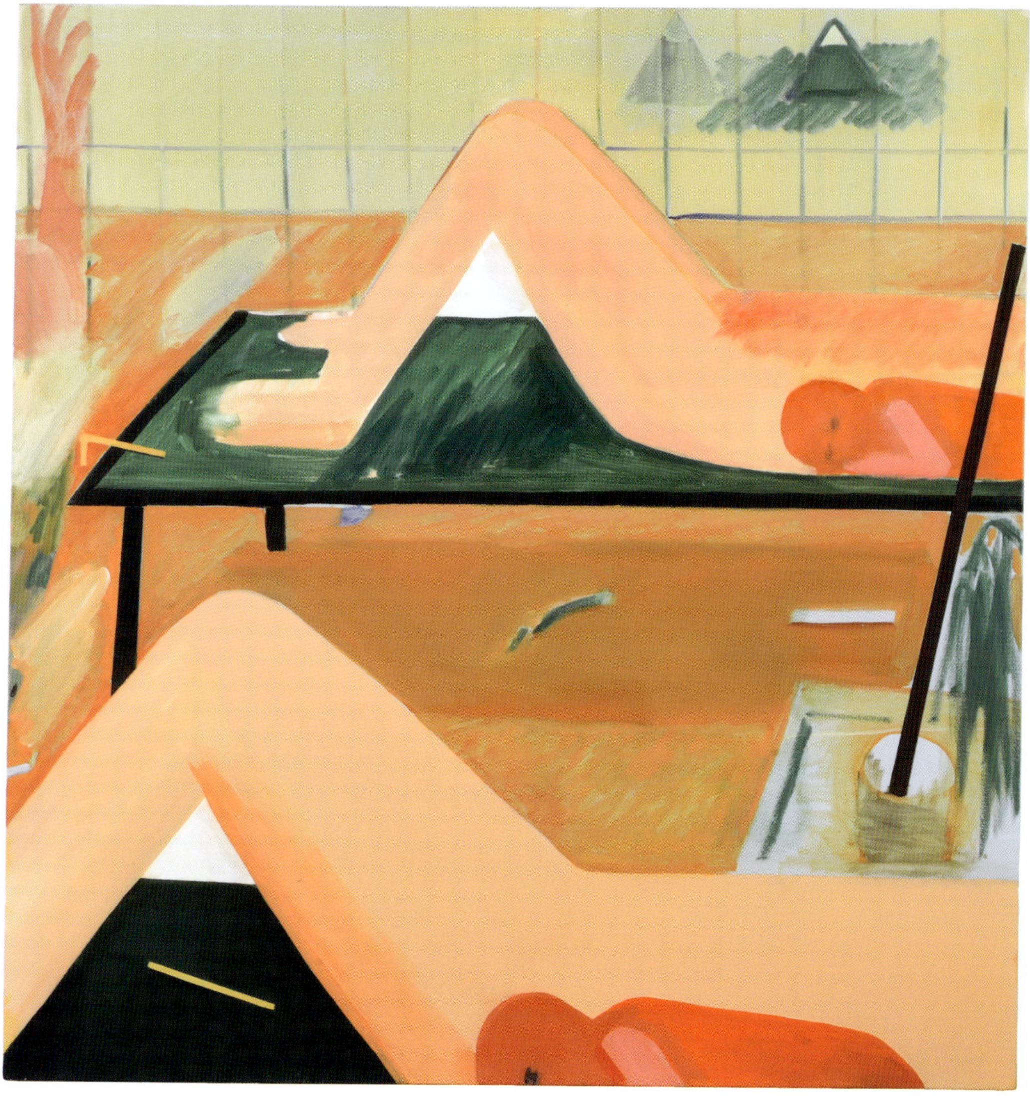

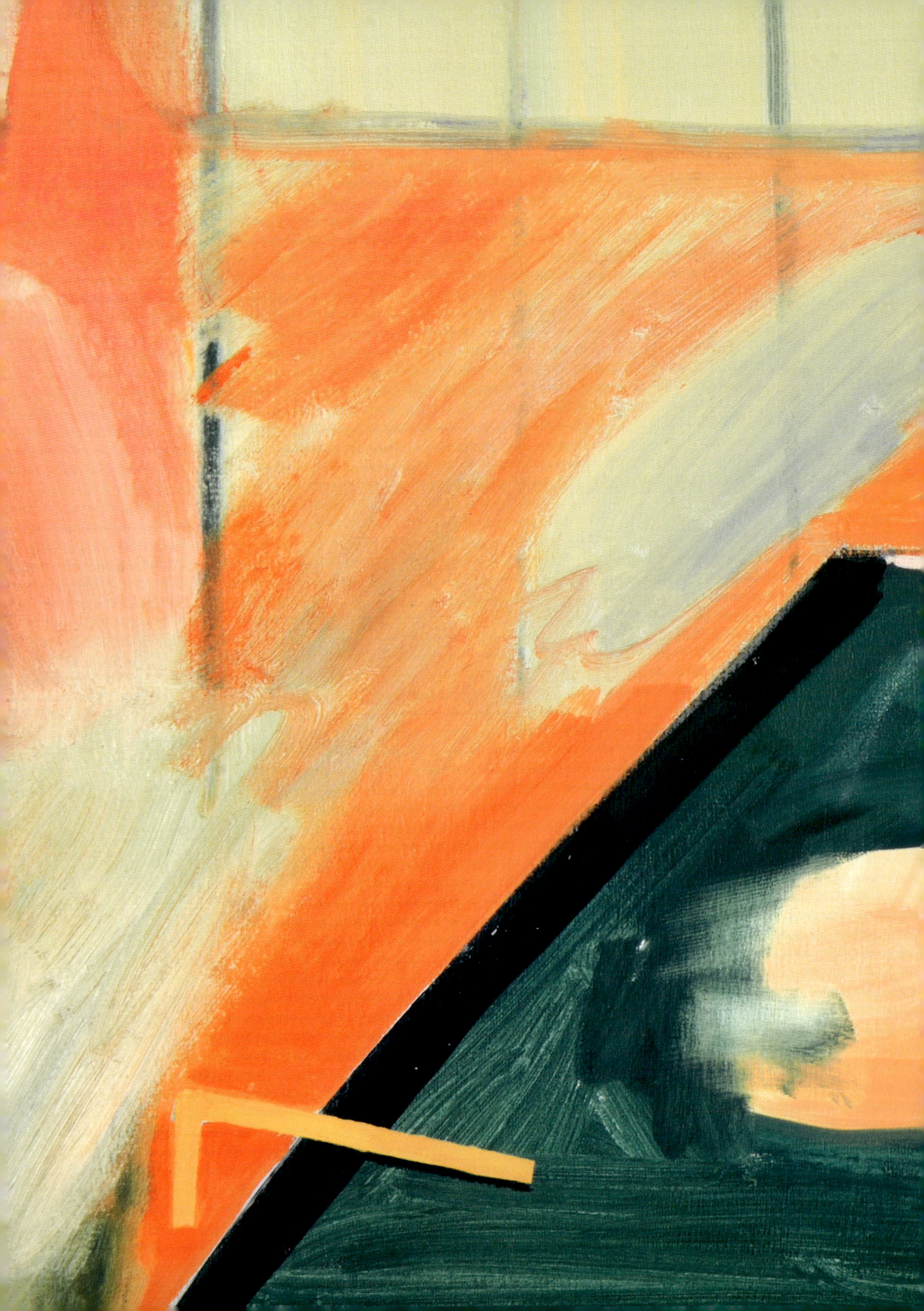

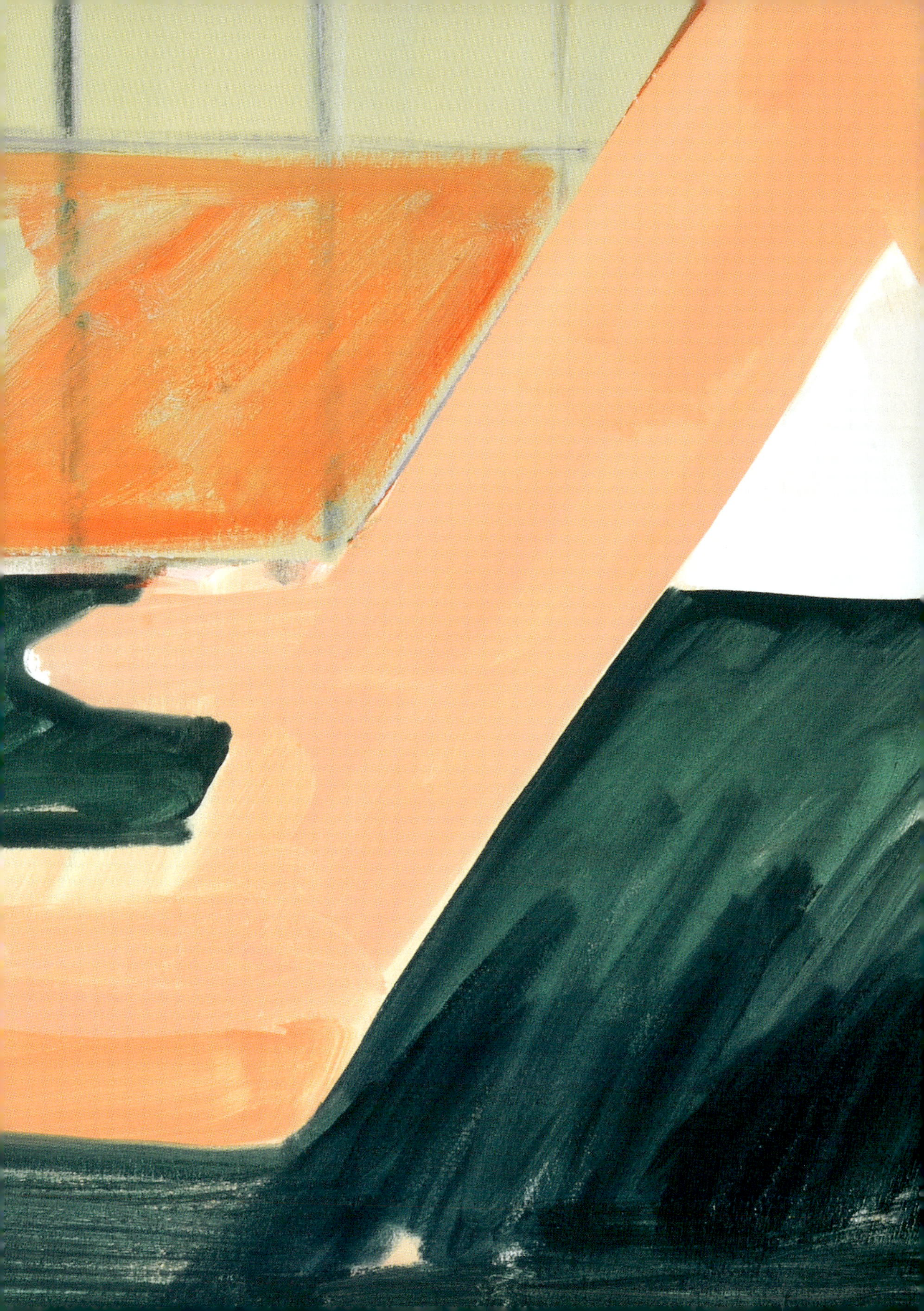

Benjamin Jamie

Dissolver

2015
Oil, distemper, wax and charcoal on canvas
150.2 x 130.2 cm

My paintings explore the boundaries between the grotesque and the saccharine and seek to turn the mundane into the unusual. Inspiration comes from many sources, be it studio detritus, fly-tipping, transhumanism or fast food, and although based somewhere in reality, my paintings are fairly undisturbed by the real world. This allows me to create notional, metamorphic spaces, and to fabricate an idealised past or future which can be populated with allegorical figures and objects.

Biography

Benjamin Jamie was born in 1978 in Nottingham and is based in London. He studied at the University of Gloucestershire 1999-2002 and on the Turps Art School Painters Studio Programme 2014-16. Recent group exhibitions, all London, include *East London Painting Prize* Strand East 2014, *Teleology* Husk Gallery 2014, *Interim Show* Turps Gallery 2015, *Malvern Show No.4a*, Malvern 2015, *Summer Show* Turps Gallery 2015, *Pay No Attention To That Man Behind The Curtain* Blain|Southern 2015, *Flash Salon* Bond House Gallery 2015, *Turps Goes West* Edel Assanti London 2015. Final *Turps* show Turps Gallery 2016.

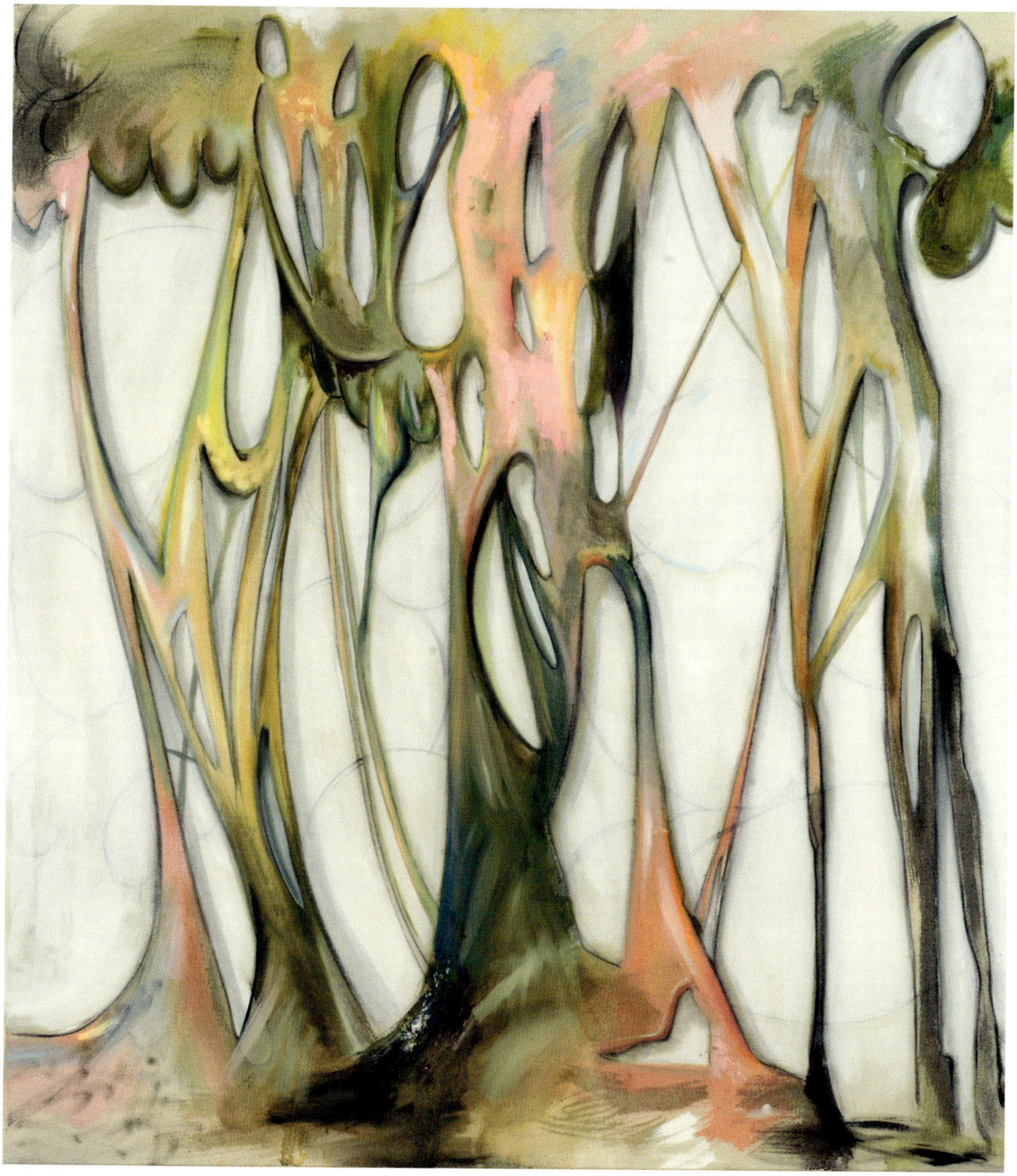

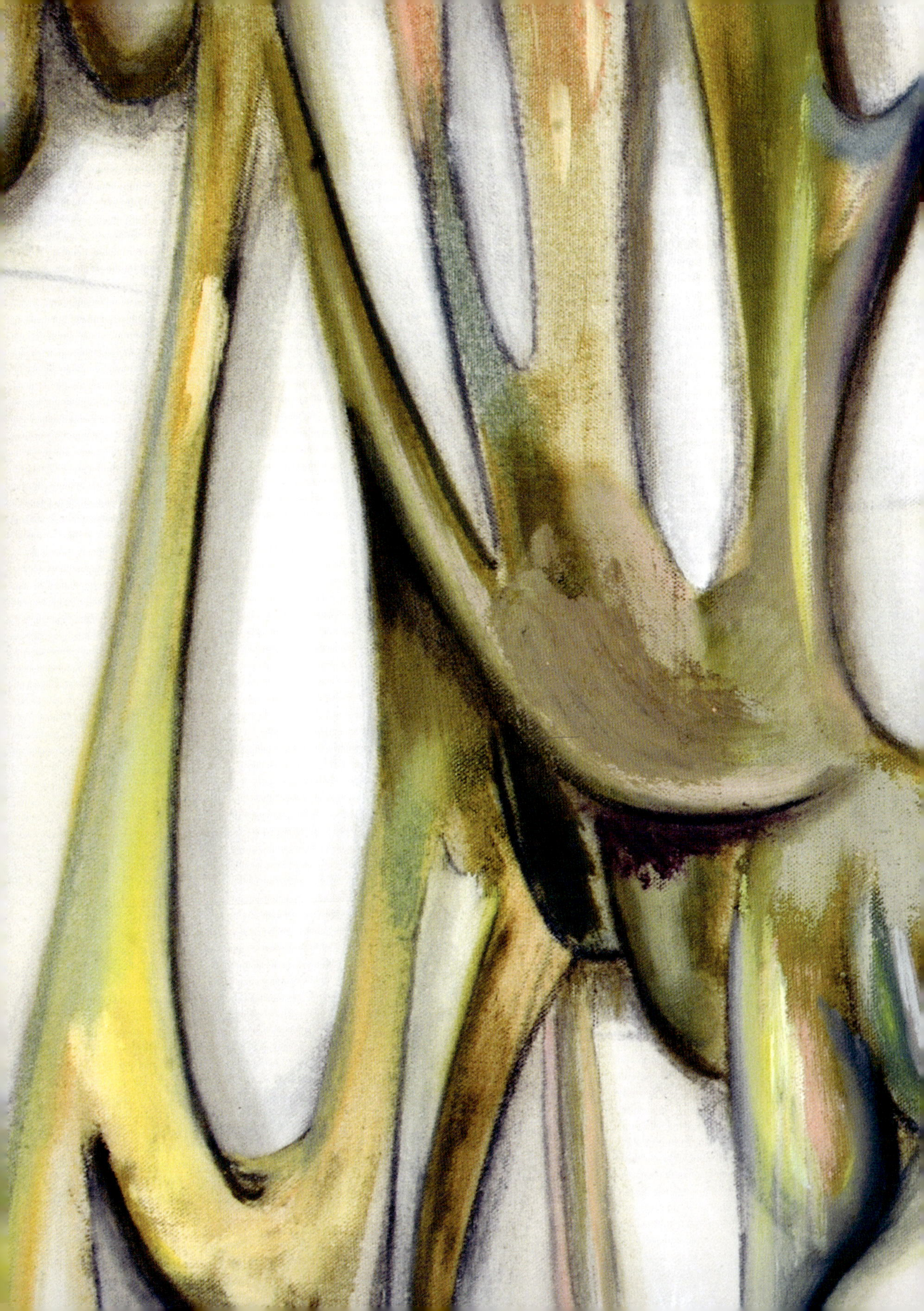

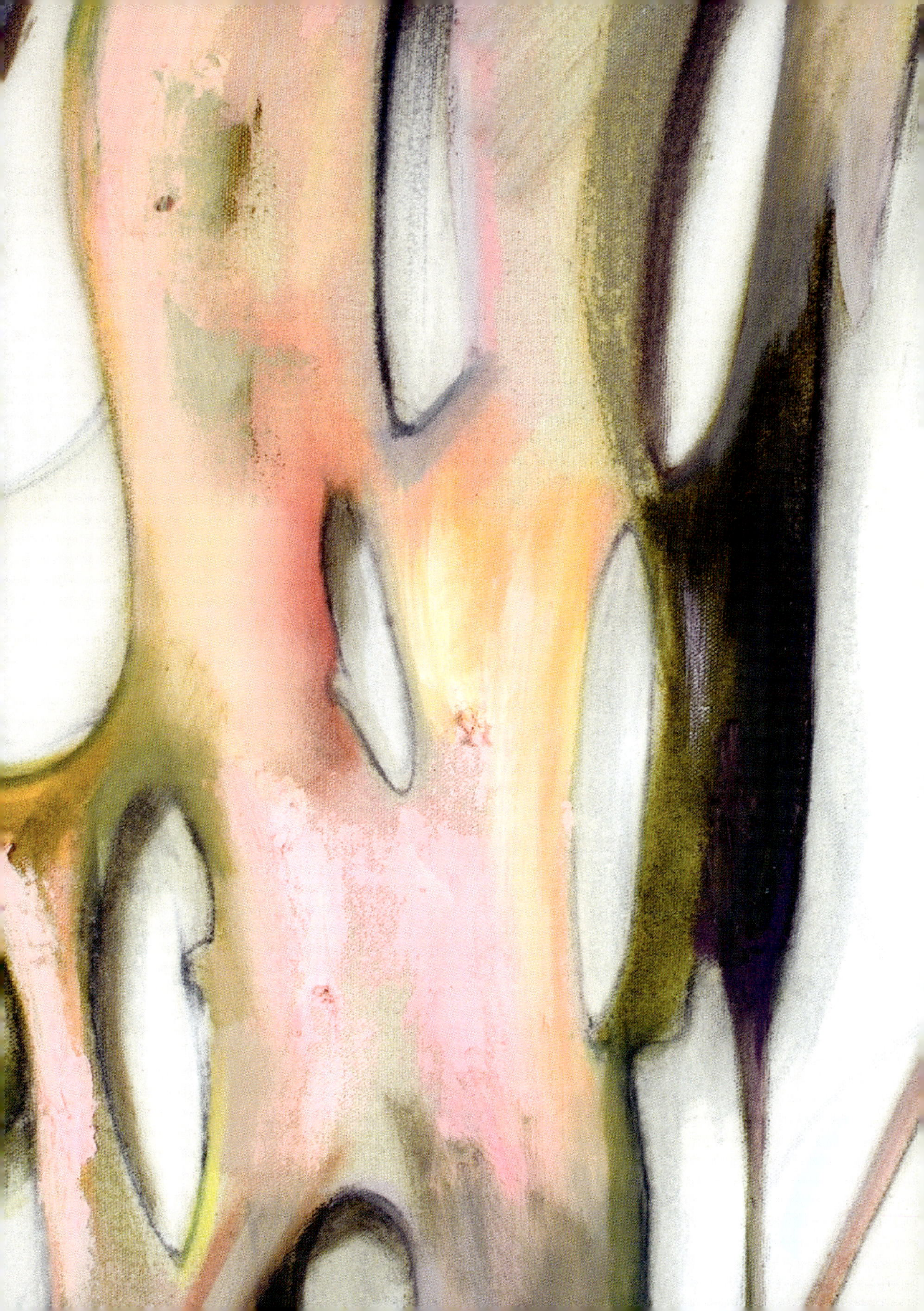

Selma Parlour

One, The Side-ness of In-Out

2015
Oil on linen
61 x 51 cm

My paintings are meticulously rendered through soft films of transparent oil so that imagery looks drawn or printed. Central to my invented vocabulary are: the frame, flatness, surface, transparency, *trompe l'oeil* illusion, repetition (with variation and displacement), and bands and units of isolated colour. In my interrogations of the technical problems of the medium, I frequently conceive of painting as a two-dimensional stage space that curtails fictive distance as it represents it.

Photographic reproductions of abstract painting often include the contextual space of the gallery. *One, The Side-ness of In-Out* draws on this convention to place abstract shapes in a 'room'. By way of a horizon line, two versions of the 'same' shape illustrate the two divergent spatial organisations accredited to painting: abstract (freely floating) or figurative (beholden to gravity). In turn, we can see each shape as either a painting or a sculpture. The repetition asks which is the referent and which the art, while the narrative considers painting's form as inclusive of, and reliant upon, the architecture of its surroundings.

Biography

Born in 1976 in Johannesburg, Selma Parlour attended De Montfort University Leicester 1995-8, University of Reading 1999-2002, Goldsmiths College London 2008-14. Exhibitions (London unless stated) include *Bloomberg New Contemporaries 2011* S1Artspace Sheffield/ ICA, *270112 Abstractions* LGLondon 2012, *Creative Cities Collection* Barbican 2012, *Selma Parlour & Yelena Popova* Horton Gallery New York 2012, *The Shape of Things* The Dot Project 2015, *The Shapes We're In* Bread & Jam 2015. Solos are *Selma Parlour* MOT International 2012, *Paradoxes of the Flattened-out Cavity* Dio Horia Mykonos 2015. Forthcoming: site-specific commission at The House of St Barnabas (from October 2016). In Thames and Hudson's *100 Painters of Tomorrow.*

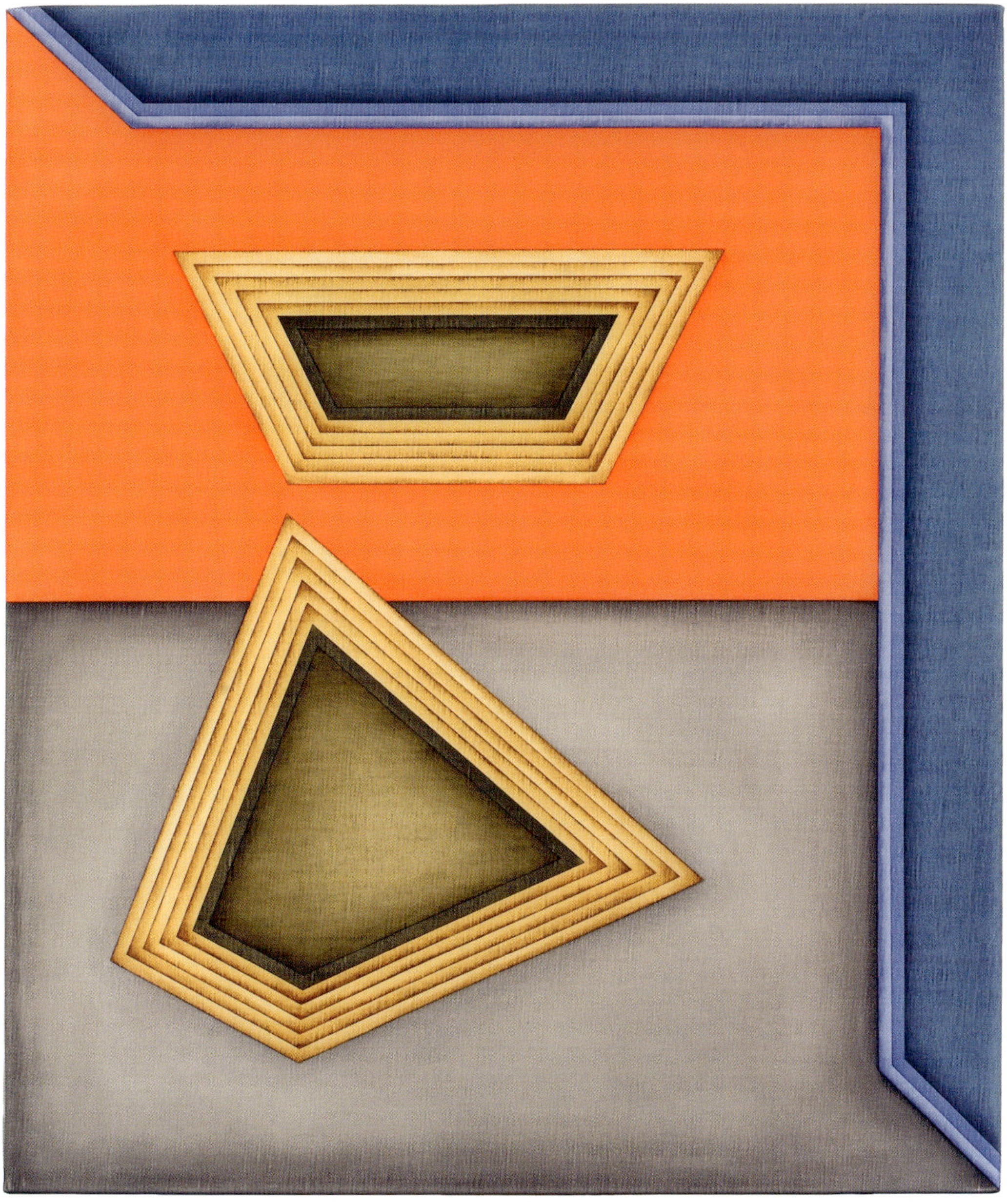

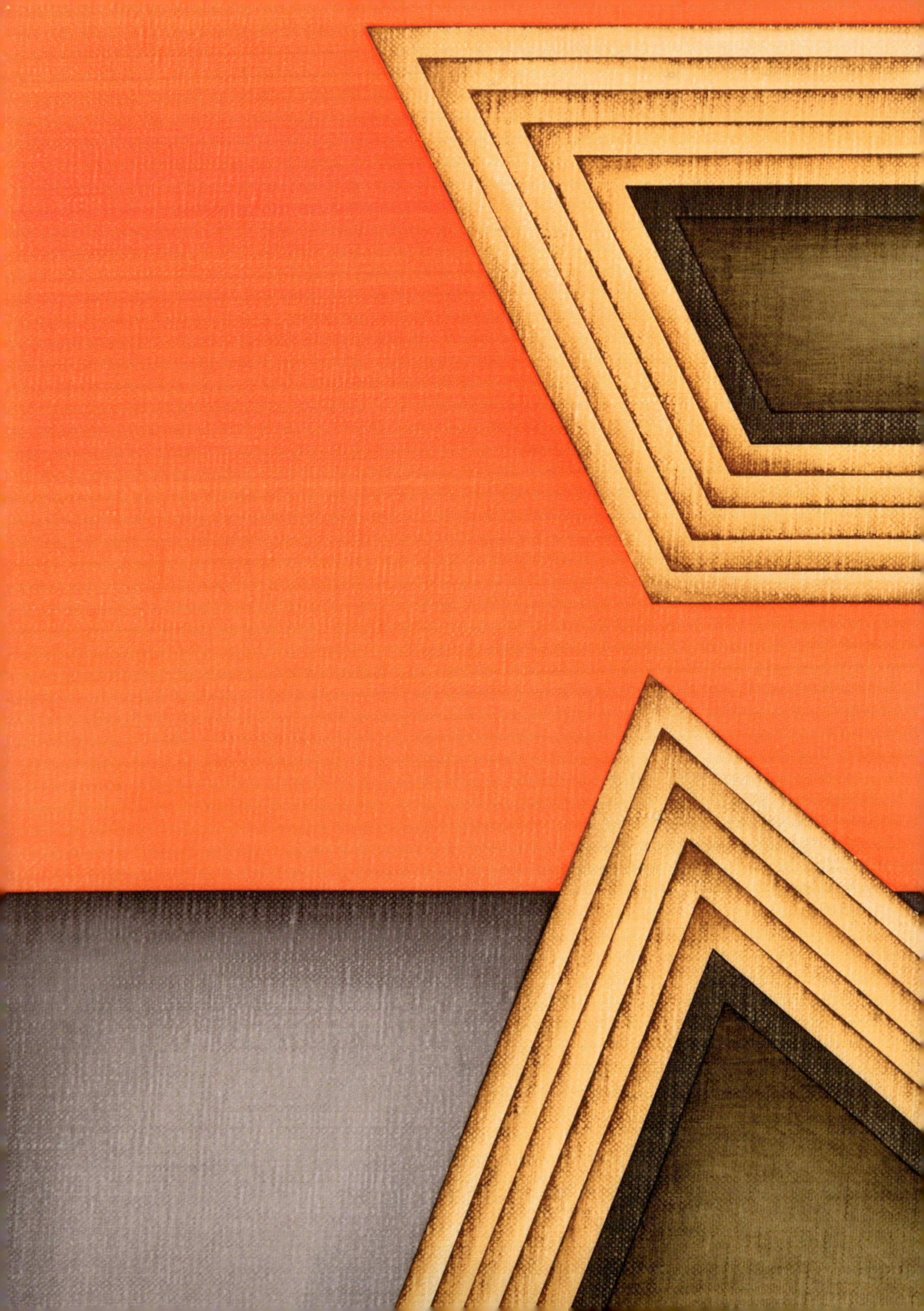

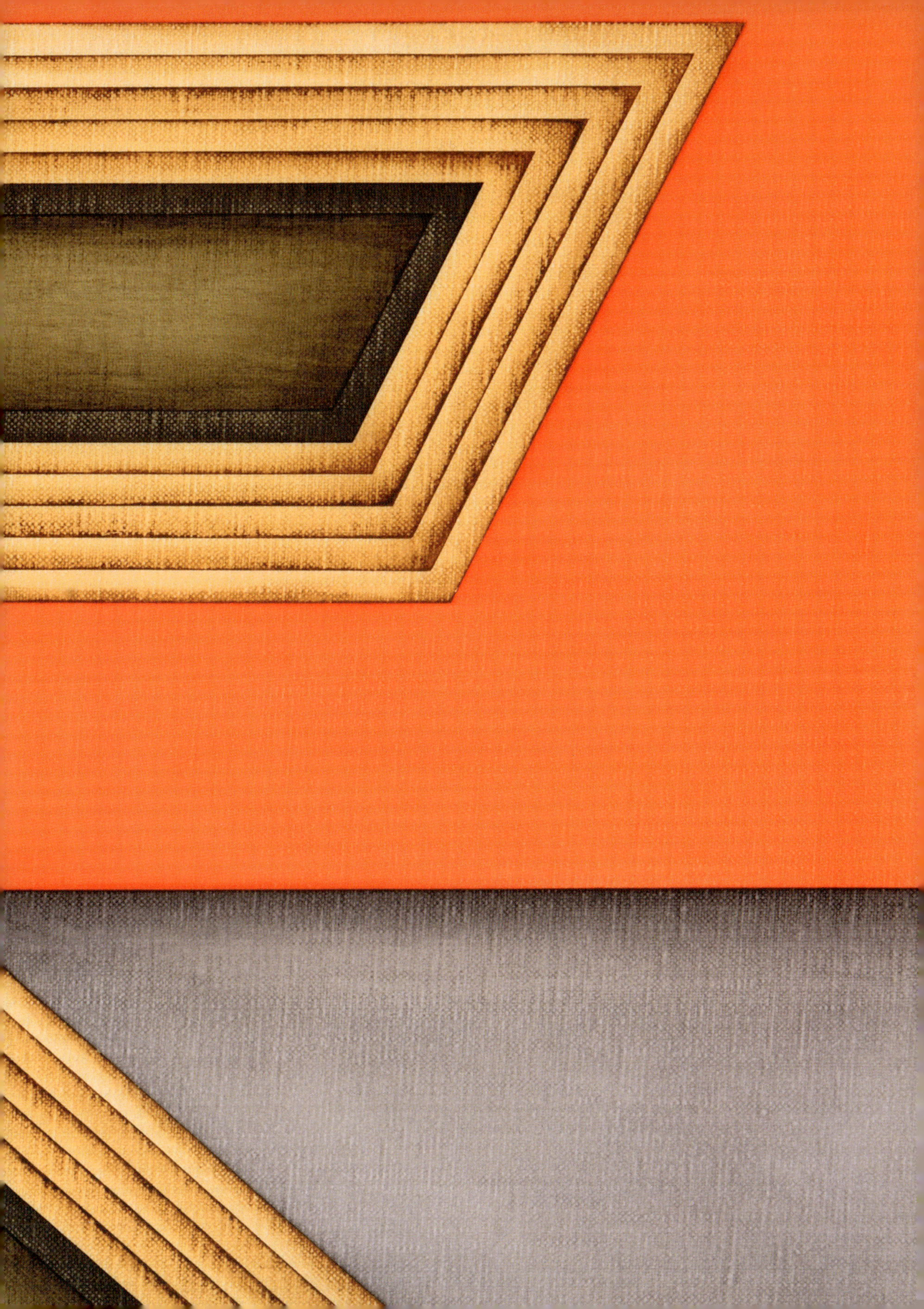

Artists

Tristan Barlow
Karl Bielik
Julian Brown
Nici Bungey
Bernard Charnley
Julie Cockburn
James Collins
Gemma Cossey
Ben Cove
Graham Crowley
William Dick
Sarah Dwyer
Bella Easton
Róisín Fogarty
Michael Ginsborg
Juliet Goodden
Steph Goodger
Christopher Hanlon
Linda Hemmersbach
Thom Trojanowski Hobson
Ira Hoffecker
Benjamin Jenner
Gareth Kemp
Nicholas Kulkarni
George Lloyd-Jones
Enzo Marra
Lee Marshall
Sneh Mehta

Nicholas Middleton
Nancy Milner
Frank Minoprio
Steve Moberly
Donal Moloney
David Murphy
Ewan Murray
Laurence Owen
Mandy Payne
playpaint
Alex Rennie
Tim Renshaw
Lizi Sánchez
John Stark
Duncan Swann
Shaan Syed
Emma Talbot
Julia Warr
Richard Kenton Webb
Simon Williams
Mary Wood

Tristan Barlow

Truck Stop Swamp

2015
Oil on linen
190.3 x 160.4 cm

My paintings are visual fictions with concrete reality; pictorial dialogues and spatial possibilities of experiences, observations and constructions. My work relies on a combination of pictorial integrity and the material building of surface and texture through paint. The spaces created within the paintings exist within a current of silent tension and deceptive stillness. The compression and expansion of spatial tensions and figurative cues create an autonomous work while alluding to a broader historical dialogue within painting.

Biography

Tristan Barlow was born in Jackson, Mississippi in 1990 and lives and works in London. He studied at the University of Southern Mississippi 2008-2012, New York Studio School of Drawing, Painting and Sculpture 2012-13, and the Slade School of Fine Art 2013-15 (awarded Barto dos Santos Memorial Award 2015). Recent exhibitions include the *Red Mansion Art Prize Exhibition 2015* Slade Research Centre London, *Creekside Open 2015* (selector Lisa Milroy) A.P.T London, *Slade MA/MFA/PhD Degree Show* Slade London 2015. Prizewinner *Red Mansion Art Prize* 2014. Residencies include *Vermont Studio Center Residency* Vermont USA 2013, *Red Gate Residency* Beijing 2014.

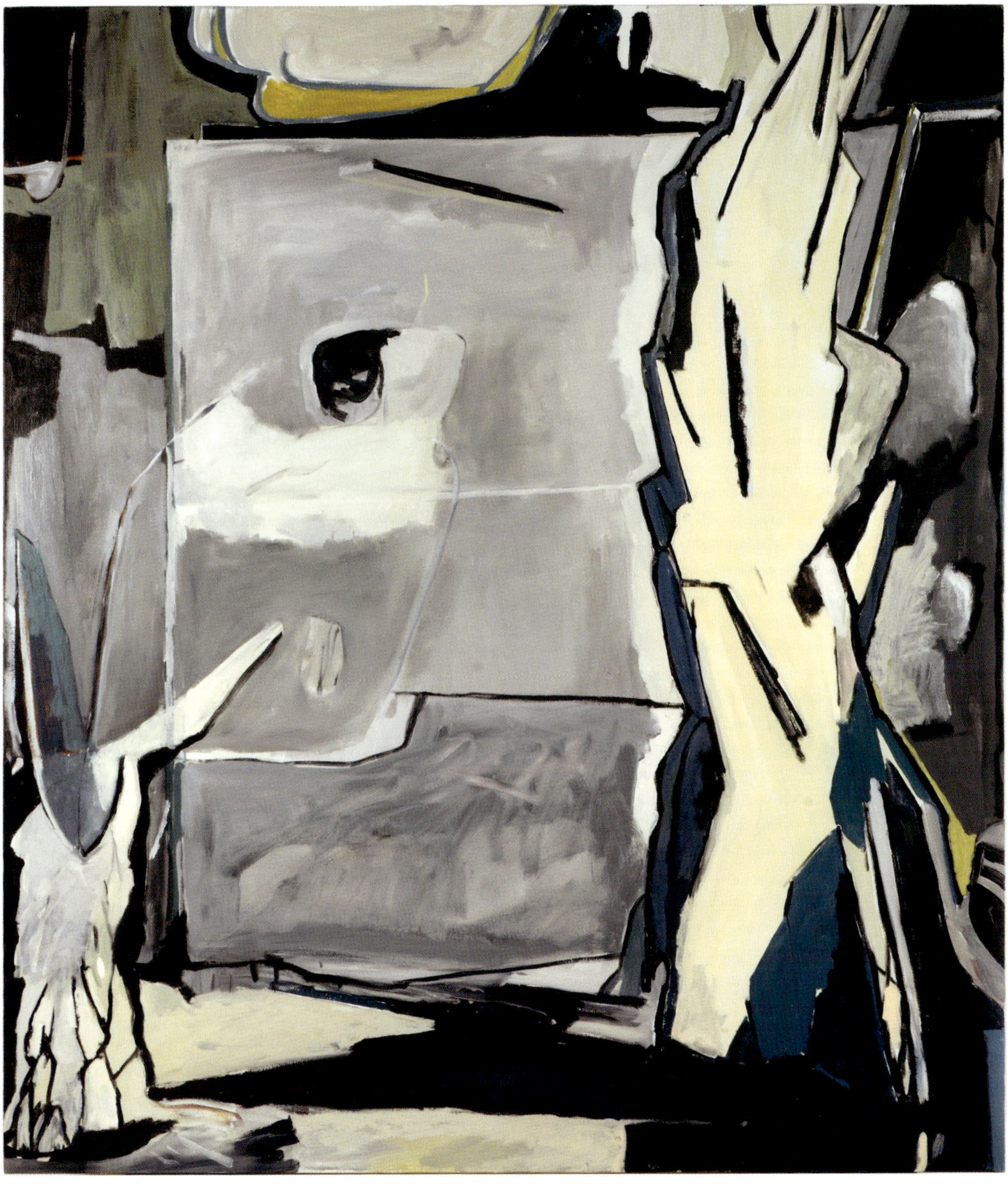

Karl Bielik

Sunday

2015
Oil on canvas
175 x 160 cm

Working on a multitude of paintings and drawings at a time, my brew of abstractions are developed in batches. Irregular canvases cover the studio walls and floors, and I shift from one painting to another, experimenting playfully with mark making.

Formal lines taken from photographs and diagrams contrast with loose, oily wounds, and thick emulsions offset light glazes and dribbles.

Also in contrast to this emotive imagery, banal solitary words form the titles, tempering and balancing the melancholy character of the paintings.

Biography

Born in Bradford in 1967, Karl Bielik studied at Halifax College 1987-9 and Stockport College 1989-91. He writes and performs in *Lark* and is Founder and Director of Terrace Studios and Gallery, London, where he is based. Exhibitions include *Creekside Open 2011* (selector Phyllida Barlow) A.P.T London, *The Marmite Painting Prize III* The Nunnery London 2011, *What I Like About You* Parallel Art Space New York 2013, *Eight Painters* Kathryn Markel New York 2014, *Infinity : One* dalla Rosa Gallery London 2014, *The London Open 2015* Whitechapel Gallery, *Contemporary British Drawing* Xi'an Academy of Fine Arts Xi'an Province China 2015.

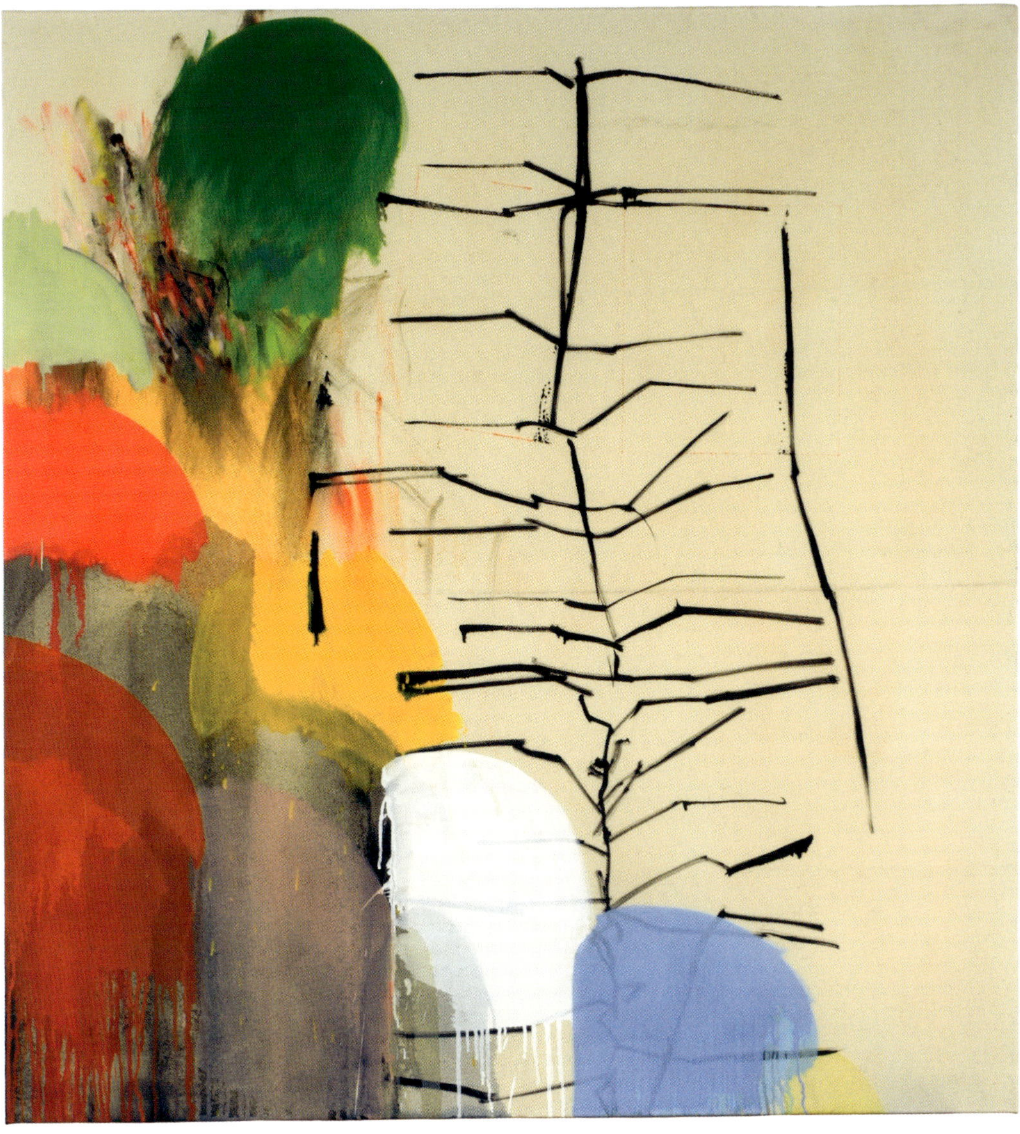

Julian Brown

A Fairytale of Gdansk

2015
Acrylic on linen
60.1 x 60.3 cm

My mind meanders to a scene from my childhood home of a humble landscape painting made by my mother shortly after she fled Poland, around the time of the Warsaw uprising.

I remember observing the painting like a love letter to her past. Etched into the landscape was a world of folklore, tradition and a longing to return to land then under Communist rule.

The composition of floating boats, trees and crescent moons still resonates in my subconscious, as does the collection of family artefacts and brightly-coloured *wycinanki* paper cut-outs that hung on the surrounding walls.

When I consider this I become aware that embedded deep into my psyche is not only a synthesis of western painting styles but also a continuation of a rich cultural tradition that animates this fairytale of abstract thought.

Biography

Julian Brown was born in Oxford in 1974 and is based in Brighton. He studied at Liverpool John Moores University 1993-6 and the Royal Academy Schools London 1998-2001. Exhibitions include *EMERGENCY⁵* Aspex Portsmouth 2011, *Marmite Prize for Painting IV* Central Art Gallery Tameside (touring) 2012/13, *@paintbritain* Ipswich Art School Gallery 2014, *Contemporary British Drawing* Xi'an Academy of Fine Arts Xi'an Province China 2015. Solos include *Julian Brown* The Mayor's Parlour London 2013, *Julian Brown* The Crypt at St Marylebone London 2014, *A Sense of Wonder* York College Gallery 2016. He is represented in the Falmouth Art Gallery, Abbot Hall and Priseman Seabrook Collections.

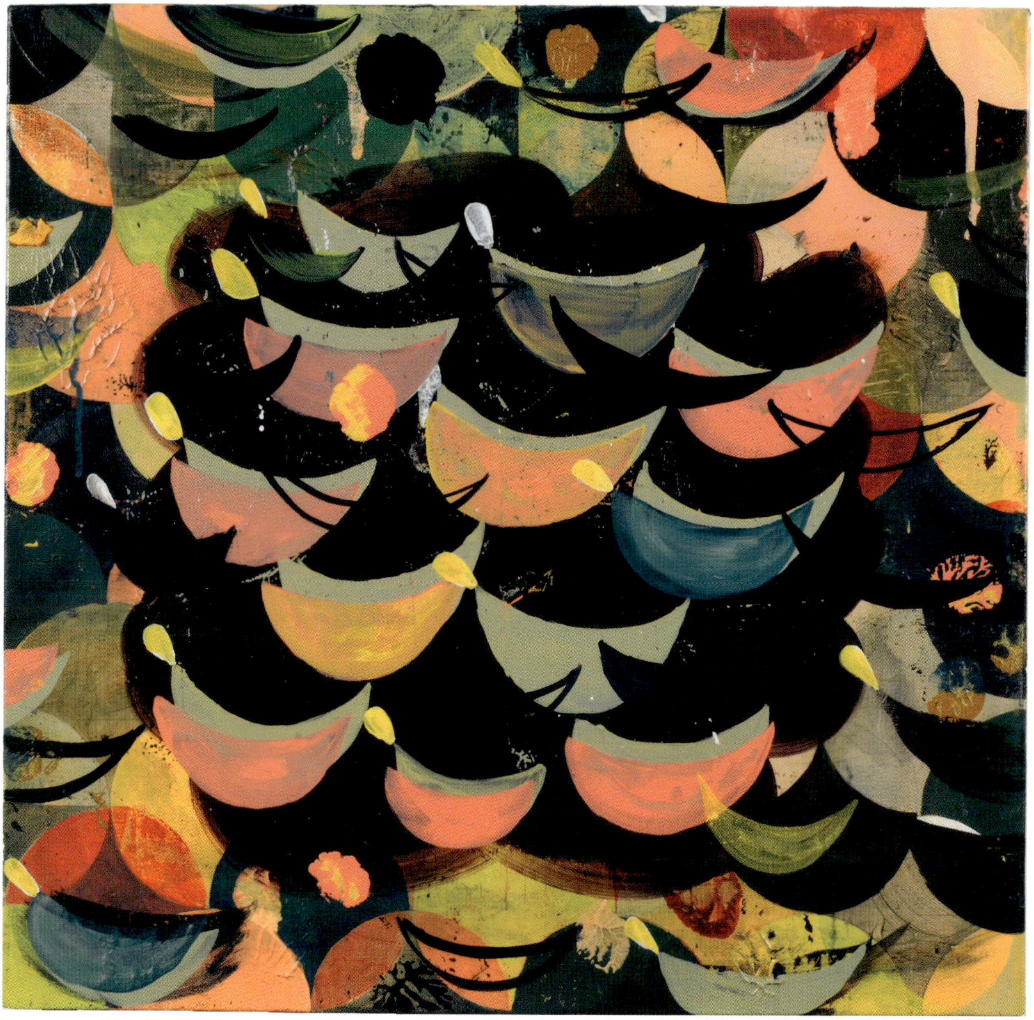

Nici Bungey

The Expiring Frog

2014
Acrylic on paper
43.2 x 38.2 cm

In 2014 I started a series of paintings using old book pages. *The Expiring Frog* is one of the first pieces I created. The pages are not only my canvas but become part of the painting.

There is a sense of freedom to begin with. The work can take any form – it's an open situation. I find basic shapes and relationships then gradually move deeper in, working with the colours, their proportions and combinations. I enter into the painting, feel its changes in weight. It is a matter of both revealing and concealing: a fold makes an edge and conceals an area. Each step has its own logic but at the same time it's an intuitive process. This is about the past and present, emotion and energy. The surfaces of my work are only the uppermost visible, the skin of the painting. These pieces grow and there is always a moment when the tension of their making is suddenly resolved.

Biography

Born in Germany in 1967, Nici Bungey is based in Haslemere. She studied at Schule für Gestaltung Basel 1991-3, London College of Printing 1993-6 and Winchester School of Art 2007-8. Exhibitions (London unless stated) are *F9* The Chocolate Factory 2011, *Sedici* (group) and *Transcience* (solo) Shed Petersfield 2012, *Libero* and *Suspension* One Padget Street 2013, *House on Fire* Embassy Tea Gallery 2014, *UND* (two person) Gallery Muse Petersfield 2014, *Summer Exhibition 2015* Royal Academy, *Art on a Postcard* Revue Gallery 2015, *The National Open Art Exhibition* Harrogate International Visual Arts Expo 2015, *Approaching the Edge* (solo) Revue Gallery 2015.

Bernard Charnley

When the stars threw down their spears

2015
Oil on canvas
91.8 x 122 cm

This title was reached by chance and, I like to think, by a kind of recognition across time. I'm interested in how a title or language can shape reception of a work, and so Googled arbitrary title lists. This William Blake line from *Songs of Experience* intrigued me and the apocalyptic spirit of his poetry, with its recognition of the human devastation of his time, also connected. My painting exists perhaps in the same territory, even though over 200 years later. It depicts an extraordinary event in an undefined landscape, with implications of disaster. And yet there is also, arguably, an exuberance at work in the interplay of colour and light and in the act of painting.

The painting is also one of a series marking a change of direction in my handling of paint and subject matter. Colour, glazing and scumbling take an active role and the play between disruption and place becomes visible.

Biography

Bernard Charnley was born in Reading in 1948. Attended Leeds College of Art 1966-8, London University Institute of Education 1977-80. Studied philosophy with the Open University 2001-4. Exhibitions include *Identity* The Art Organisation Nottingham 2007, *SALON* D2 Gallery Leipzig 2008, *Interrogation: Walsall* New Art Gallery Walsall 2009, *Common Ground Art Trail* (AirSpace project) Hanley Park Stoke-on-Trent 2010, *Kiss Me Quick* Harbour Arm Gallery Margate 2011, *Airvent* AirSpace Gallery Stoke-on-Trent 2011. Solos include *A Different Kind of Beauty* Harrington Mill Studios Nottingham 2009, *The Instability of Spaces* (AirSpace Dialogue Box) Airspace Gallery 2009, *Signs Of Disorder* Rugby Art Gallery & Museum 2014.

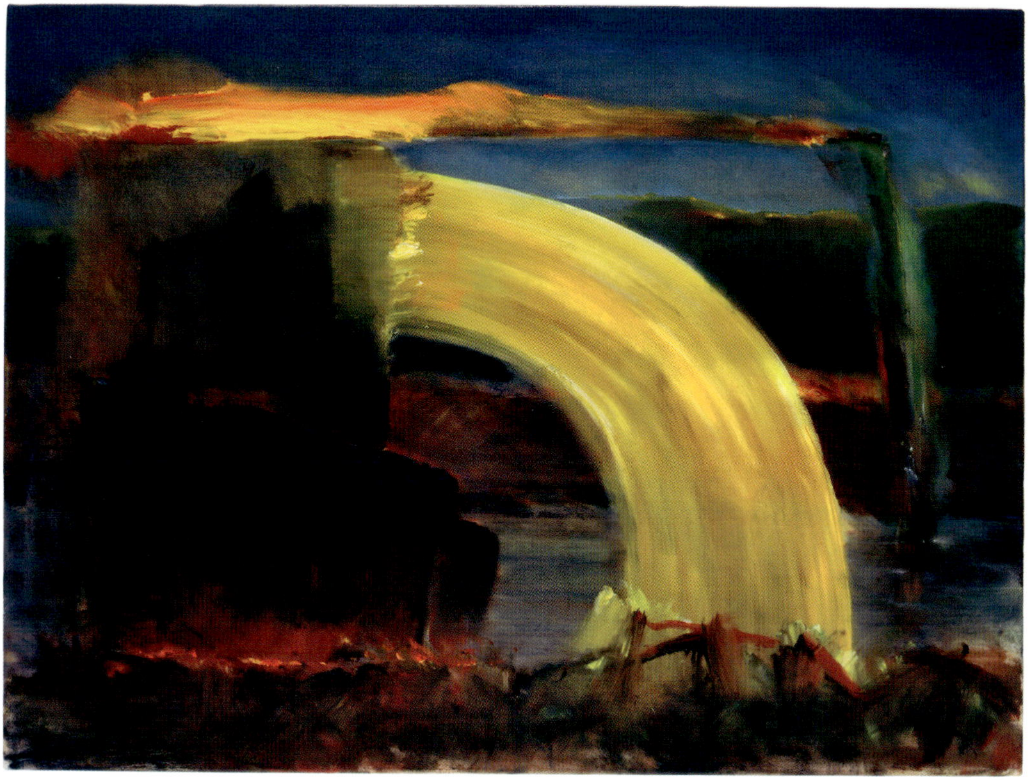

Julie Cockburn

The Playground

2015
Plasticine and acrylic paint on altered book cover
22.4 x 28.3 cm

My usual practice involves carefully controlled and labour intensive collage and embroidery and making *The Playground* was an antidote to this. Working on an abstract painting is liberating for me and I found myself trying to strike a balance between this opportunity to indulge in creative play and the discipline of formal composition. Although there are echoes of collage and sculpture here (the familiar adding and subtracting of material, cutting, breaking down and re-assembling), this work holds its own for me as a painting. I find myself captivated by it.

I have painted with Plasticine, a three-dimensional material that either sinks into or stays proud of the picture plane. The beautiful stains it left on the cardboard were unexpected. Right at the end I took a risk and cut the piece in half – I didn't have anything to lose. I then discovered that when you randomly cut a rectangle in two and put the halves back together in reverse, they make a perfect rhomboid. My willingness to follow my playful intuition was rewarded with a satisfying mathematical resolution.

Biography

Born in 1966 in London, Julie Cockburn studied sculpture there at Central Saint Martins 1993-6. Exhibitions include *RIFF/T* Baltic39 Newcastle 2013, *'Of Green Leaf, Bird, and Flower': Artists' Books and the Natural World* Yale Center for British Art New Haven 2014, *Soft Target* M + B Los Angeles 2014, *Morphisisation* A.P.T London 2014, *Jerwood Drawing Prize* 2007, 2010, 2015 Jerwood Space London (touring), *FOUND* New Art Gallery Walsall 2015. Solos are *Portraits and Landscapes* Flowers Gallery (Cork St) London 2012, *Slight Exposure* Yossi Milo Gallery New York 2013, *Waiting Room* Flowers Gallery (Kingsland Rd) London 2014. Included in *John Moores Painting Prize 2012.*

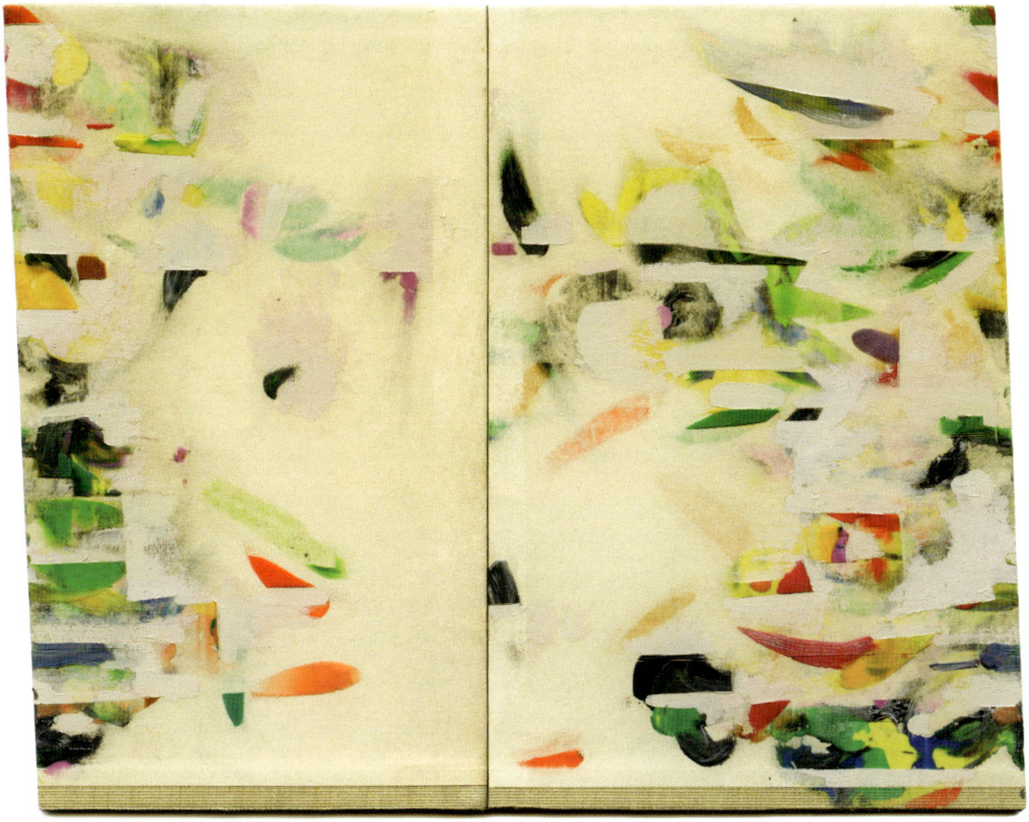

James Collins

Floyd

2015
Oil on canvas
206.4 x 160 cm

I view painting as pragmatic yet romantic, and the relationships that occur on the canvas as essential. Although this is an intuitive process, I find it is fundamentally highly informed in an equal measure.

My practice explores perceptions of pictorial space and the extent to which figuration can be used as a tool for pictorial inquiries. I am interested in the notions of 'quality' or 'legitimacy' in painting, and I propose to examine questionable tropes and trends that occur in painting.

I often deliberately incorporate what is usually incidental visual information, such as gradients or excessive volumes of drips, in order to highlight their presence when such apparitions often pass as only collateral charm. Motifs gradually develop between painting to painting, and some parts of one painting that could be seen as unnecessary may develop into an integral part of the next, as a manifestation of indifference to the value assigned to each component.

Biography

James Collins was born in Darlington in 1992. He lives and works in London and studied there at Wimbledon College of Art 2012-15 and the Royal College of Art 2015-17. Recent exhibitions (London unless stated) include *Demimonde* (Slate Projects/Mottahedan Projects) Amberwood House 2015, *The Blank Back Of A Sign* The Front Room 2015, *Piercing the Veil* Simmons & Simmons 2015, *Bloomberg New Contemporaries 2015, Backlit* One Thoresby St & Primary Nottingham/ICA London, *Dark Ages* Geddes Gallery 2016, *Work-in-Progress Show* RCA 2016, *Four Painters* (Slate Projects) The Averard Hotel 2016. A solo show *Threeworks* was at Three Works Weymouth 2015.

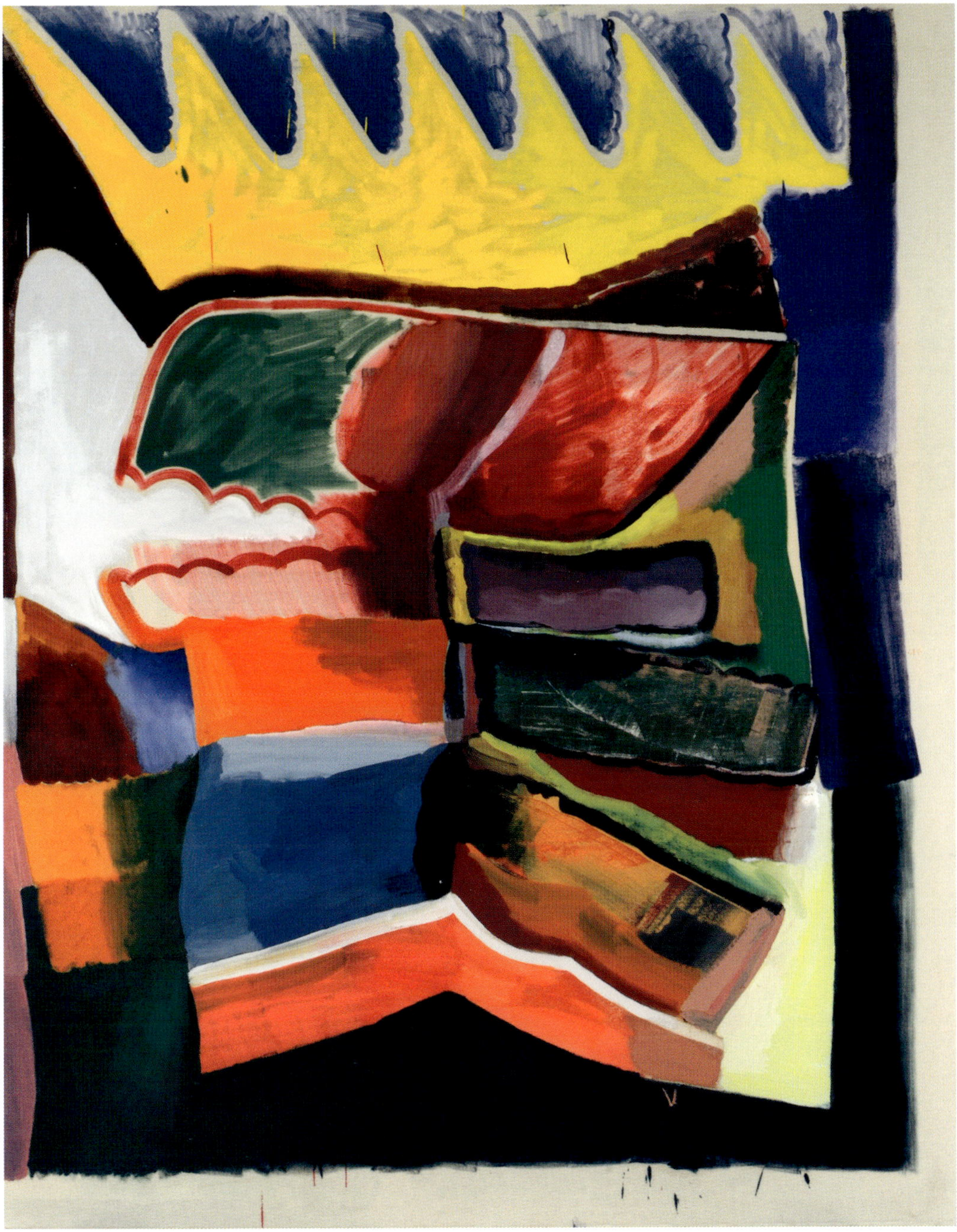

Gemma Cossey

Halves II (Continuum)

2015
Acrylic, water-based pigment paint and gesso on canvas
101.3 x 101.5 cm

This painting is part of a series entitled *Continuum* which explores scale, repetition and the relationship between parts and the whole. Repeated marks and gestures are gradually constructed using white and near-black. The overall balance and interaction between mark making and background only appear to make sense on completion of the chosen process, and often differently from how I imagined. One intention is to create distinct viewing experiences: the calm minimalism of a distant gaze and something else revealed or discovered when the work is experienced at close hand.

In recent paintings the use of a brush-tipped paint pen has allowed me to paint a continuous line across a large surface, one that is fast-flowing enough to travel over the texture of acrylic on canvas. Beginning with a line that follows the canvas edge, the lengthy process then establishes its own rhythm, and although controlled by a set of rules, in a sense the painting develops arbitrarily. This is an ongoing interest, exploring the relationship and conversation between two processes – one that is intended and planned, and another that is allowed to evolve intuitively or serendipitously. Often ideas begin with playful experimentation but are regulated by parameters and constraints.

Biography

Born in Bridgwater in 1974, Gemma Cossey studied at Somerset College of Arts & Technology 1992-3, De Montfort University Leicester 1993-6 and, 1998-2000, at De Montfort, Fontys Academy Tilburg, Granada University Spain. Exhibitions (London unless stated) include *Jam Tomorrow* A.P.T 2012, *Motorcade/FlashParade National Open 2012* M/FP Bristol, *Discernible* Zeitgeist Arts Projects 2013, *Creekside Open 2013* (selector Paul Noble) A.P.T, *Pistols & Pollinators II* (an Accident & Emergence project) The Albert Kilburn 2013, *Drawn* RWA Bristol 2015, *Autocatalytic Future Games* no format 2015, *Griffin Gallery Open* 2015, *Lines for Agnes* The Crypt at St Marylebone 2015, *The London Group Open* Cello Factory 2015.

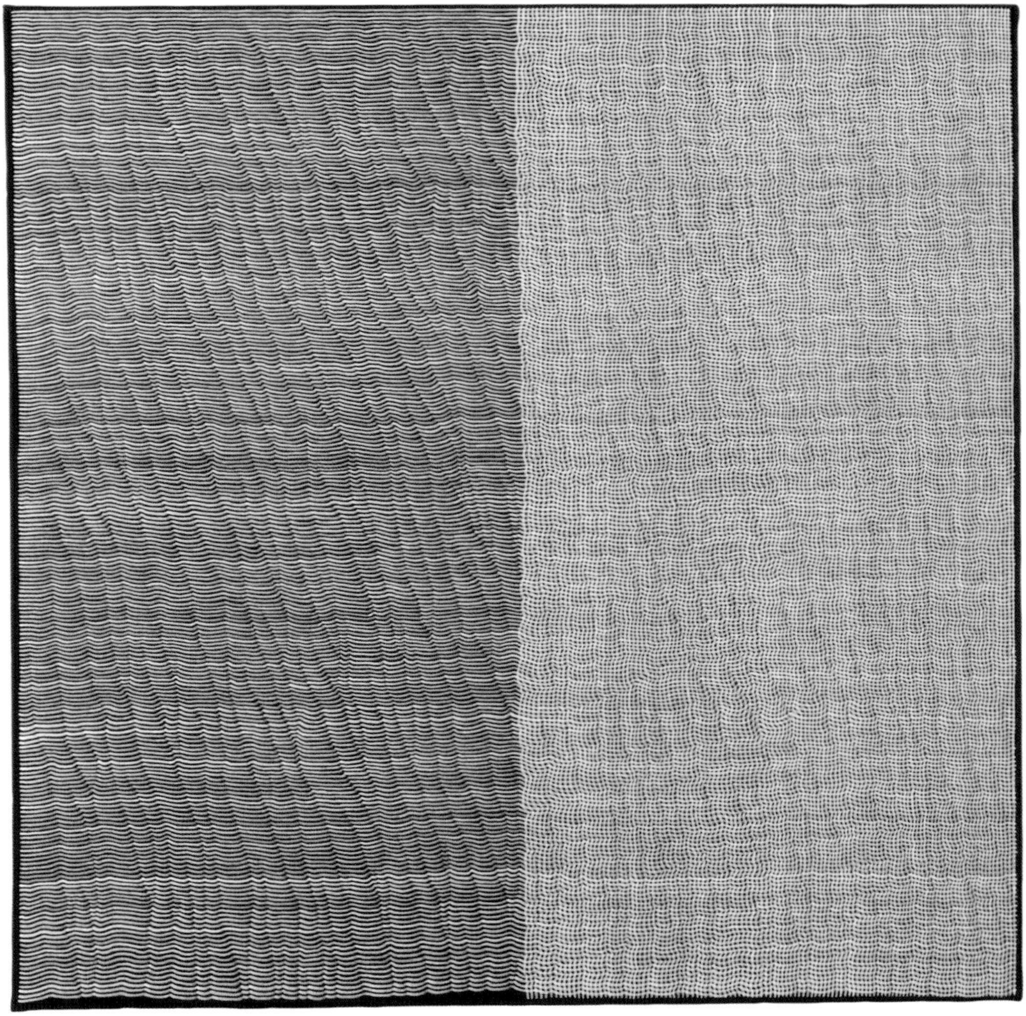

Ben Cove

Freeloader

2014
Acrylic on panel
40 x 40 cm

The paintings embrace multiple forms of representation, moving between mimesis and abstraction – things to hold onto amongst the uncertainties. A bank of images that includes architecture, furniture, artefacts, product design and depictions of the body serve as source material. These images are selected both for their formal interest and for the position of authority they come to occupy through shifting narratives and processes of association and assimilation. Little is translated directly from these images. Forms are evoked in order to render something that seems valid, dumb, familiar, discordant and alien.

In order to work against habitual instincts, the paintings begin with little pre-planning and evolve through a process of often drastic editing. These failed gestures are embraced as a necessity and are visible in the surface. What remains is clearly constructed, a fiction built on a series of narratives resulting in something that perhaps only makes sense to itself.

The John Moores Liverpool Exhibition Trust and John Moores Project Team offer condolences to the family and friends of Ben Cove. We thank them for their permission to show the painting Ben submitted before his death, in memory of his talent and dedication to the practice of painting.

Biography

Ben Cove (1974-2016) was born in Wiltshire. Studied Architecture, University of Nottingham 1995-8, Fine Art Sheffield Hallam University 1998-2001 and Goldsmiths, University of London 2006-8. Exhibitions (London unless stated) include *East London Painting Prize* Strand East 2014, *Tomb, Shrine, Survey-Marker, Spare Part* Enclave 2014, *Indefinable Cities* AirSpace Gallery Stoke-on-Trent/Art Takahashi Hikone Japan 2015, *A Putting Down of Roots* Gallery 1C03 Winnipeg 2015, *Ben Cove & Kate Terry: Plane to Line to Point* dalla Rosa 2015, *The London Open 2015* Whitechapel Gallery, *In Schönheit Auferstehen* Galerie Patrick Ebensperger Berlin 2015. Solos include *Vernacular Hangover* Acme Project Space 2013, *Modern Language* Peter von Kant 2015. Forthcoming solo at Aspex Portsmouth 2016.

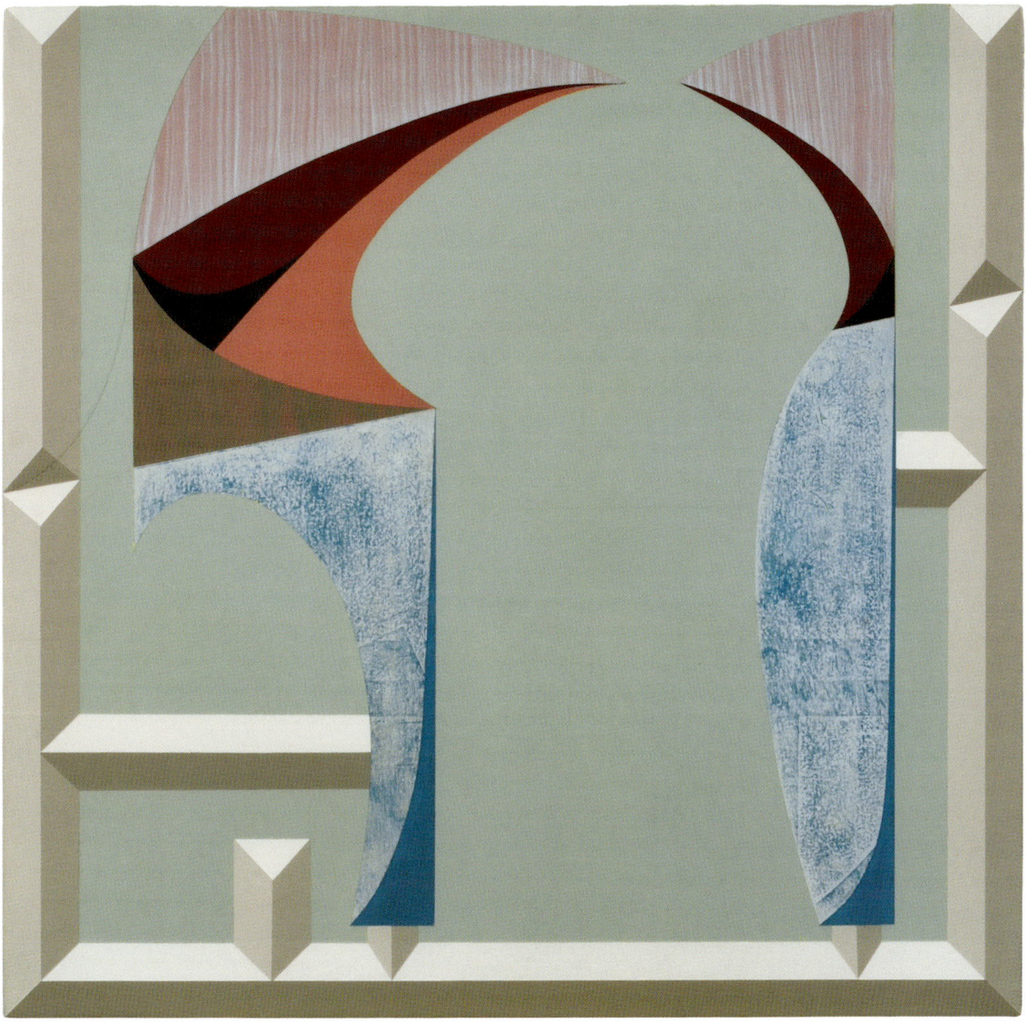

Graham Crowley

Blue Drift 4

2015
Oil on canvas
92 x 122 cm

Reflections and shadows have always fascinated me. They epitomise illusion, in that they don't exist in any concrete sense. This marks them out as 'the stuff of painting' – visible and intangible, familiar and incoherent.

As a child I witnessed the flooding of Canvey Island in 1953. The experience has never left me. These memories have recently been reanimated by our growing awareness of climate change and the increased prevalence of flooding. Water is ubiquitous, essential and beguiling. It is also deadly.

As I get older there are fewer certainties. Apprehension becomes a way of life. I need to acknowledge this sense of unease. The play between light and illusion creates a sense of misapprehension and disorientation.

Painting allows us the opportunity to contemplate a particular moment in a world of contingency and change. Just as fear can be exhilarating, so tranquillity can be disturbing. Painting may be static but thought is constantly shifting.

Biography

Born in Romford in 1950, Graham Crowley attended London's St Martin's School of Art 1968-72, Royal College of Art 1972-5. In 1982 became artist-in-residence Oxford University and Fellow of St Edmund's Hall. Professor of Painting RCA 1998-2006. Exhibitions include *Reality: Modern and Contemporary British Painting* SCVA Norwich/Walker Art Gallery 2014/15, *Anti-Social Realism* Charlie Smith London 2015. Solos include West Cork Arts Centre Skibbereen 2008, *Graham Crowley* Cross Gallery Dublin 2014. Martin Holman's book *Graham Crowley* 2009. Graham's book *"I don't like art"* 2015. In several public collections. In eight *John Moores Painting Prize* exhibitions (joint second prize 1987, prize 2006) and a juror in 2008.

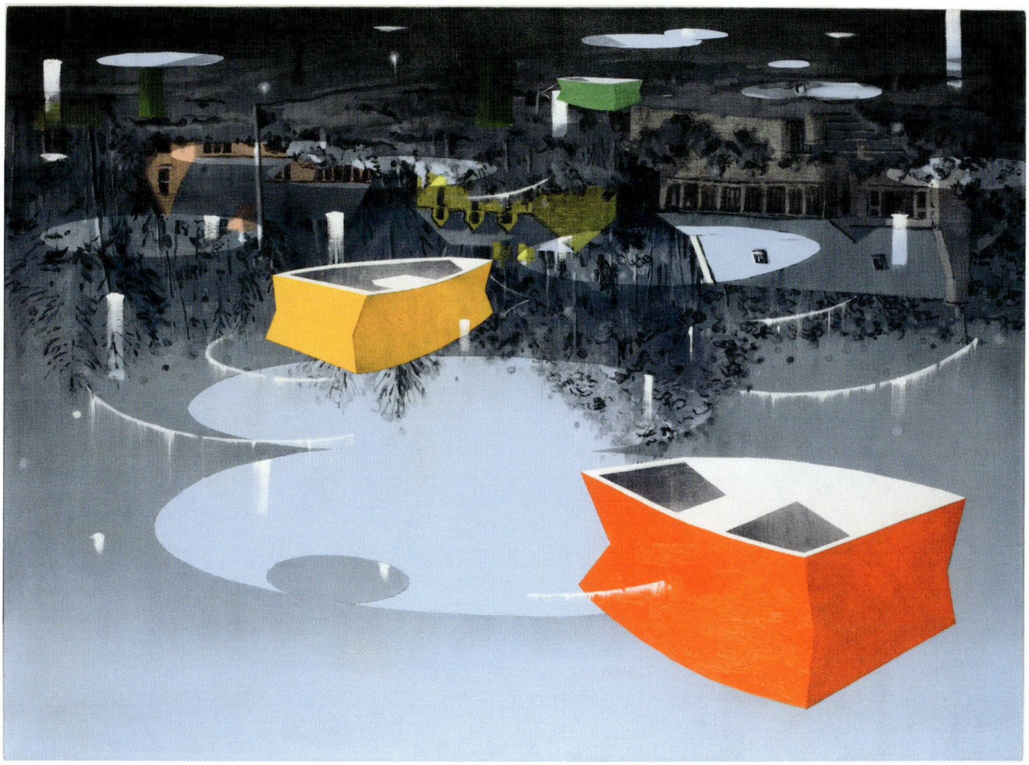

William Dick

Oldal II

2015
Mixed media on paper
154.5 x 149.5 cm

I have always accepted the notion that there are two distinct forms of abstract painting, namely geometric and organic. Given this, my work explores the questions that arise from examining a minimalist structure in an expressively painterly way, to produce objects which embrace the purest language of painting. These works transcend the illustrative, treating drawing as a mark making process. By offering themselves as physical objects, paradoxically they are able to create in the mind of the spectator an imaginary, ambiguous, atmospheric world that is wholly located in the abstract language of painting.

I commence with the fundamental balance between line and colour and have drawn on ancient symbolic shapes from my Scottish heritage. The apparent appropriation of forms found in Celtic and other ancient art represents an attempt to create an historical context for my modernist language beyond the confines of the Western tradition. Regarding colour, I begin from an observation of geological form and the very substance of the land – of dust, sand, mud and rock – as well as the outcrop of local street furniture or architecture. I also look to the weather, and the effects of weathering, along with the extreme and exotic colours of lichen, peat and mosses.

Biography

Born in Glasgow in 1950, William Dick studied at Glasgow School of Art 1971-2, Duncan of Jordanstone College of Art Dundee 1972-7, St Martin's School of Art London 1977-8. Awards include Pollock-Krasner Foundation USA 1989, British Council Moscow/Russia 1992, Adolph & Esther Gottlieb Foundation USA 2001. Residencies/workshops include Bemis Foundation Omaha 1989/90, Crawford Arts Centre St Andrews 1991, Triangle Artists' Workshop New York 2004, Yaddo Artists' Residence Saratoga Springs New York 2006, Artists' Workshop Szeged Hungary 2015. Solos include Pier Arts Centre Stromness 1990, Limerick City Art Gallery 1996, UNESCO Gallery Amman 2001, forthcoming Lillie Art Gallery Milngavie 2017. In public collections worldwide.

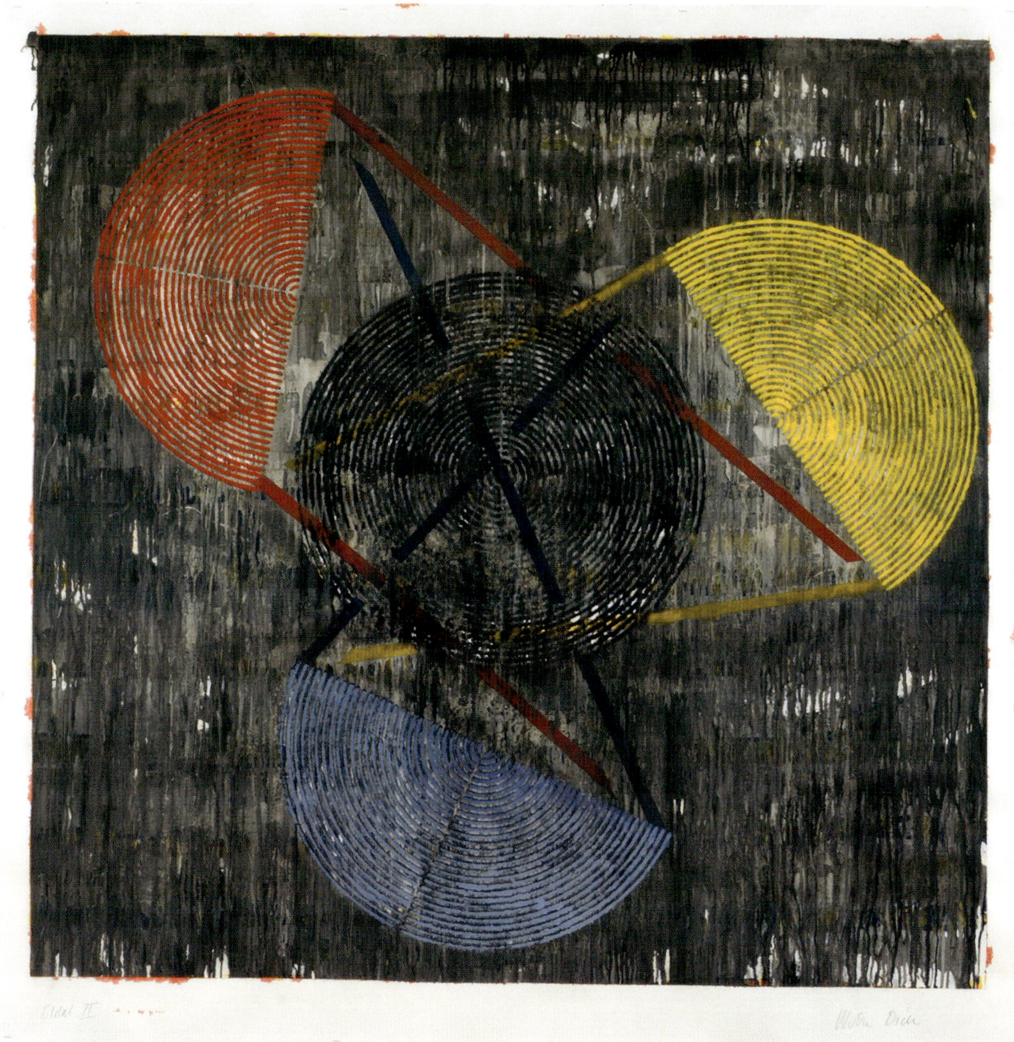

Sarah Dwyer

Potrero

2015
Oil on linen
142 x 132.4 cm

My process of conceiving an image is rooted in the line, and always retains the impulsive nature of drawing. A scratched mark might suggest the contours of a landscape, a stream carved out of a hillside, a figure, or a portrait. The form that finds its way through always settles back into an unresolved entanglement, where the pictorial narrative is in constant flux.

Citing many different literary sources, poetry, folkloric traditions and mythology, the written word at times can be the key to tracing the path etched out in the paintings. Pictorially, one can find kinship with the European history of landscape painting, stretching back to the Romanticism of Caspar David Friedrich, and onwards to the more localised landscape painters of St Ives, as well as the tenets of Surrealism and New York School high modernism.

The act of painting is a cathartic one for me. This work is suggestive of personal and shared histories, drawing on myth, religion and psychoanalysis, in order to grasp the real within the imaginary. Like the memory of a dream, *Potrero* exists on the outskirts of understanding, occupying a space between physical reality and the subconscious.

Biography

Born in Cork in 1974, Sarah Dwyer studied Environmental Economics York University 1993-6, Fine Art Staffordshire University 1999-2001, Painting Royal College of Art London 2002-4. Exhibitions include *ARTfutures* Bloomberg Space London 2007, *Daily Miracles* Josh Lilley London 2009, *Fear, Lo and Behold* Salon de Vortex Athens 2011, *New Order II* Saatchi Gallery London 2014, *I shall stay the way I am because I do not give a damn...'* Lombard Freid Gallery New York 2014. Solos include Kevin Kavanagh Gallery Dublin 2011, *Falling into Positions* Josh Lilley 2012, *Whip-poor-will* Josh Lilley 2014, *Sunk Under* Jane Lombard Gallery New York 2015.

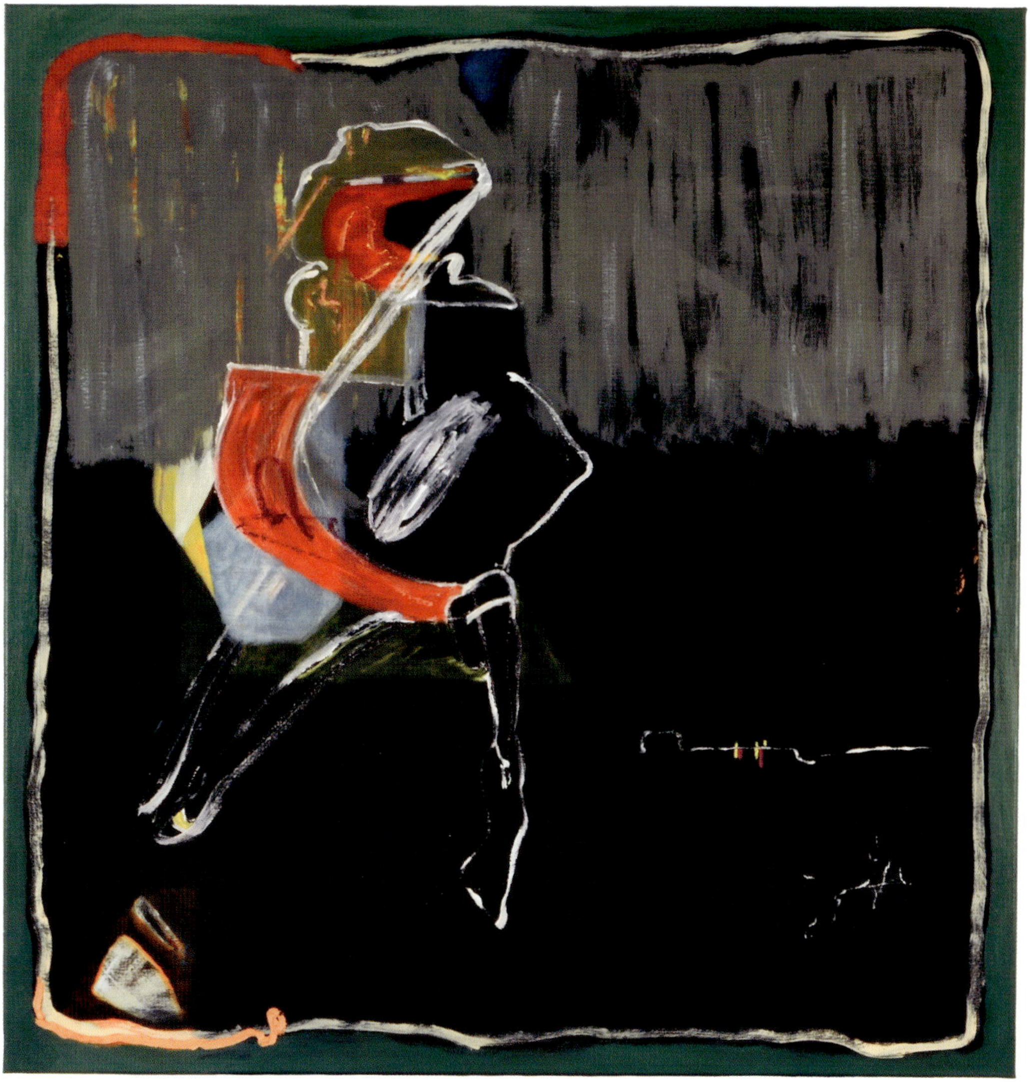

Bella Easton

Passageways

2015
Oil on 88 pieces of linen
230.2 x 168.2 cm

Passageways is one of a series of large paintings formed from small-scale drawings of real places, reconfigured into an immersive fabrication made from a geometric framework of 88 painted linen panels.

The intimacy of this domestic interior is fragmented, and the process applies a further distorting and distancing. Each section is made by applying thin layers of oil paint over a long period of time, during which the panels are pinned to the studio wall. Pressure and touch are used to offset the paint marks between them in order to create mirror images. These symmetrical dissections are equals and rely on each other to co-exist. My method is a kind of controlled spontaneity generating abstract effects into a figurative ground. Each section has its own personality, so that when the panels are spliced together, harmonies and dissonances arise, forming relationships.

For me, making a painting is a journey of complementary opposites. I employ actions that are contradicted or opposed until equilibrium is reached. That system may be set up to seek perfection but is interrupted by an interference of incongruous glitches and borrowed light. A scratched, disturbed space begins to emerge, giving clues to some other memory, time and place.

Biography

Born in Epsom in 1971, Bella Easton attended Winchester School of Art 1990-3, Royal Academy Schools London 1997-2000, City and Guilds of London Art School 2000-02. Exhibitions include *Summer Exhibition 2013* (invited artist), *2015* RA London, *The Opinion Makers* (curator) Londonewcastle Projects London 2014, *Flowers of Romance* White Conduit Projects London 2015, *Griffin Gallery Open* London 2015, *Illegitimate Objects* Mathematics Institute Oxford 2015, *Collateral Drawing* (curator, with Paul Carey-Kent) rosalux Berlin & (curator, with John Stark) UCS East Anglia 2015, The *Future Can Wait* Art Bermondsey Project Space London 2015, *Spaced Out* ENIA Gallery Athens 2016, *Foreign Affairs* A Brooks Art, Art Athina Athens 2016.

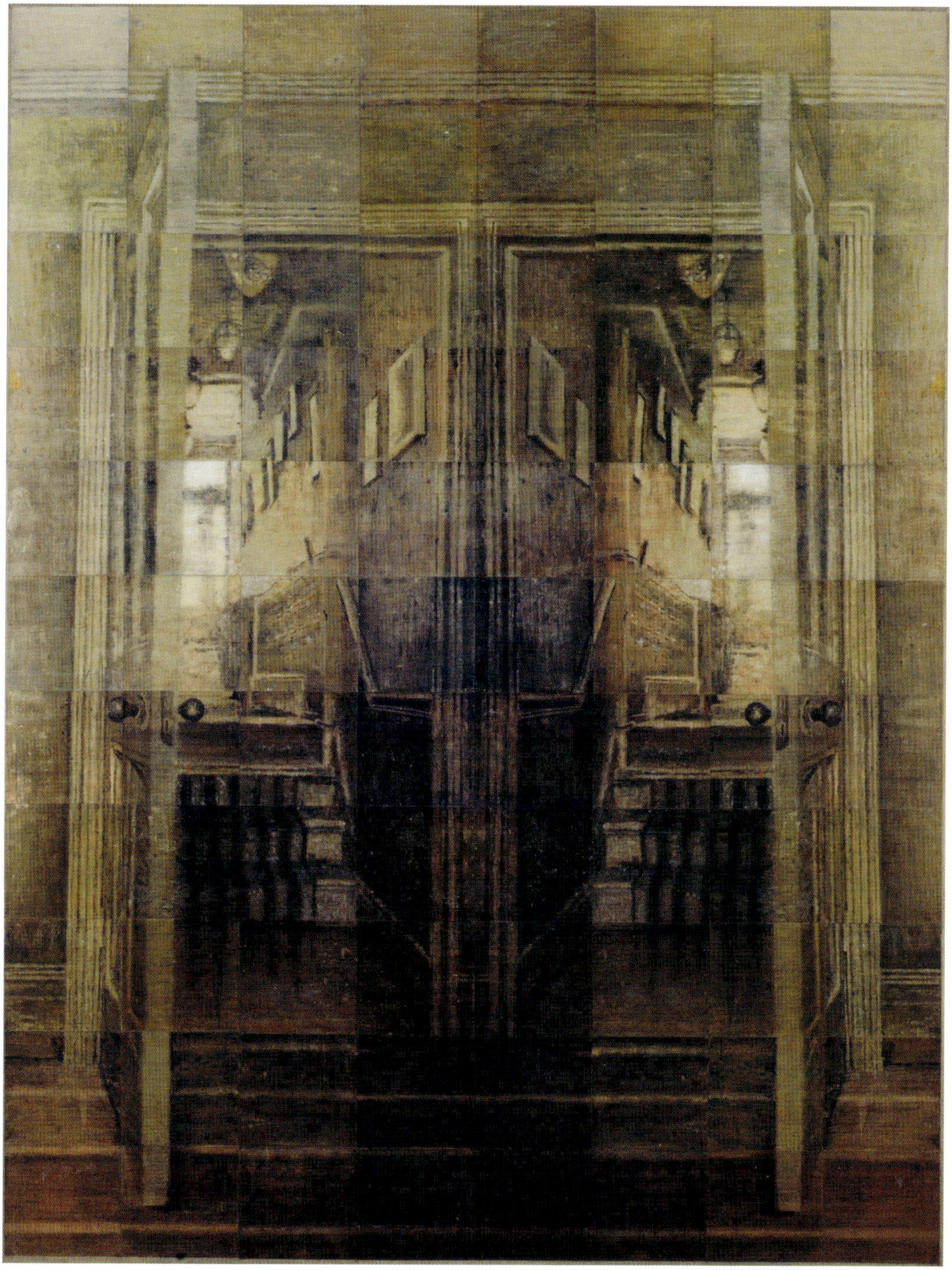

Róisín Fogarty

Goofy Foot

2015
Oil on canvas
61 x 81.5 cm

Goofy Foot combines imagery from an outdoor basketball court in Walworth, south London, with a village skate park in mid-Sussex. Both are places that I visit frequently and I am often struck by similarities between children from these two locations, even though their wider surroundings can sometimes seem worlds apart.

I like looking at the mathematical structure and clear division of space within recreation grounds and playing fields. These areas provide me with a ready-made framework for observing colour at play within space. There is something satisfying about the clearly defined contours of the ramps and the markings of the court as they delineate the distance, tracking perspective and cooling in hue.

As a painter, I enjoy the problem of using two dimensions to convey an experience of time and space in the physical world. I find the dynamics of movement and the complexities of spatial awareness fascinating. And I am intrigued by left-footedness, a genetic trait that might run in my family.

Biography

Of Irish nationality, Róisín Fogarty was born in South Korea in 1973 and grew up in Sussex. She studied at Worthing College of Art & Design Sussex 1992-3 and De Montfort University Leicester 1993-8. She undertook the Turps Art School Correspondence Course 2013-14, and the Turps Painters' Studio Programme 2014-16. Group shows (London unless stated) are *ZAP Summer Exhibition* ASC Gallery 2013, *Made Space* 5th Base Gallery 2013, *Correspond* Turps Gallery 2014, *Spring Interim* Turps Gallery 2015, *Malvern Show* No.4a Malvern 2015, *Turps Goes West* Edel Assanti 2015, *Works in Progress* Turps Gallery 2016.

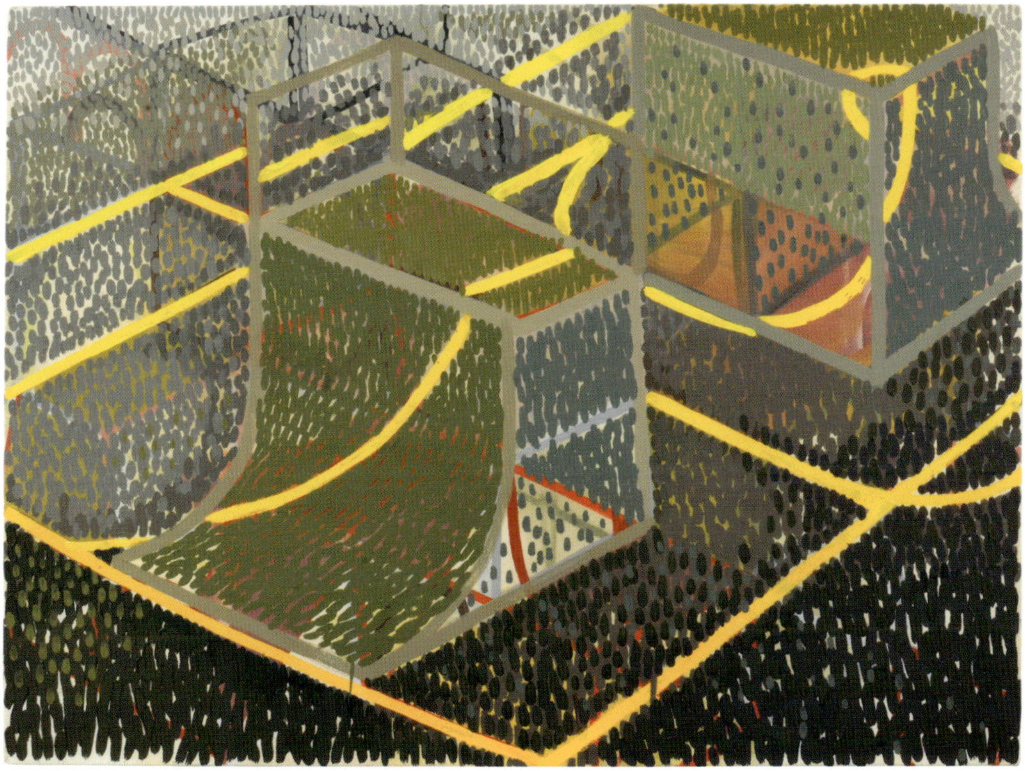

Michael Ginsborg

From Package to Picture

2015
Acrylic, paper and cardboard on linen
30.7 x 40.8 cm

My work is generated from a collection of images on paper. Some of these have been made by me, such as drawings, photographs and collages, and some are found images such as diagrams, words or other printed matter.

The package referred to in the title of this piece is exactly that – a flattened out cardboard box, a portion of which was glued to the canvas at the outset.
I work with a process of extended improvisation, slowly adding layers of paper and paint in different configurations. The finished picture is not consciously produced with reference to a motif existing in the world, but I want it to look as if it might have been.
I welcome this ambivalence as an essential part of my working process. It is never entirely replaced by certainty. The picture is finished when it speaks with its own voice, even if I can't hear exactly what it is saying.

Biography

Born in London in 1943, Michael Ginsborg studied there at Ealing School of Art 1964-5, Central School of Art and Design 1965-8, Chelsea School of Art 1968-9. Solos (London unless stated) include *New Paintings* Lisson Gallery 1969, *Serpentine Painting '73* Serpentine Gallery 1973, *Recent Paintings and Drawings* Acme Gallery 1980, *Recent Paintings and Works on Paper* Benjamin Rhodes 1986, *Playing The Great Harp* Benjamin Rhodes 1993, *Dances With Michael* The Drawing Gallery 2005, *Percorsi Londinese Opere su Carta* Immaginaria Arti Visive Gallery Florence 2008, *Collage* Wills Lane Gallery St Ives 2008. Mark Rothko Memorial Award 1978, Gold Medal International Biennale of Contemporary Art Florence 1997.

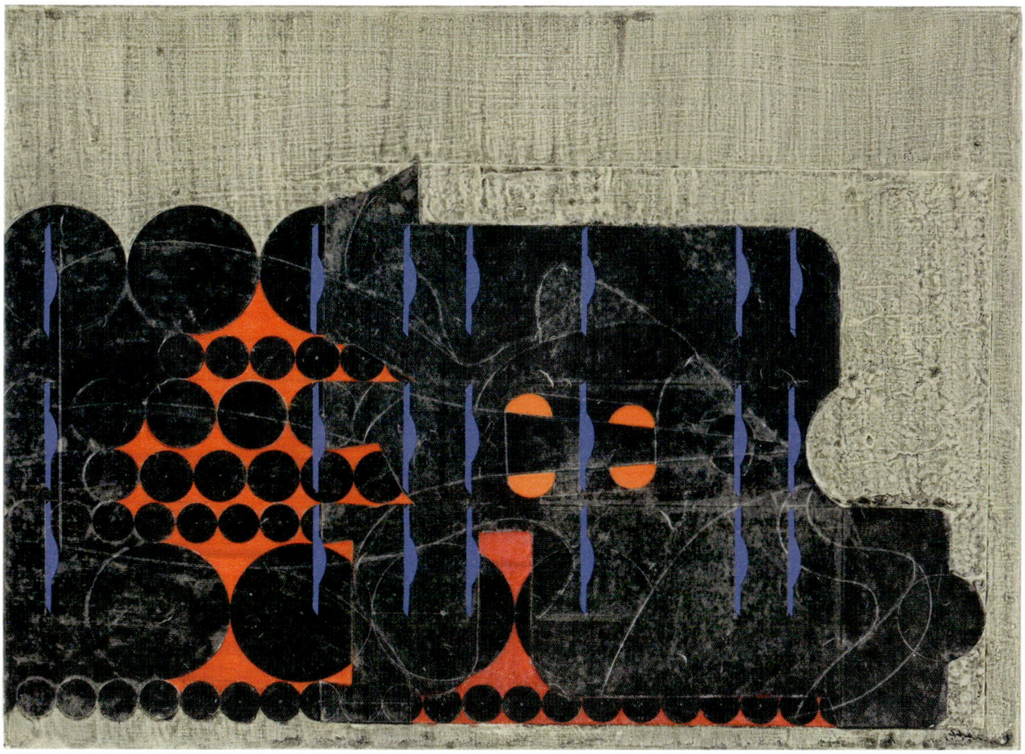

Juliet Goodden

Kedleston Road

2014
Oil on linen
40 x 25.2 cm

Since relocating from Harrow to the East Midlands I have continued to explore the visual influences of different communities on urban and suburban environments. I am interested in the ways in which the presence of other cultures impacts upon our notions of identity. By drawing and painting in mosques, churches and temples, I document diverse places of worship and the people who use them.

Kedleston Road was painted from my car. The 1972 Anglican Church of St Alkmund is visible though the front windscreen, while reflected in the rear view mirror, a group of boys are walking past a mosque. By overlapping the subject matter in this way, the painting acts as a commentary on contemporary multiculturalism.

We see things in short bursts when walking, driving, or talking on the phone. The layers of paint, texture and colour in my work reflect the piecing together and layering of experiences and cultures that are central to everyday urban life.

Biography

Born in Colchester in 1957, Juliet Goodden attended Central School of Art and Design London 1975-8, Nottingham Trent University 2011-13. Residencies Nottingham Lakeside Arts 2014/15, Derby Cathedral 2015. Exhibitions include *Summer Exhibition 1997* Royal Academy London, *Juliet Goodden /Tony Snowden /Kate Strafford* Rainyday Gallery Penzance 2004, *Dot Searle & Juliet Goodden* Rainyday 2009, *Ashenhaus* Backlit Nottingham 2013, *Civic Faith* 367 Station Rd Harrow 2014, *University Summer Exhibition* Djanogly Gallery Nottingham 2015, *Gatherers* (curator) ArtsmithLIVE Derby 2015. Solos *Juliet Goodden* (with Geoff Rigden) Francis Graham-Dixon London 1982, *Indian Spring* Commonwealth Institute London 1985, *Juliet Richardson Goodden: New Paintings* FG-D *1988*. Forthcoming *New Work: Juliet Goodden* Djanogly 2016.

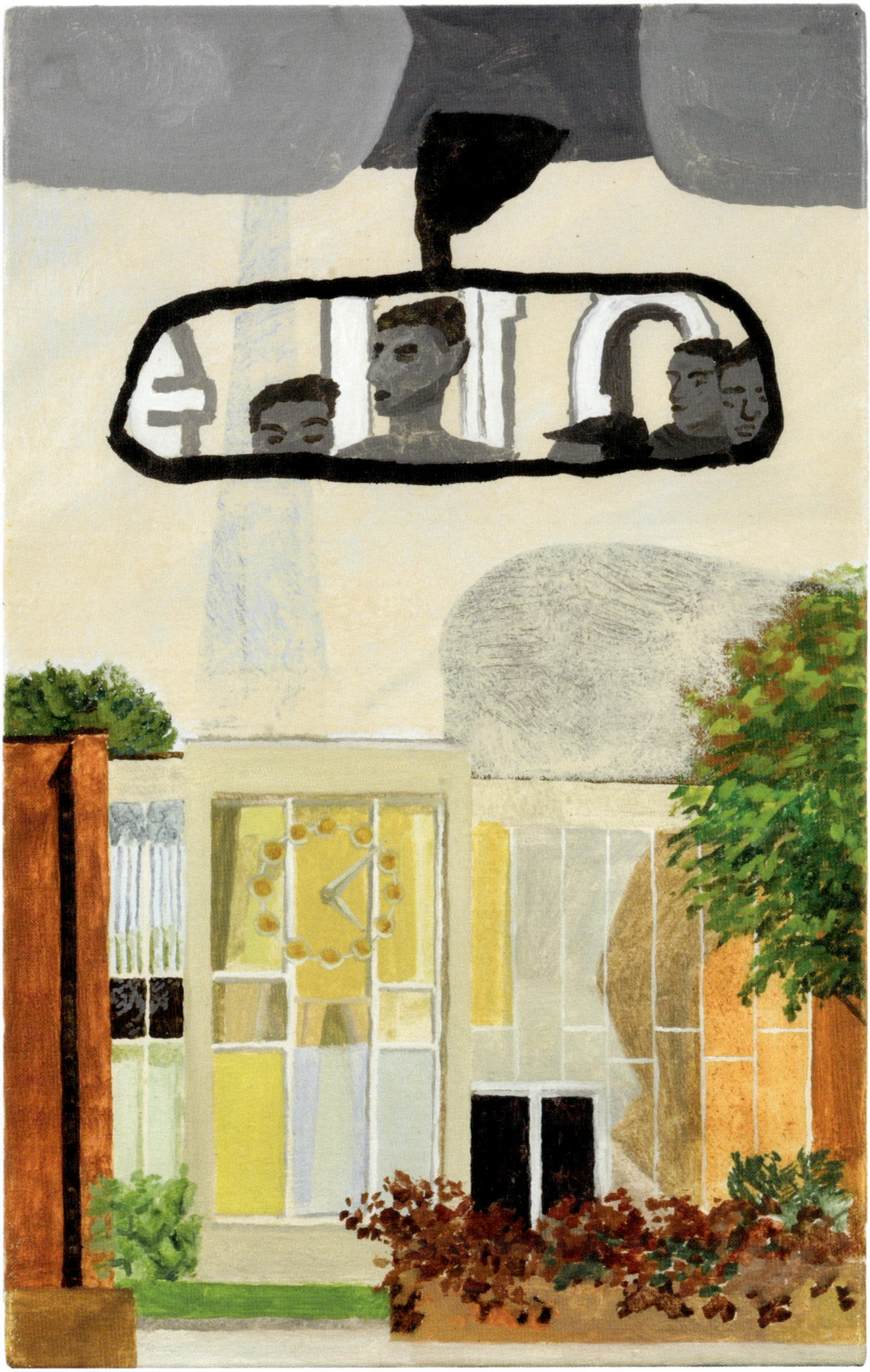

Steph Goodger

Les Non-réclamés (The Unclaimed)

2015
Oil on canvas
120 x 360 cm

An anonymous photograph entitled *Insurges Non-réclamés*, and another, attributed to André-Adolphe-Eugène Disdéri, *Communards in their coffins* (and sometimes called *Insurgents killed during Bloody Week*), show dead Communards lying in their coffins. These men of the Paris Commune of 1871 are lined up vertically, carefully arranged for the photograph. Photographers of the Commune capitalised in different ways on the capacity of the medium for posing and staging. It appears that the Commune, and subsequently the Government, after it regained Paris, recorded the dead for identification purposes. In the book *Peuples Exposés, Peuples Figurants*, Georges Didi-Huberman describes these morbid scenes as reunions, representing the community of the Commune itself. The *figurants* are those without name – history's anonymous 'extras'. In the photographs they are brought into uncommonly sharp focus, exposed individually within the group. My painting elaborates on the staged nature of the two photographs. The ever shifting speculations about the images fuel the intrigue over the many baffling details they contain. There is too, a general sense of emptiness, of watching people fading from the world. Such a painting is unresolvable. At best it is able to bring into being some of the rich contrasts and oppositions present in the subject.

Artist's source credits: Photograph: *Insurgés Non-réclamés*, 1871. Gernsheim Collection, Harry Ransom Center, University of Texas at Austin; Photograph: *Communards in their coffins*, 1871. Disdéri, André-Adolphe-Eugène. Musée de la Ville de Paris, Musée Carnavalet.

Biography

Born in Kent in 1974, Steph Goodger attended Kent Institute of Art and Design 1991-2, Surrey IAD 1992-5, University of Brighton 1997-9. Exhibitions/projects (London unless stated) include *Threadneedle Prize* Mall Galleries 2012, *The London Group Centenary Open* (Winsor & Newton Prize) Cello Factory 2013, *I'd still like to speak to the Governor...*(with Julian Rowe) Brewery Tap Folkestone Triennial Fringe 2014, *National Open Art Exhibition* (South of England Prize) Somerset House 2014, *The Discerning Eye* Mall Galleries 2015, *The Open West* The Wilson Cheltenham 2015, *Of The Sea* Historic Dockyard Chatham 2016, Cherry Time ...(with JR) Elysium Gallery Swansea 2016. In *John Moores Painting Prize 23* 2004.

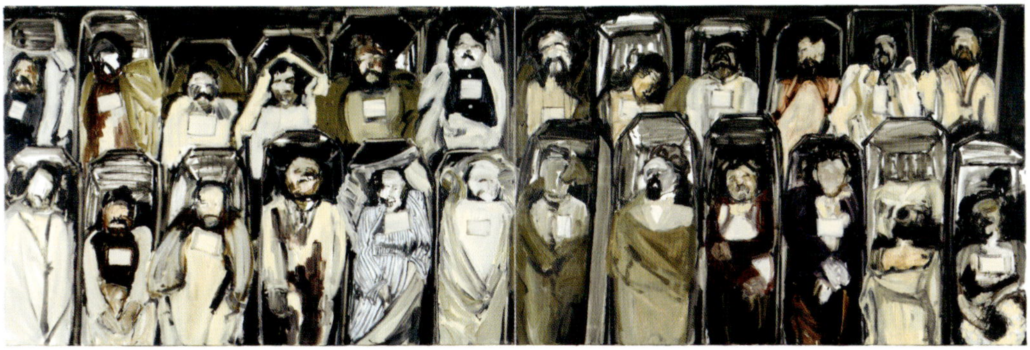

Christopher Hanlon

Untitled

2015
Oil on linen stretched over board
61 x 44.5 cm

One of the reasons I'm attracted to screens is due to the shallow space they create, forming a natural reconciliation between figuration and abstraction, depth and flatness.

In much of my practice I usually select images as much for their formal potential as for any suggested content and meaning in order to maintain openness for both the viewer and myself.

Often I find myself drawn to images that occupy a feeling of boredom, or blankness, which paradoxically has the potential to transport us elsewhere.

Biography

Christopher Hanlon was born in Poole in 1978. He studied at Brighton University 1999-2002 and the Royal College of Art London 2006-8. Exhibitions include *Bloomberg New Contemporaries 2008* A Foundation Liverpool/Club Row London, *Featuring* Galerie Chez Valentin Paris 2009, *Pokerface* Koraalberg Antwerp 2010, *Polemically Small* Torrance Art Museum California 2011, *Carousel* Slate Projects London 2014. Solos, Domobaal London unless stated, include *Because You Stood Still* 2009, *Disseminatus* 2012, *Chamber* 2014, *Christopher Hanlon* (invited by Emma Dexter) Timothy Taylor Gallery 2010, *Christopher Hanlon* Edel Assanti London 2015.

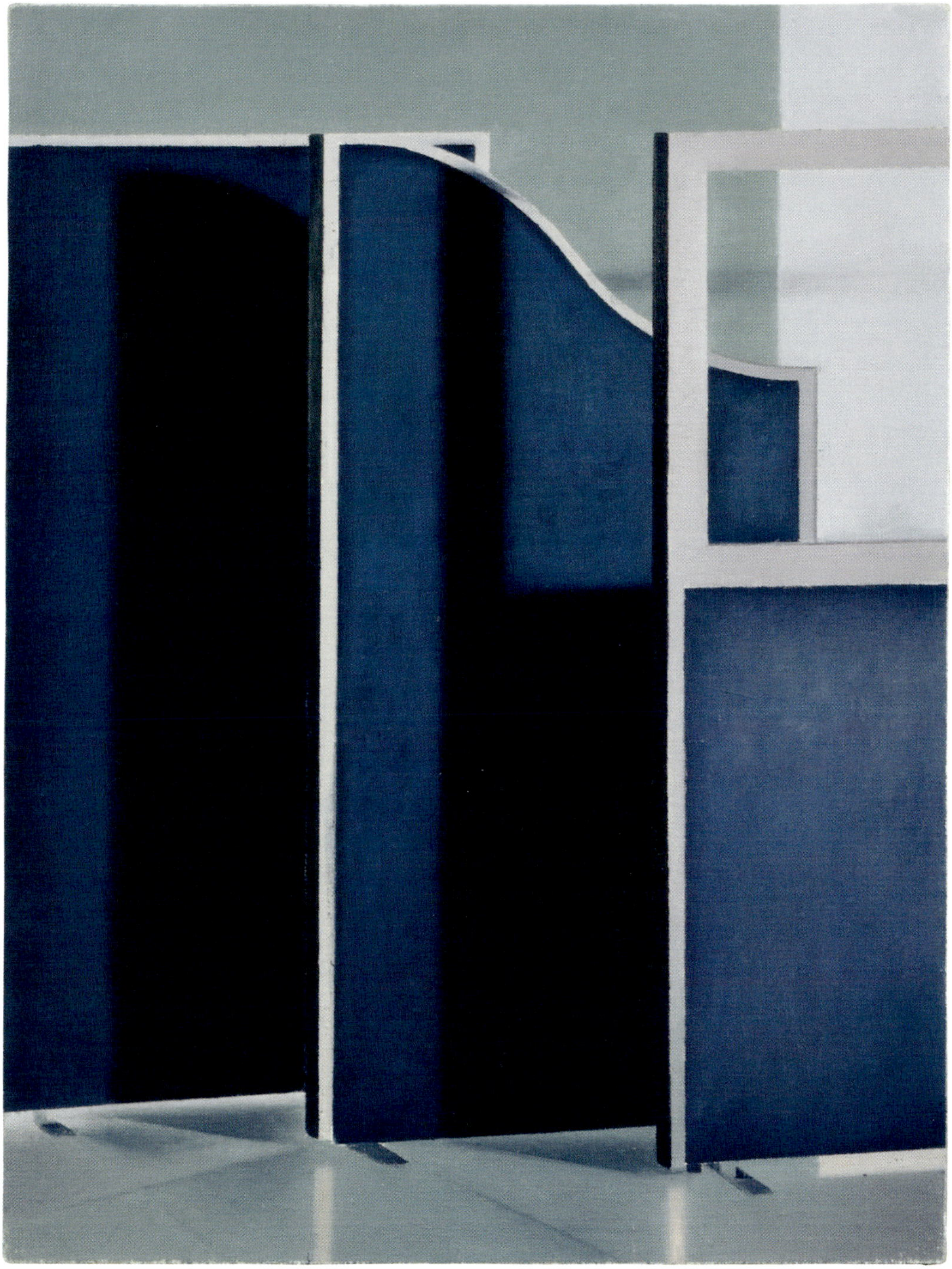

Christopher Hanlon

Linda Hemmersbach

January

2015
Oil and distemper on linen
30.5 x 51 cm

At the beginning of 2015 I spent a few quiet days in a remote cottage on the Norfolk coast. The vast, flat expanses of dunes and marshes, interwoven with the sea, reminded me of the North Sea in Germany, which I used to visit often as a child. Walking in the silent, barren landscape triggered a concentrated attentiveness to my surroundings.

January marks a month of introspection and reflection, of letting go and being in-between. It is a time of moving forwards into unknown territory, which can be daunting, but also hopeful, filled with new possibilities.

Painting *January* was a surprise for me and in retrospect marked the beginning of a new way of working, discovered through stripping back and slowing down. It is a very simple painting, yet rhythmic, and perhaps meditative. The horizontal format accentuates the experience of stretched inner time and mental expansion. The three intersecting lines offer resting points, or anchors in the landscape of the mind, where moments of clarity drift into consciousness, yet remain elusive.

Biography

Born in Cologne in 1984, Linda Hemmersbach studied at Central Saint Martins London 2004-08 and Wimbledon College of Art 2009-10. Exhibitions include *It's Very Quiet Here* Gowen Contemporary Geneva 2014, and 2015: *So Many Constellations* (curator) Mayor's Parlour Gallery London, *On Silent Mode* FOUR Vienna, *Anonyme Zeichner* Kunstverein Tiergarten/Galerie Nord Berlin, *Painted Surface* Surface Gallery Nottingham, *Bankley Open Call 2015* (shortlisted) Bankley Gallery Manchester, *Anonymous Drawings* artQ13 Rome. Solo show at Footfall Art London 2015. Artist-in-residence *The Trelex Residency* Switzerland 2014, *The Bothy Project* Isle of Eigg 2014, *Gamli Skóli* Hrisey Iceland 2015. Participant in *TRACING Paper* mentoring scheme Paper Gallery Manchester.

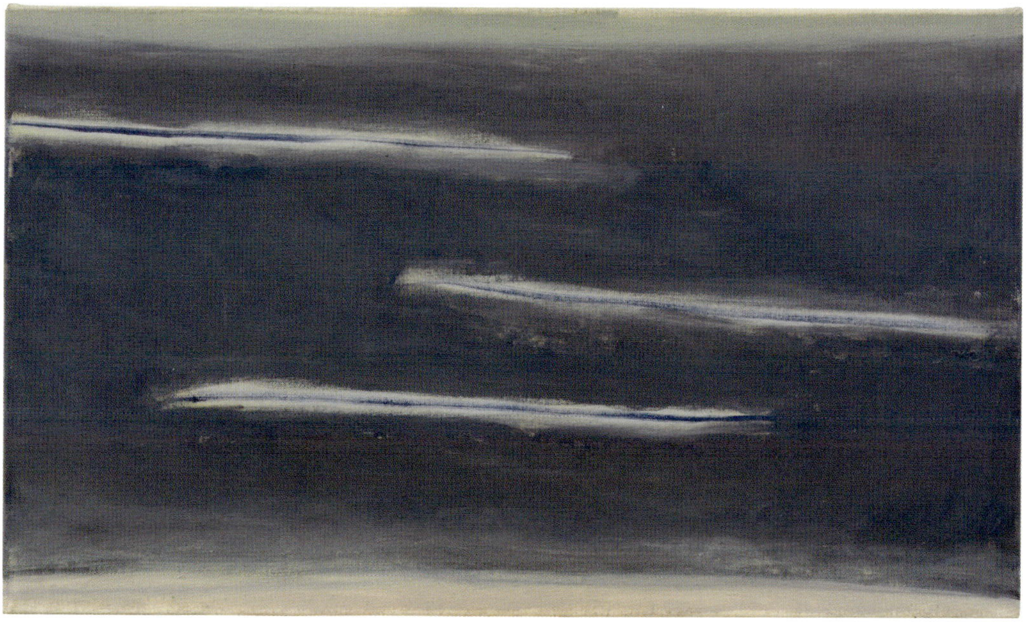

Thom Trojanowski Hobson

It's a Circus Out There

2015
Oil, acrylic and spray paint, pencil, pen and ink on canvas
140.8 x 106.6 cm

PAINTING HAS ALWAYS BEEN AN AUTOBIOGRAPHICAL, EMOTIONALLY CHARGED, HONEST THING, WHICH, LIKE THE CHARACTERS AND SYMBOLISM IN MY PAINTINGS, I STRUGGLE TO KEEP FROM TEETERING OVER THE EDGE. LIKE THE WORLD WE LIVE IN, THEY COULD TOPPLE UPON THEMSELVES IN A SELF-DEPRECATING, AWKWARD MESS. I DRAW HEAVY INSPIRATION FROM BANDS LIKE TELEVISION, WIRE AND TALKING HEADS, AND OTHER PUNK AND POST-PUNK POETS, ARTISTS AND WRITERS.

THE WORD 'VOYEURISM' HAS ALMOST BECOME TABOO IN TODAY'S ART WORLD, MAKING ME EVEN MORE EARNEST IN SHOUTING LOUDER. AS EVERY PAINTING IS FINISHED I CARE LESS ABOUT WHAT PEOPLE THINK OF HOW I FEEL ABOUT MY PERSONAL RELATIONSHIPS, MY COMMENTS ON PEOPLE'S RELATIONSHIPS WITH EACH OTHER AND MY CRITICISM OF MAN'S RELATIONSHIP WITH MOTHER NATURE.

MATERIALS, MEDIUM, FORMAT AND THE SURFACE ON WHICH A PAINTING IS MADE ARE UNIMPORTANT. USING ANYTHING AT HAND IN THE STUDIO AT THE TIME IS VITAL, KEEPING THE ENERGY HIGH AND THE MARK MAKING ALIVE, INSTINCTUAL AND TRUE.

THE TELLING OF STORY AND HURT AND STRUGGLE AND LOVE WILL ALWAYS SIT HIGHER IN MY PRIORITIES ABOVE TECHNIQUE AND HIGH-BROW CONCEPTUAL THEORY. THIS STATEMENT MAY SUGGEST THAT I HAVE A BLASÉ ATTITUDE TOWARDS PAINTING, BUT IT IS MY ALL-CONSUMING EVERYTHING. MY ONE DRIVING FORCE, ALONG WITH HATE AND LOVE.

Biography

Thom Trojanowski Hobson was born in Kidderminster in 1988. Based in London, he studied there at Wimbledon College of Arts 2012-15 and The Slade School of Fine Art 2012. Group exhibitions include, in 2014, *Second Eight* Brixton East London, *#100aires* Dray Walk Gallery Truman Brewery London, *Milla Eastwood & Thom Hobson* (two-person) Brixton East, *Hans Brinker Budget Trophy* Hans Brinker Hotel Amsterdam, and in 2015, *Secret 7"* Somerset House London, *Third Six* Brixton East, *Degree Show* Wimbledon College of Arts, *Synaesthesia* Asylum Studios Suffolk, *Exhibition of Art* (The Cone Sisters collaboration) Asylum Studios, *Affordable Art Fair* Battersea Park London.

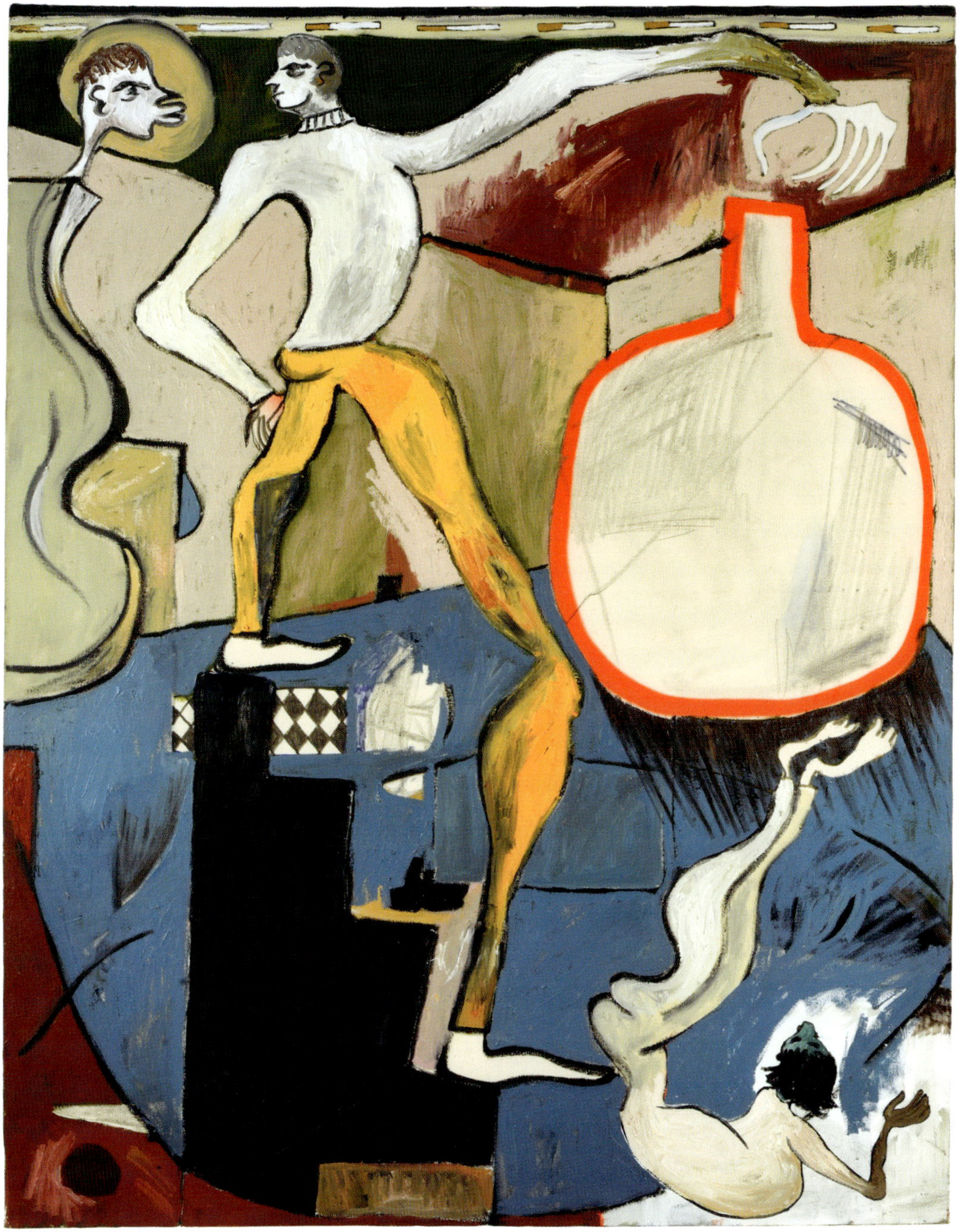

Ira Hoffecker

Camp Moschendorf II

2015
Acrylic, ink and resin on birch wood panel
101.5 x 76 cm

My paintings are informed by the different identities cities take on over a period of time. I am also interested in how different societies transform and change city spaces across the centuries. My work examines the relationships between people and cities by responding to constant change, reconstruction and restoration in the urban landscape.

Decay, erasure, covering, revealing and rebuilding take place at the same time. I see my process of covering as a metaphor of forgetting and suppressing the past. The process of revealing and sanding the surface down alludes to remembering and coming to terms with historic events. In many of my paintings I use layers of resin which physically separate one layer of paint from the previous one. Those layers are equivalent to the archaeological strata in the evolution of a city. Places are overlaid with multiple histories, layers of paint cover and obscure, but each coat is also informed by the previous layer.

This painting shows Camp Moschendorf (Lager Moschendorf) at the German border to Czechoslovakia, a former Nazi forced labour camp, which from 1945 became a refugee camp. Today there is a factory building at the site. None of the former camp buildings have been preserved.

Biography

Born in Hof, Germany in 1963, Ira Hoffecker studied at Vancouver Island School of Art 2008-2013, University of Gloucestershire 2014-15, Transart Institute Plymouth University (2016-present). Group shows include *Urban Reflections* The Front Gallery Edmonton 2013, *Berliner Bilder* Galerie Leo.Coppi Berlin 2015, *Journey Elsewhere* (with Abbie Phillips) Menier Gallery London 2015, *High Street Layers Project* The Wilson Cheltenham 2016, *Urban Settings* (with Jo Kley) Galerie Hoffmann Rheda-Wiedenbrueck 2016. Solos *Urban Settings* Sewell Centre Gallery Abingdon 2015, *Urbane Welten* Freiheitshalle Hof 2015, *German Identities* Zack Gallery Vancouver 2016. *Works in Print Graduate Art Prize 2015* (shortlisted), *Abstract Exhibition 2015* (1st prize) FCA Vancouver, *takt* residency Berlin 2016.

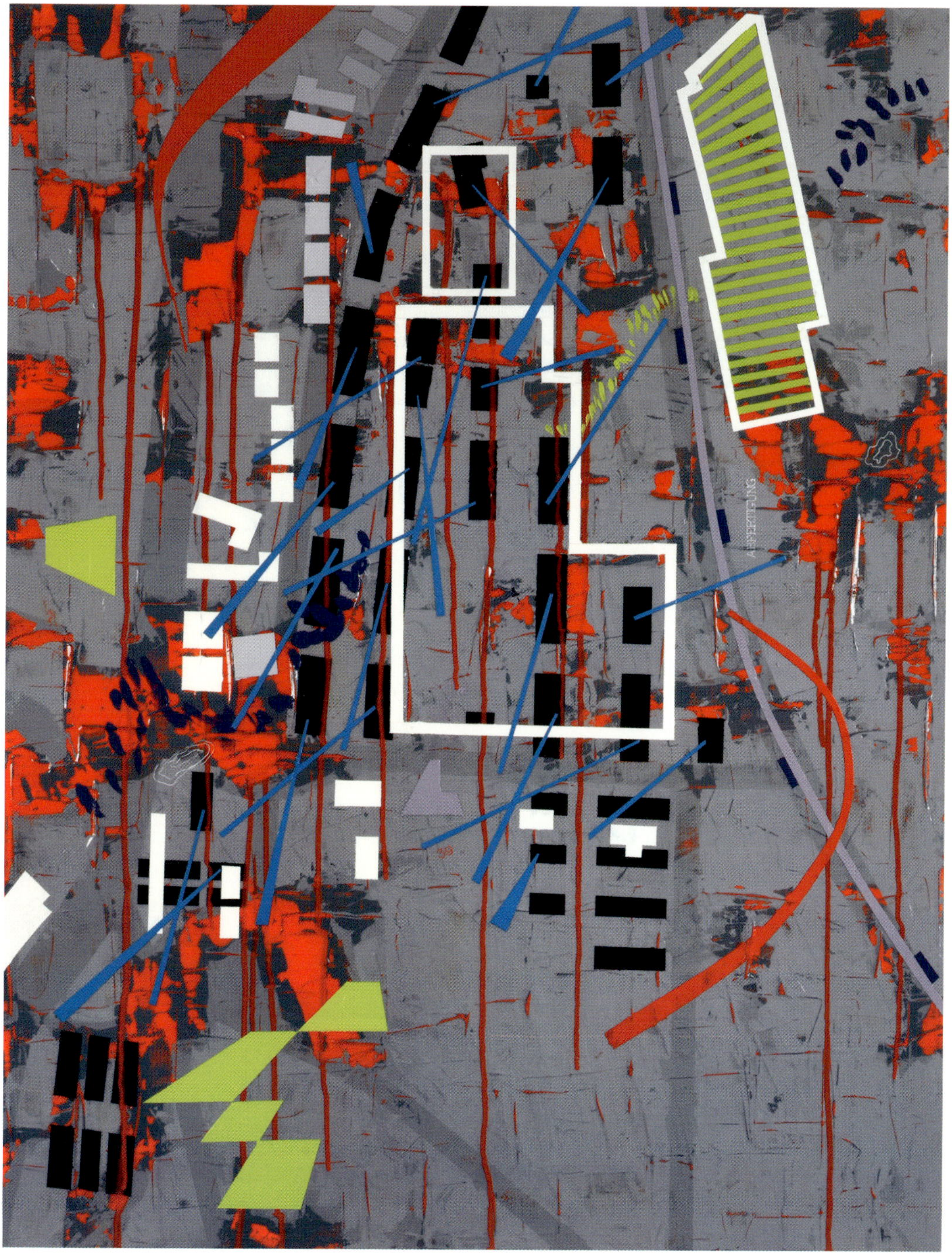

Benjamin Jenner

Flicker 3

2015
Pencil, pen, ink, tempera and gouache on paper
158.8 x 148.2 cm

Flicker 3 describes an image of an image of a form set in a landscape of green puddles and an encroaching dark sky.

The depicted form in the image's centre appears in a vertical tableau that shares pictorial incidents, green puddles and black wavy lines similar to those displayed in the wider landscape in which the tableau sits.

It is from a series of paintings and plaster casts that show a lighthouse's Fresnel lens from a number of different angles and in the process of emitting light.

The painting's construction, measured and structured in its articulation of a cluster of interlocking, faceted, sharp-edged surfaces, is also strikingly totemic, surrounded by an amorphous halo-like form.

The notion of an object represented in a tableau sitting within a landscape is meant to be both literal and metaphorical. It is intended to point towards a wider context, itself a kind of landscape – in this instance, the series of paintings and plaster casts of which *Flicker 3* is a crucial part.

Biography

Born in Dover in 1981, Benjamin Jenner studied in London at Wimbledon School of Art 2001-04 and the Slade School of Fine Art 2007-9. Prizewinner *Red Mansion Art Prize* 2008 (with residency Beijing 2008 and exhibition Slade London 2009). Exhibitions (London unless stated) include *Contested Ground* 176/Zabludowicz Collection 2009, *Bloomberg New Contemporaries* A Foundation London/Cornerhouse Manchester 2009, *The Invention of Painting* C4RD 2011, *Translate/Transcribe* The Central House of Artists Moscow 2011, *Drawing Biennial 2013* Drawing Room, *Creekside Open 2013* (selector Paul Noble) A.P.T, *Summer Exhibition 2013* Royal Academy. Solo *From No Fixed Point* The Foundry Gallery 2014.

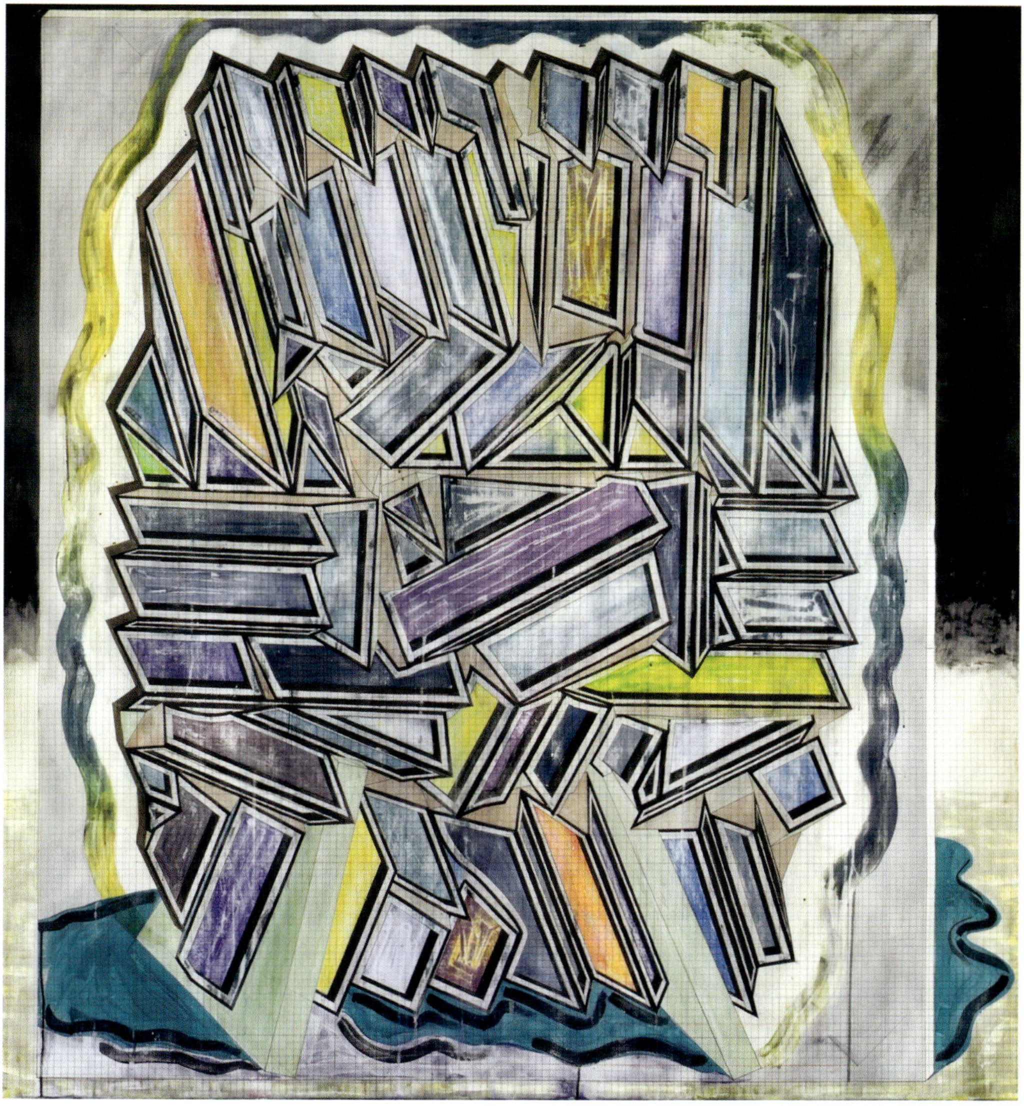

Gareth Kemp

This Could Be Eastern Europe

2015
Acrylic on canvas
50.8 x 76.2 cm

This is one of a series of fictional landscapes referencing the work of Caspar David Friedrich. The series also draws upon my memories of growing up in a remote part of Wales. The title comes from a song by The Wild Swans, '*The Coldest Winter For A Hundred Years*' – music is often an important and complementary reference point for me.

I spend many hours carefully planning the assemblage of elements in each painting, a process of mentally cutting and pasting between photographic sources. This method results in repetitions and occlusions, recurrences of motifs and, frequently, a blurring between foreground and background. My paintings are built up in layers. The paint in each zone within a composition is given a consciously different treatment.

Together with the autobiographical significance that they carry, the finished works address my experience of the process of their painting and the decisions I have taken along that path, embracing that which is rigorously thought through, unplanned, or sometimes accidental.

Biography

Born on the Wirral in 1972, Gareth Kemp is Liverpool-based. He studied at Staffordshire University 1992-5 and the University of Liverpool 1995-7. On the Turps Art School Correspondence Course since 2014. Exhibitions include *Liverpool Art Prize 08* Novas CUC Liverpool 2008, *Next Up: Liverpool Art Now* Bluecoat Liverpool 2008, *The National Open 2010* Minerva Theatre Chichester, *The Manchester Contemporary* Axisweb 2013, *Threadneedle Prize 2014, 2016* Mall Galleries London, *The Discerning Eye* Mall Galleries 2014, *Correspond* Artworks Halifax 2016, *Lynn Painter-Stainers Prize* Mall Galleries 2016, *Early Warning* &Model Gallery Leeds 2016, *Let's Make a Better World* Cello Factory London 2016.

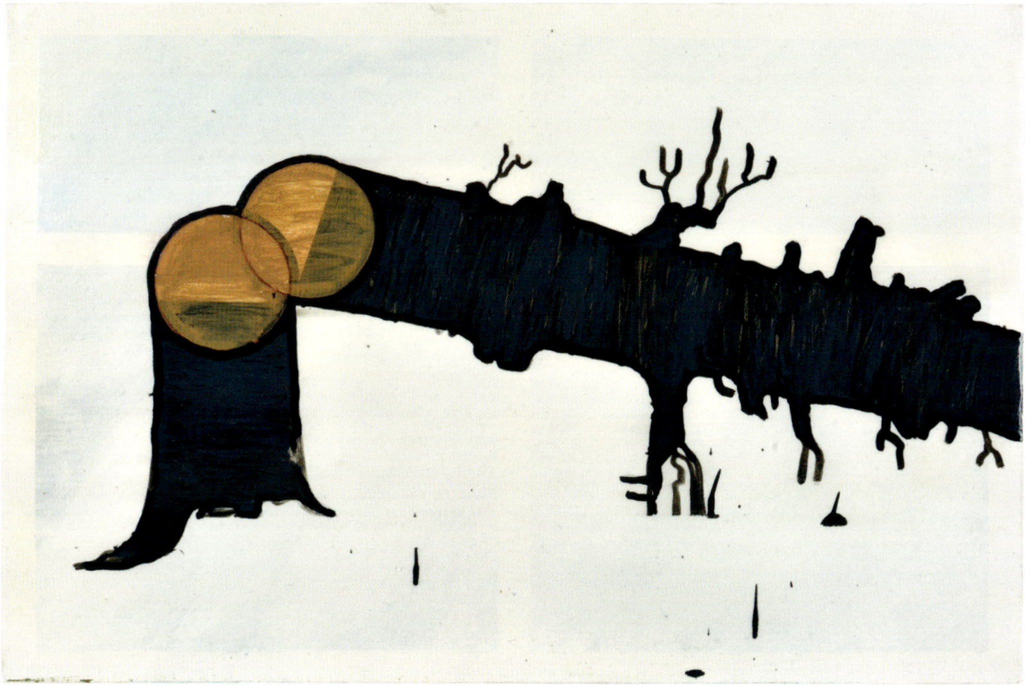

Nicholas Kulkarni

Untitled

2015
Oil on linen
165.2 x 180.4 cm

In a new body of works, I have been exploring the responses that can be invoked when perceiving coloured patterns placed in a perspective space within the flatness of a picture plane.

In this painting the composition is formed of two interlaced chequered patterns with a void section that remains as a field of colour. The elements of the patterns are distorted as they extend further from the centre line, but always maintain their definition, even as they recede towards the vanishing point.

Despite the repetition of the pattern, the perspective makes each check unique in terms of its form and dimensions. Even though the checks appear uniform, no mechanical means of reproduction have been used to paint them, a process which makes hours pass by as if they were minutes. For me, the number of checks is beyond quantification. It is a sense of their mass and the elapsing of time taken to paint them that I regard as important.

As a whole the elements create a third pattern, one which is an optical effect and that exists in the eye of the viewer alone, a pure illusion.

My aim is to evoke from a structure of order and logic a response of disorientation and uncertainty coupled with a state of questioning as to the intent behind this act.

Biography

Nicholas Kulkarni was born in Heswall in 1971, and has lived and worked in London since 1994. He studied at Northbrook College of Art and Design 1990-1, then the University of Northumbria, Newcastle upon Tyne 1991-4, winning two prizes including the TG Stephenson's Purchase Prize. Group shows (London unless stated) include *48 and rising...* Raw Gallery 1994, *Whitechapel Open* Whitechapel Gallery 1996, *Newcastle X* University of Northumbria Newcastle 1999, *Deptford X* Acme Studios 2001. In the *John Moores Painting Prize 2014*. Works in various collections, including the University of Northumbria and North Tyneside Council.

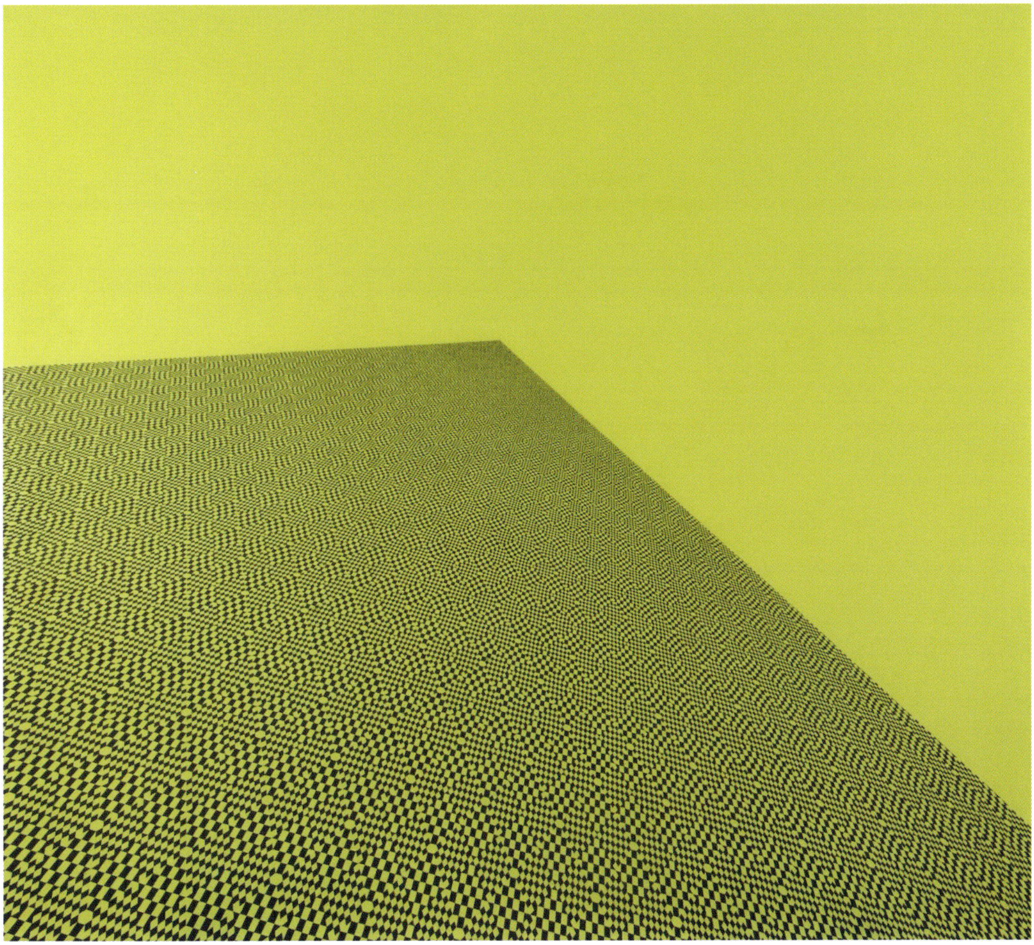

George Lloyd-Jones

Round Tables (2)

2015
Oil on canvas
137.5 x 158 cm

A painting, like a chosen subject, should innately, subconsciously and instantly seize my attention. Once this first connection is made there is time for conscious links and thoughts to be explored and exchanged between the image and the self.

This year I have decided that the way to create successful paintings must be through similar means to the way I view them – with subconscious immediacy followed with deeper exploration. This requires the pathway between first contact with the subject and the canvas to be as short as possible to facilitate and use that immediate excitement. I have created a fully functional and mobile studio space in a lorry, in order to commit to and fully immerse within my practice and subject matter. With a studio on wheels, I can find the excitement and take the studio directly to it.

Biography

Born in Bristol in 1992, George Lloyd-Jones studied at the University of Falmouth 2010-11 and the University of Brighton 2011-14. Exhibitions include *CPRE Oxfordshire Landscape Competition* (winner) Town Hall Gallery Oxford 2009, *Herding Cats* Yolo's Café Brighton 2012, *In-Transition* Grand Parade South Gallery Brighton 2013, *Undiscovered Talent* No.5 Cavendish Square London 2013, *Black, White and other Colours* SVA/Ale House Stroud 2014, *The Other Art Fair* (with Young Artist Partnership) Old Truman Brewery London 2014, *The Ruth Bochard Self-Portrait Prize 2015* Piano Nobile London, *Off the Wall* ACP Gallery Painswick 2015. Solo *Coloured Spaces* The North Wall Oxford 2013. Creator, the BoonRig mobile art studio.

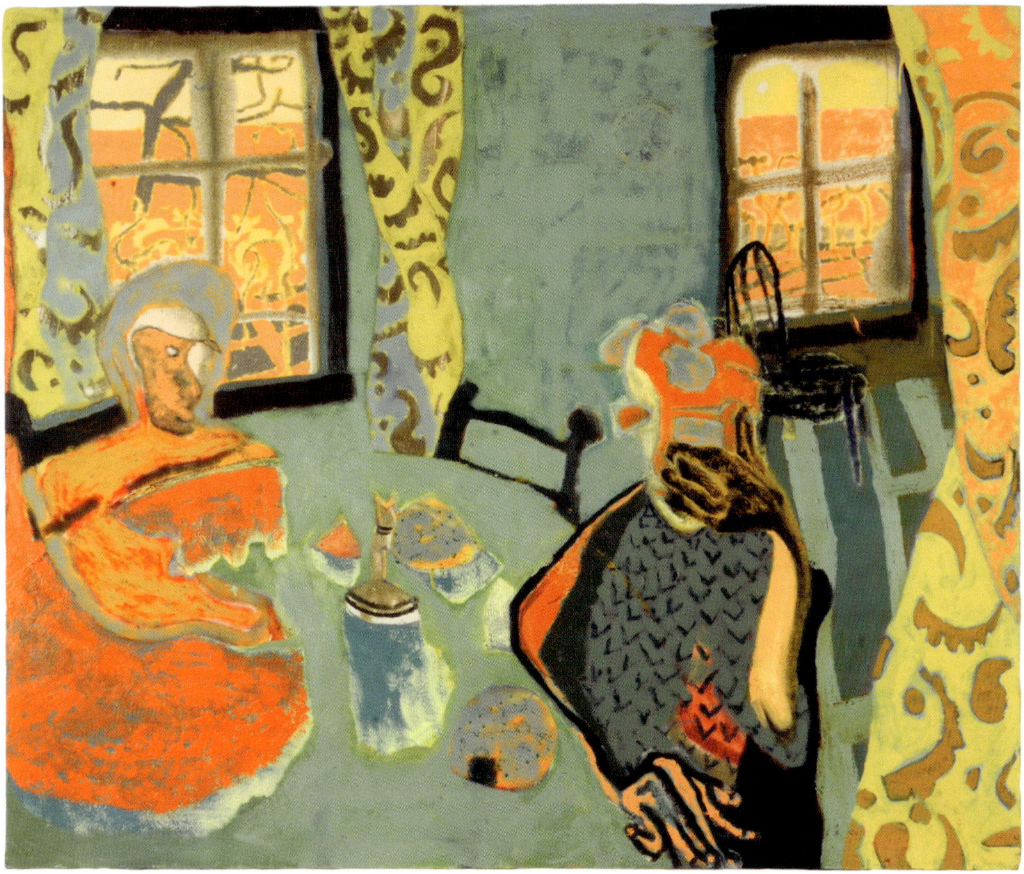

Enzo Marra

Invigilator (John Virtue)

2015
Oil on canvas
52 x 51.5 cm

My works are explorations of the art world, whether it be the artist, the studio, the gallery, the auction, the observer or the invigilator. They are executed in a manner that is suggestive, excluding extraneous details, and with a limited palette, in order to allow the viewer to interact with the finished paintings and complete the image in their own mind. The action of the brush over the surface, and the furrows within the pigment which it leaves behind, are as relevant in the final image as the subject matter they portray.

This piece is based on photographs I took at the Towner Art Gallery in Eastbourne. The seated invigilator appears dwarfed by the proportions of the John Virtue painting at his side. In capturing the observing invigilator in a painting, I have attempted to reverse the viewer's gaze onto the protective dynamic of the gallery. A usually silent and often overlooked figure is entwined with the mammoth works they are expected to serve and to protect.

Biography

Enzo Marra was born in Bournemouth in 1975, studying there at Shelley Park Art College 1993-5, then at the universities of Reading 1995-9 and Brighton 1999-2001. Group exhibitions include *This space we are* The International 3 Manchester 2014, *TROIKA!* Hillsboro Fine Art Dublin 2014, *Controcanto* Yellow Artist Run Space Varese Italy 2015, *Creekside Open 2015* (selector Richard Deacon) A.P.T London 2015, *The London Group Open* Cello Factory 2015, *Life Lines* Ellsworth Gallery Santa Fe 2016. Solos include *Wall, Floor and Table Sun* Pier House Gallery Chatham 2015, *Adorations* Hooligan Art Dealer London 2015. Exhibited in *John Moores Painting Prize 2012*.

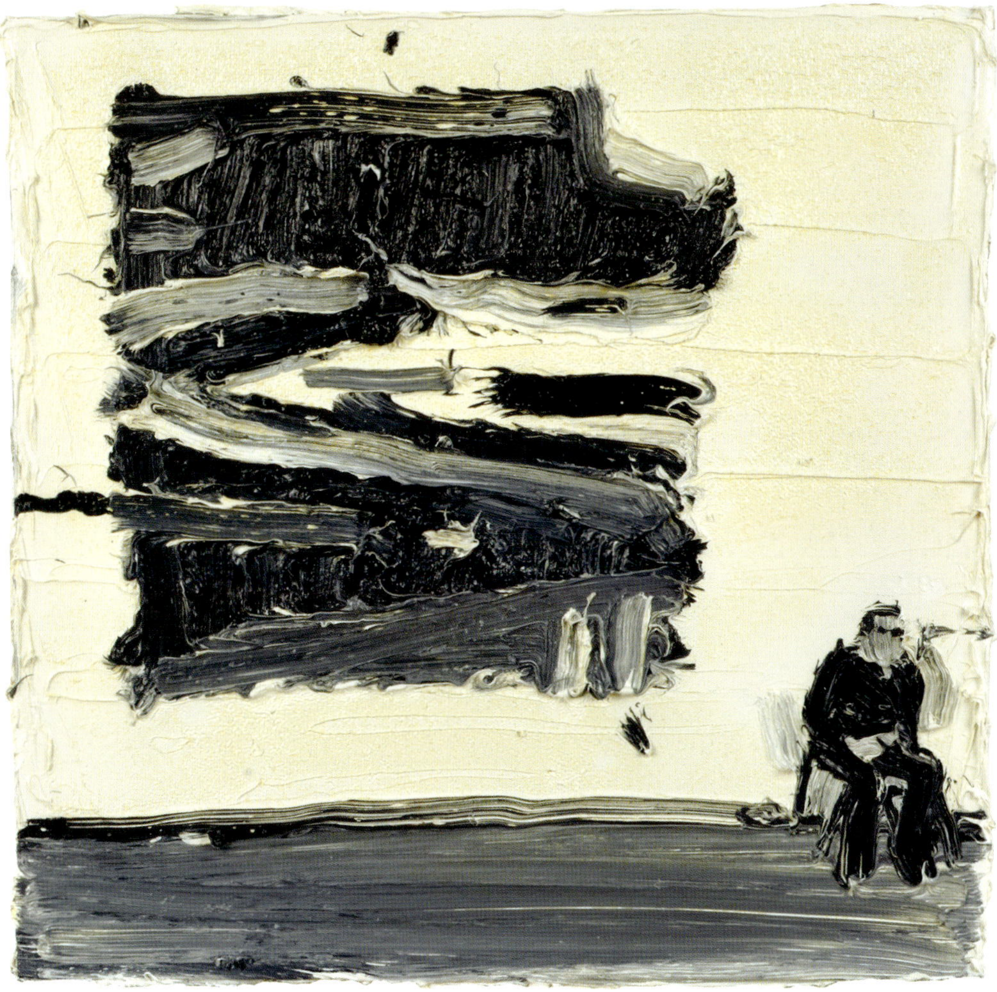

Lee Marshall

Midnight I

2015
Acrylic on canvas
116 x 81.5 cm

I prefer to see a painting as more of a screen than a window upon the world, with my paintings being just as influenced by the process of using image editing software or creating computer generated imagery as they are informed by the language of painting. Alongside this, they are a means to explore the depiction of space and form within the two-dimensional plane of the canvas, conveying playful compositions that are constructed spontaneously during the initial drawing stage of my work through a combination of layering, rendering and manipulating forms in the virtual space of the picture plane.

Midnight I is part of a recent body of work in which the palette has been reduced to two colours used against black. This approach was initially intended as an exercise in rendering shape and volume through an economic use of colour. It has developed into a bold graphic direction for my paintings, which is embedded with a nostalgic air of neon lighting and arcade screens. Whilst there is no intended narrative, I like to equate viewing *Midnight I* with the experience of stumbling into an artist's studio at night, lit only by the lights from signage on the street outside.

Biography

Lee Marshall was born in Cambridge in 1986 and is based in London. He attended Norwich School of Art and Design 2005-8. Exhibitions (London unless stated) include *Expanded* Wysing Arts Centre Cambridge 2009, *A Thing is a Thing is a Thing a Thing* The Minories Colchester 2012, *Cosmo's Levels* The Sunday Painter 2012, *This Glitch* The Blyth Gallery Imperial College 2013, *Demimonde* (Slate Projects/Mottahedan Projects) Amberwood House 2015, *In Schönheit Auferstehen* Galerie Patrick Ebensperger Berlin 2015, *Autocatalytic Future Games* No Format 2015, *Cybernetic Meadow* (Slate Projects) The Averard Hotel 2016, *MIND OUT-Manufactured Space and Constructed Transformations* A.P.T 2016. Solo *Salutations!* Outpost Gallery Norwich 2009.

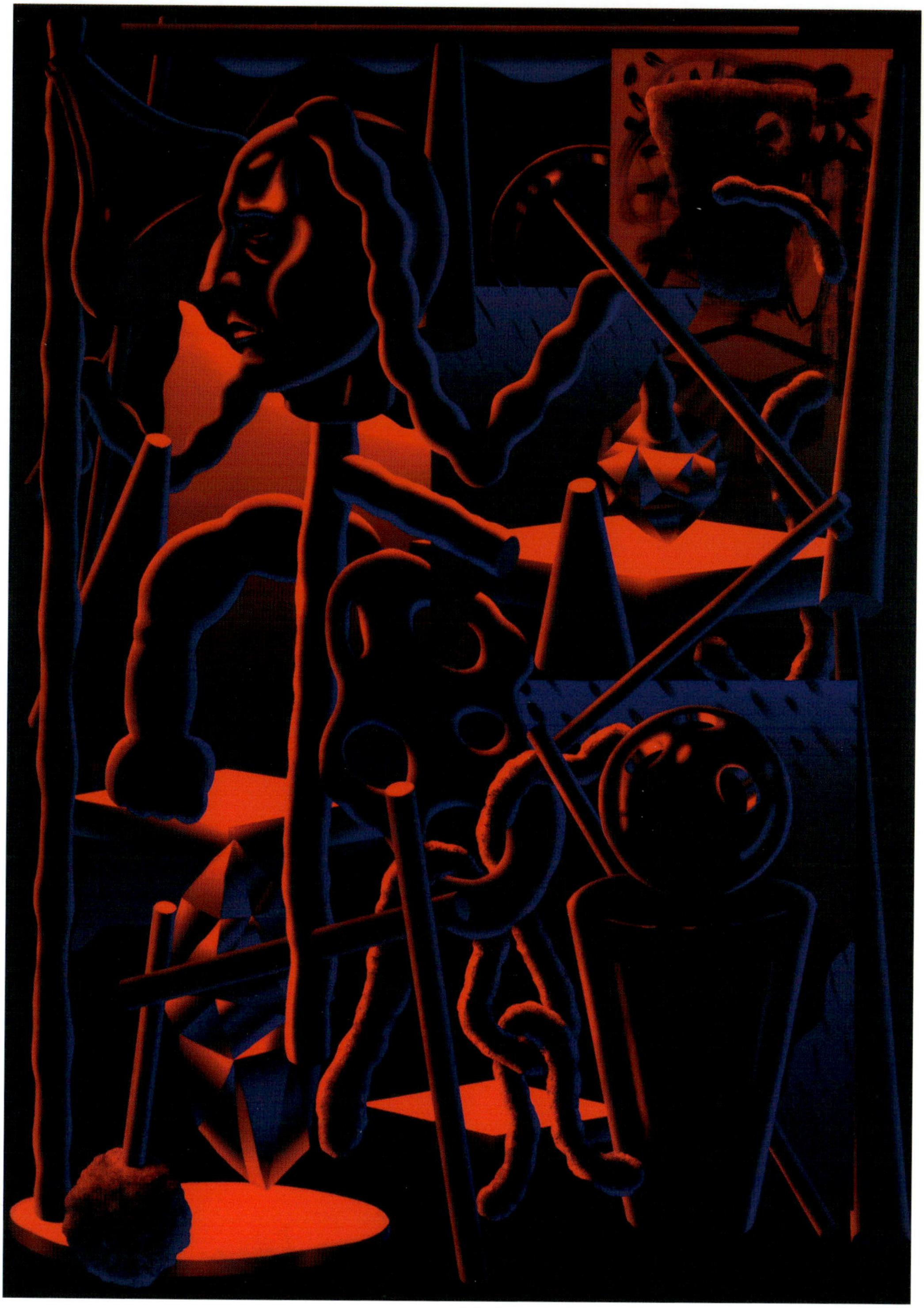

Sneh Mehta

Him & Her

2015
Acrylic on canvas
71 x 91.3 cm

Him & Her is a psychological portrait of a couple's relationship. The nuances and undercurrents in their life together are explored. I do this through the relational sensations of colour and the physical qualities of an assortment of marks. The specific life story of a well-known couple was my source material.

I may do an initial sketch of the protagonists, but will not refer to it once I start painting as memory plays a vital part in the work. The blank canvas starts with layers of paint made up of colours that reflect and evoke the emotions and feelings that I want to portray. These layers are scratched through using a variety of mark making tools such as spatulas, combs and other implements. Imaginary and intuitive forms evolve and reveal themselves slowly as the process continues.

My current paintings are an exploration of the intangible within the human condition through their moods, emotions, relationships and states of being.

Biography

Born in Mombasa in 1954, Sneh Mehta is based in London. She attended Hull College of Art & Design 1974-7, Brighton University 1992-3, City & Guilds of London Art School 1997-9, Goldsmiths College London 2001-3. Exhibitions (London unless stated) include *Boundaries: Sussex Open* Brighton Museum & Art Gallery 1995, *Sussex Open* Brighton M&AG 1998, *20/20* Beverley Knowles 2006, *Marmite Prize for Painting* The Residence Gallery 2006, *Deep Inspiration* Jerwood Space 2007, *Silo and Flux* Beverley Knowles 2008, *ArtWorks Open* 2010 ArtWorks Project Space, *Summer Exhibition 2012* Royal Academy, *Beneath the Surface* Highgate Contemporary Art 2013. Solo *Morphosis* New Greenham Arts Newbury 2004.

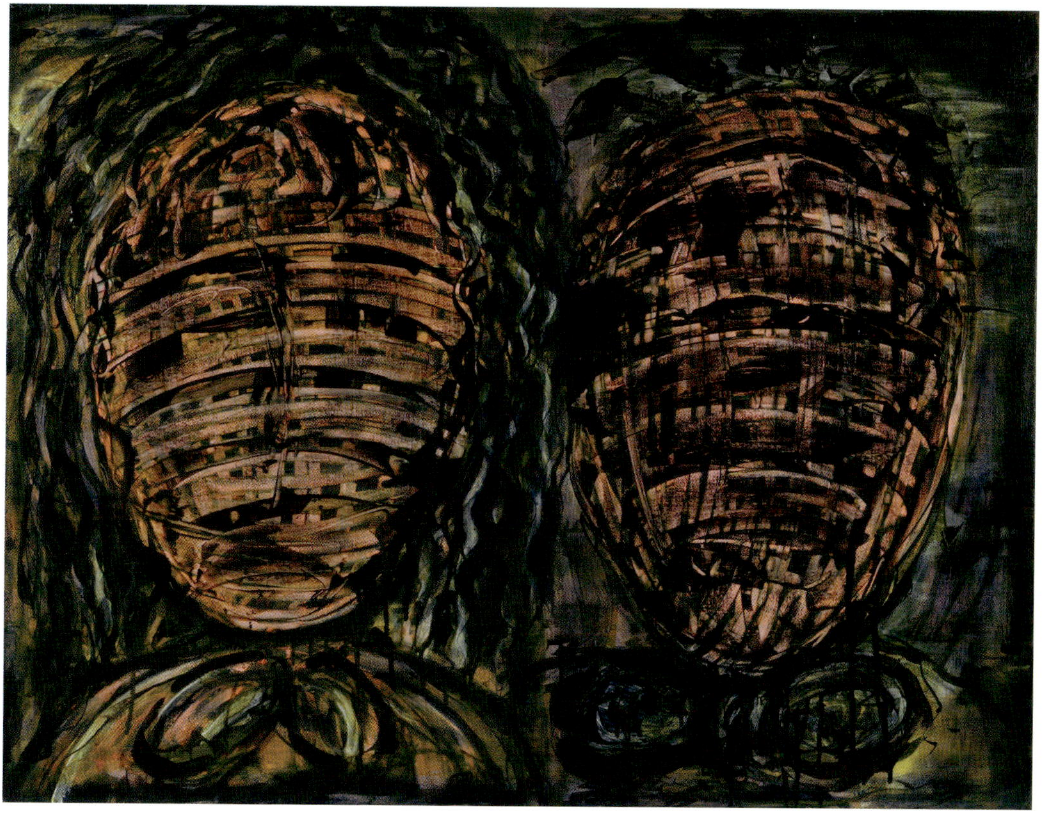

Nicholas Middleton

Figures in an Arch

2015
Oil on paper
10.2 x 15.2 cm

I have been using the postcard format to make small paintings on paper for a number of years. The constraints of size and proportions have allowed me to explore both the topographic expectations of the postcard and my use of photography as a sketchbook. This painting shows a small group of figures standing in a railway arch, picked out against the architecture by the sun. It's unclear what brings them together in this location, surrounded by litter and fly-tipping, facing into the shadows.

Biography

Born in London in 1975, Nicholas Middleton studied at London Guildhall University 1993-4 and Winchester School of Art 1994-7. Exhibitions include *Francis Bacon to Paula Rego* Abbot Hall Kendal 2012, *Towards a New Socio-Painting* Transition Gallery 2014, *@PaintBritain* Ipswich Art School Gallery 2014, *Documentary Realism: Painting in the Digital Age* The Crypt at St Marylebone London 2015. Exhibitor seven times *Summer Exhibition* Royal Academy of Arts London. Solos include *Black & White Paintings* Arch Gallery London 2010 and *Provisional Cities* The Crypt at St Marylebone 2013. In the *John Moores Painting Prize* 2004, 2006 (Visitors' Choice Prize), 2010 (Prizewinner and Visitors' Choice Prize) and 2014.

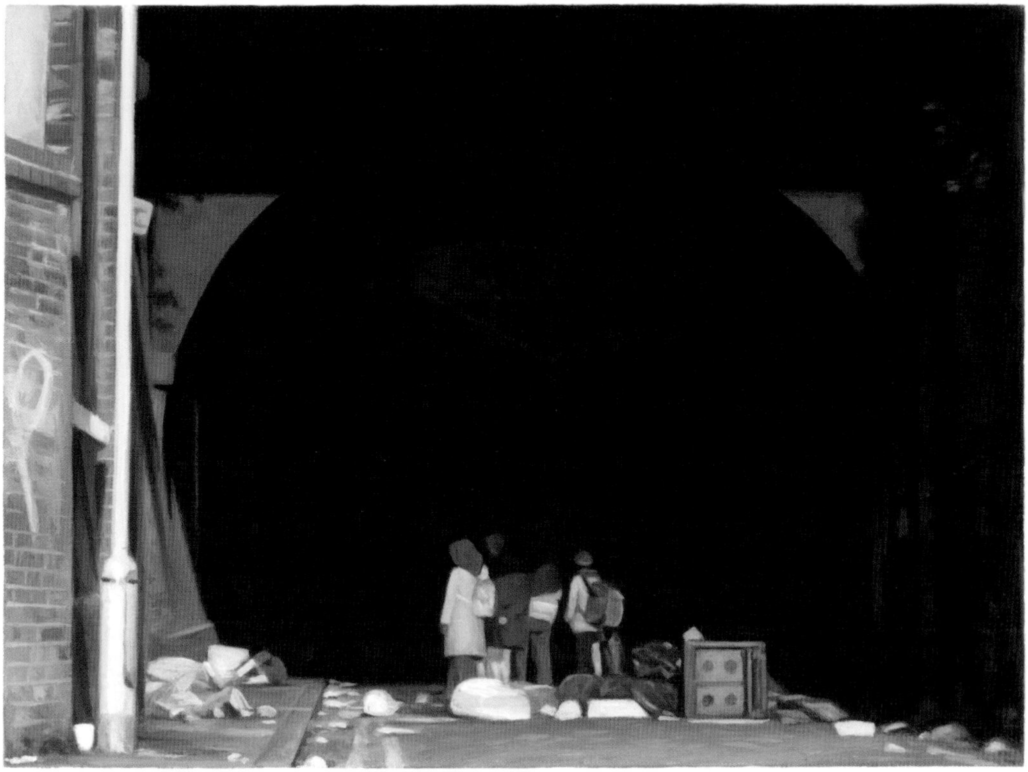

Nancy Milner

Untitled

2015
Oil on board
52 x 42 cm

My practice is to construct paintings that fix colour and form in various, tense economies. My work reflects the influence of colour field painting, pop art and gestural abstraction. When I make a painting, I begin with a series of drawings on paper, which I sift and edit to achieve a colourless draft. With these drawings as a scaffold, I contemplate how superimposed colours can generate a vital whole. The process is not pre-set. The painting grows and reshapes with the distensions of time, grasping for a legible equilibrium: a balance between colour and line, vacancy and repletion.

Biography

Nancy Milner was born in Barnsley in 1986. She studied at the University of Reading 2005-9 and the Royal Academy Schools London 2010-13 (awarded Royal Academy Keeper's Print Prize 2013). Attended British School at Rome (Abbey Scholar in Painting) 2014-15. Group exhibitions include *Premiums Interim Projects* (awarded Jerwood Purchase Prize for Painting) Royal Academy Schools London 2012, *RA Schools Show 2013* Royal Academy of Arts London, *At Home Salon* Marcelle Joseph Projects Ascot 2014, *June Mostra* British School at Rome Italy 2015, *Ittenology* (two-person, with Marita Fraser) Rook & Raven London 2016.

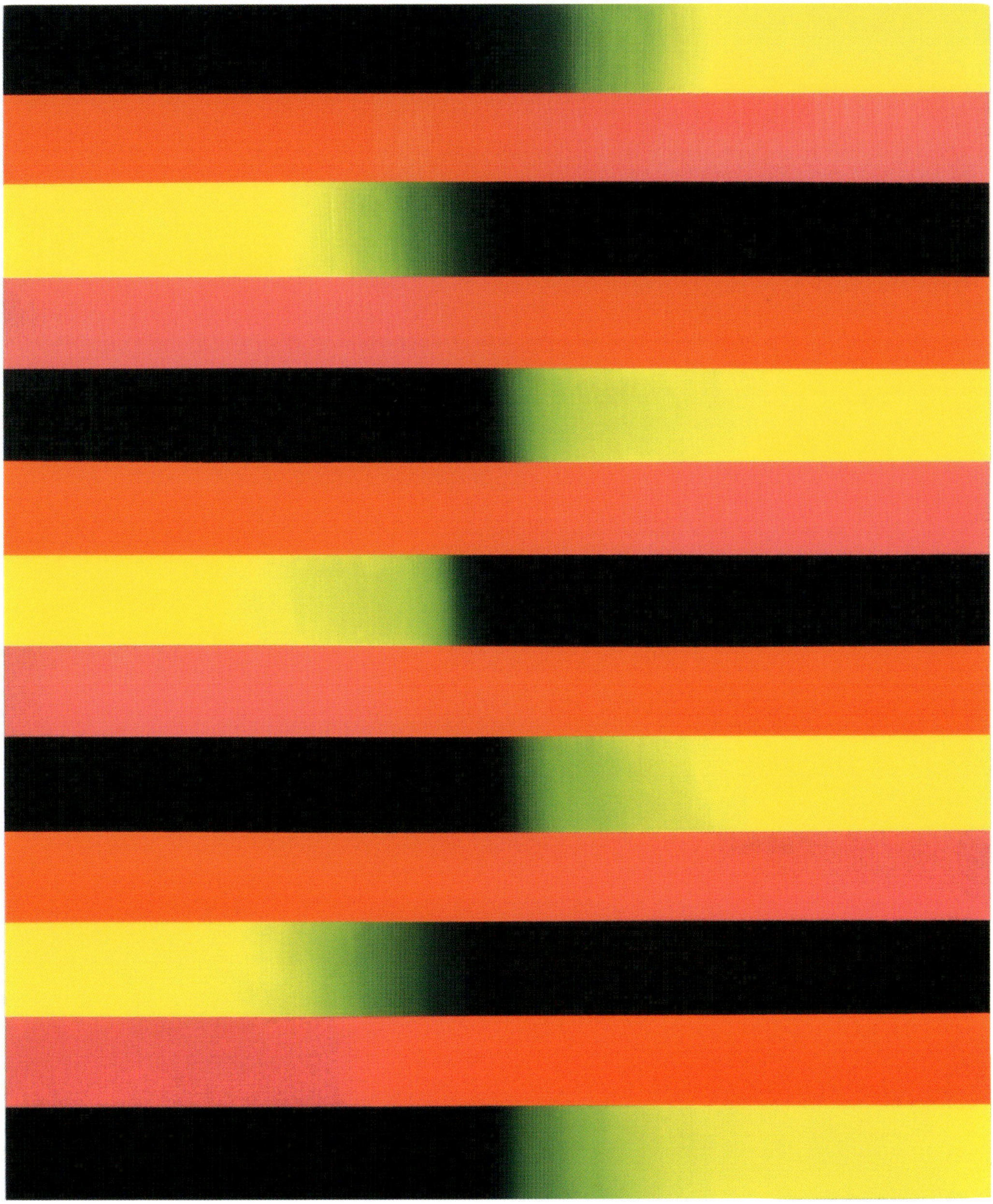

Frank Minoprio

Field Myth

2015
Acrylic and spray paint on canvas
139.3 x 101.6 cm

Spray paint ground overlaid with unplanned flaccid geometric forms and bodged perspectives worked up from unmixed colours. References to AbEx gesture, graphic design and other cosmic slop. Tension between improvised 'unknown image' played out against forms developed in previous works. Within solitude of studio ideas dissolve through painting process. Outcome unpredictable, shifting, never fixed.

Biography

Frank Minoprio was born in Wrexham in 1980 and lives and works in London. He studied at Wimbledon School of Art London 1998-2002, including an Erasmus scholarship exchange to Universidad Complutense de Madrid in 2001. Group shows include *Summer Exhibition 2006, 2007* Royal Academy London, *Postcard From My Studio* ACME Project Space London 2013, *The Threshold: Liminal Abstracts* Mayor's Parlour Gallery London 2014.

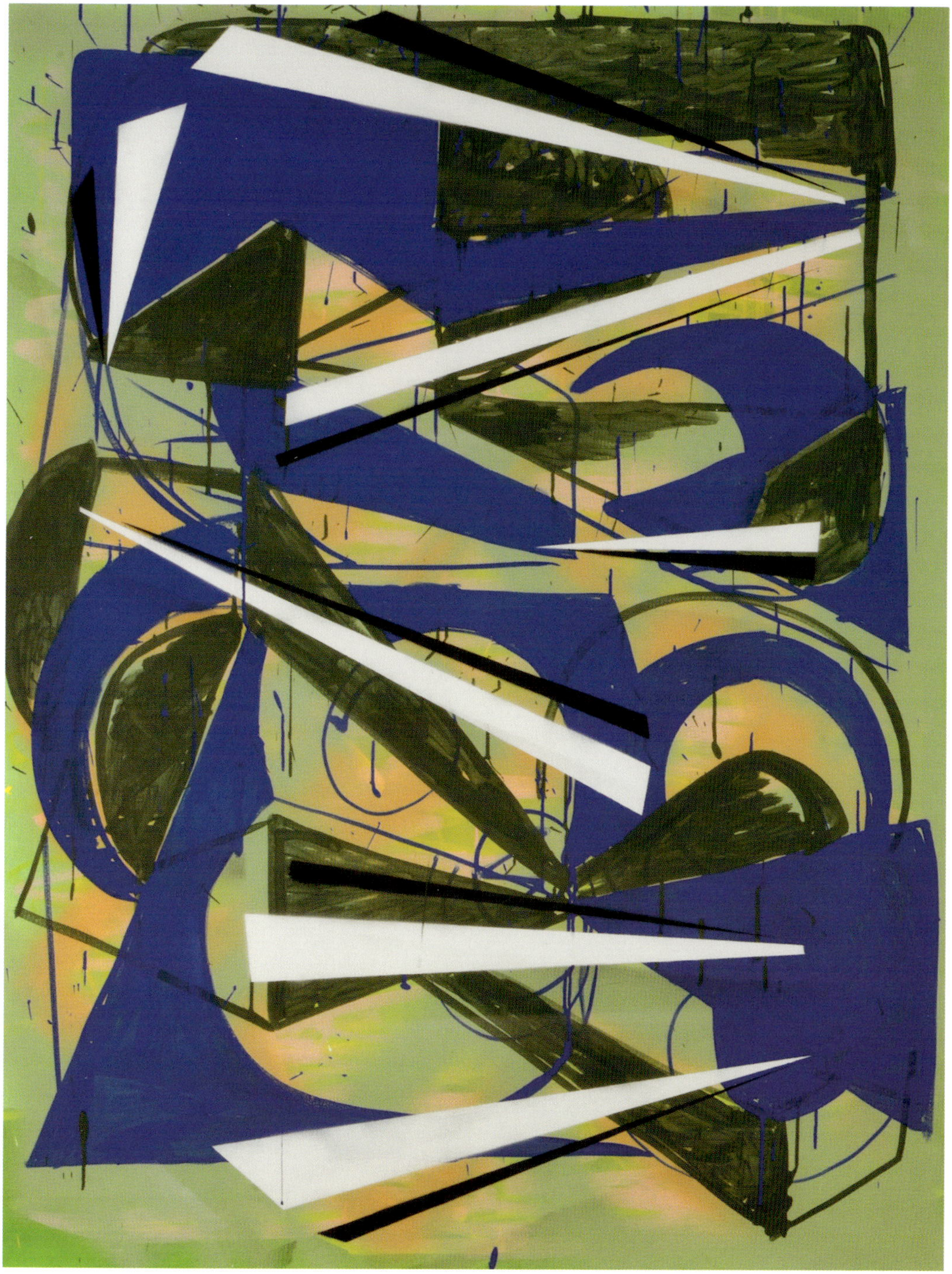

Steve Moberly

If I called this painting 'List' would you read it as such?

2015
Acrylic on polyester on board
74 x 57.5 cm

Economy of mark making has long been admired. Now we, so too, admire marks made awkwardly, not just in their economy but in their illusory counter effect, where the individual mark acts against the reading of the whole image.

If I can make a painting that asks, 'Does he or does he not know the conventions of contemporary painting?', then that is the motivation – not the faking of outsider art, rather the bastard child of outsider and insider; an attempt to shift to a process executed in wilful ignorance, lacking in consistency, marks sometimes tentative, sometimes confident.

In the tradition of the amateur scientists of the 19th century, exposing bits of the world with naive observation, such is this exploration of non-verbal communication in paint – false expertise that exhumes from within. The act of painting excavates the layers that underpin relationships. Figures interact in space in an agitated world of comfort eating, *faux pas* and social media.

It is easy to be distracted by the details of the making, perhaps stealing from abstract painters or pilfering old colour combinations from budget interior design shops, but ultimately there emerges a final result that gives away little but one's own disposition.

Biography

Born in Keynsham in 1972, Steve Moberly is based in Bournemouth and studied at the University of Bournemouth 2011-14. Exhibitions include *Best of the South West* The Pound Corsham 2014, *Platform Award* Aspex Portsmouth 2014, *Quay Arts Open* Newport Isle of Wight 2015, *Emergency 2015/16* Aspex Portsmouth 2015. Solos include *Paintings for Alleyways and Living Rooms* Nolia's Gallery London 2006, *Paintings for Alleyways and Living Rooms mrk2* No4 Southbourne 2009, *Paintings for Hallways and Caravans* Byzantium London 2009, *Steve Moberly* No4 Southbourne 2010, *Borderline Rude* Southbourne Library 2011, *Insider Planting* (awarded Best Visual Arts Event B.E.A.F) Old School House Boscombe 2015.

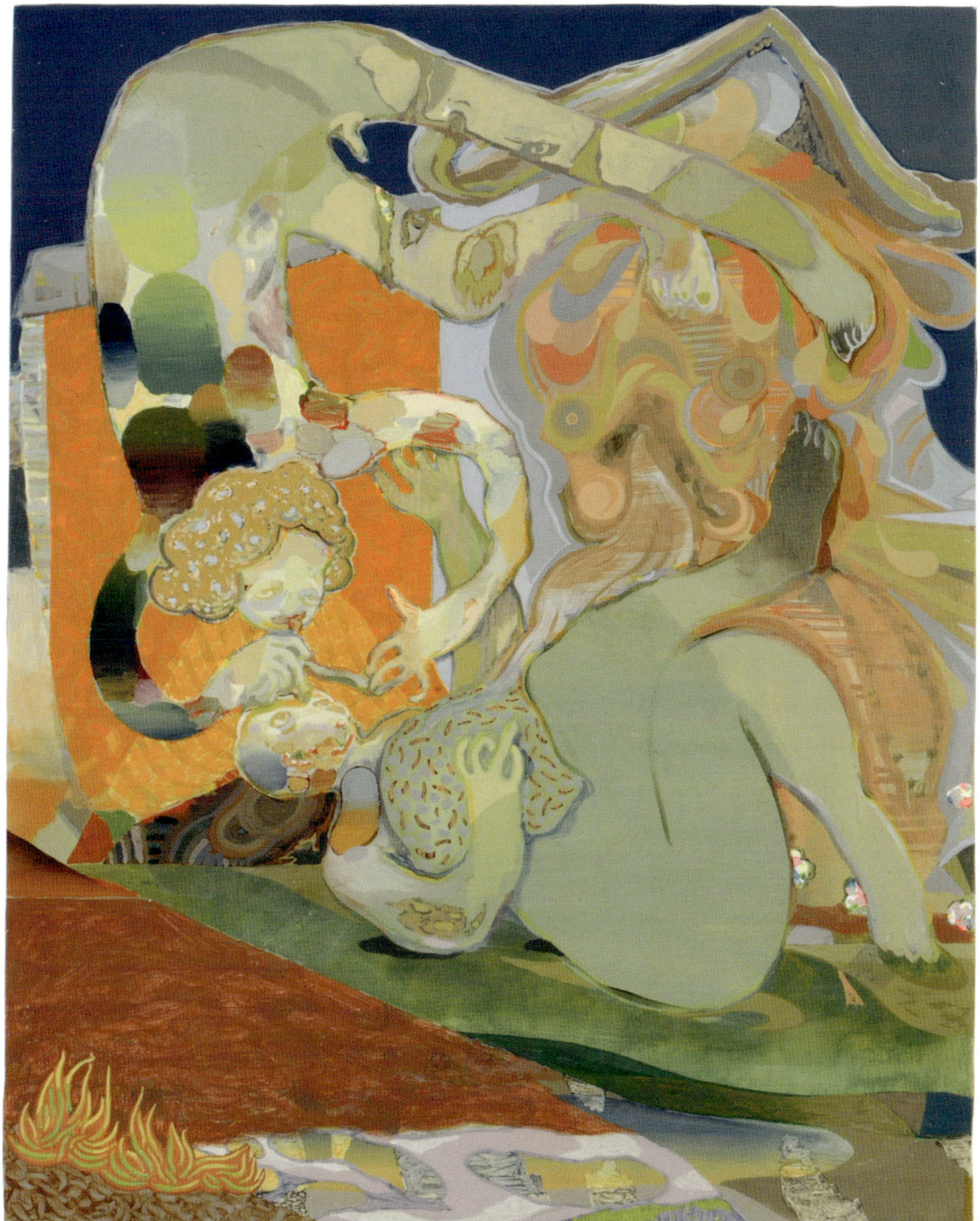

Donal Moloney

Cave Floor

2015
Acrylic on canvas over board
43.2 x 32.2 cm

I make intricate paintings that contain fragments of images from a wide variety of sources. I playfully combine and compress disparate collections of images to the point of overloading the picture plane. This 'kaleidoscope' of glistening surfaces becomes a vehicle for my interest in mixing fantastical imagery and ambiguous narratives.

Central to my practice is the use of a wide variety of media and processes to create the source imagery for my paintings. These include rapidly made drawings, sculptures and digital collages. I transform images from these sources through a protracted and slow process of painting, often taking more than a year to complete each piece. In so doing, I try to imbue these initial 'sketches' with something jewel-like and precious.

Biography

Born in Cork in 1984, Donal Moloney studied at Crawford College of Art Cork 2003-7, the Slade School of Fine Art London 2008-10 and University of the Arts London 2012-15. Exhibitions include *A Wall is a Surface* Londonewcastle Project Space London 2012, *The Painting Parade* LeandaKateLouise Projects London 2013, *Copy* Paper Manchester 2013, *Head to Head: 4 Questions 8 Paintings* Standpoint Gallery London 2014, *Under the Shadow of Natural Things* Benzie Gallery Manchester 2015, *Kaleidoscope eyes* Austin Forum London 2015, *London Irish Art* (Sol Art) Central Hall Westminster London 2015, *The Abject Object* Wimbledon Space London 2016.

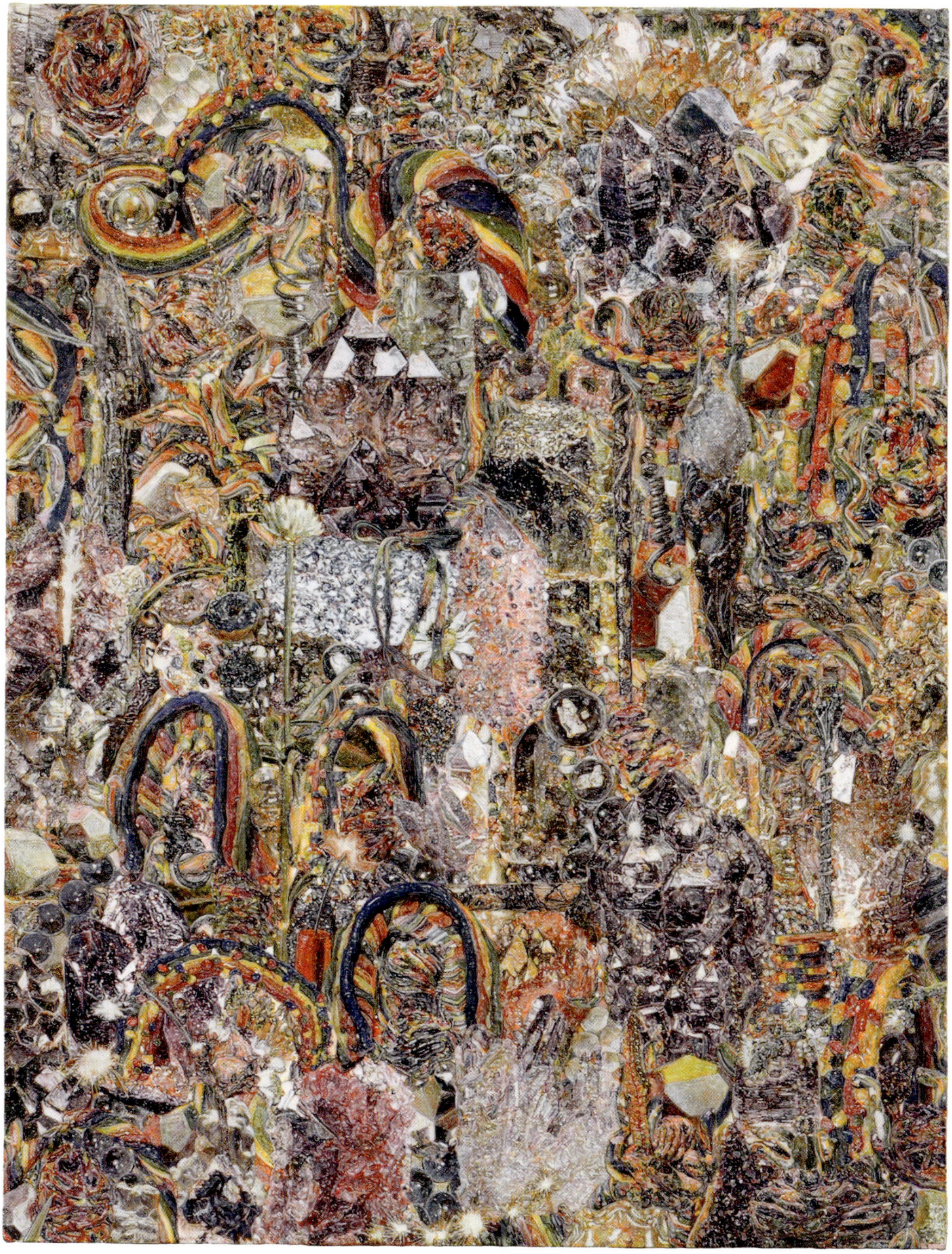

David Murphy

Long Ending (Green)

2015
Casein paint on gesso panel with surface incisions
56 x 76 cm

Across drawing and sculpture, on varying scales and in a variety of materials, my practice takes up aspects of inherently human activity that begin with the hand. Incorporating influences from architecture to anthropology, tool-making to textiles, the works are linked by their relationship to the hand-made and the hand-worked. The act of building or constructing is framed as essential and affirmative, but set against a shifting backdrop of unpredictable nature and passing time.

Since 2012 I have been heavily influenced by textile processes, an interest kindled initially by discovering a book of fibre micro-photography. The sudden consciousness that beyond the reach of our perception, textiles were complex three-dimensional structures has been highly significant for the way I think about surfaces, and has led to a large body of work exploring the 'topography' of natural forms at varying levels of zoom. Since then a textile 'language' has been a useful tool for me to examine more broadly within my practice the threshold between two and three dimensions, surface and volume.

Biography

Born in Newcastle-upon-Tyne in 1983, David Murphy attended Newcastle College 2001-2, Glasgow School of Art 2002-6, HFBK Dresden 2005. Exhibitions include *Zeichnung ohne Zeichnung* Christian Ehrentraut Berlin 2013, *KeepItReal* Bayt al-Sinnari Cultural Centre Cairo 2015, *Groundwork* New Art Centre Salisbury 2015. Solos include *New Basics* Monica De Cardenas Galleria Zuoz Switzerland 2013, *Certain Impacts* PEER London 2014, *Deep, Deeper* Monica De Cardenas Milan 2015. *Artist-in-residence* Yorkshire Sculpture Park Wakefield 2014, *Murano Glass Residency* Le Stanze del Vetro Venice 2015, *Kenneth Armitage Foundation Fellowship* 2015-17. An Arts & Heritage Public Art Commission for Dales Countryside Museum Wensleydale 2016.

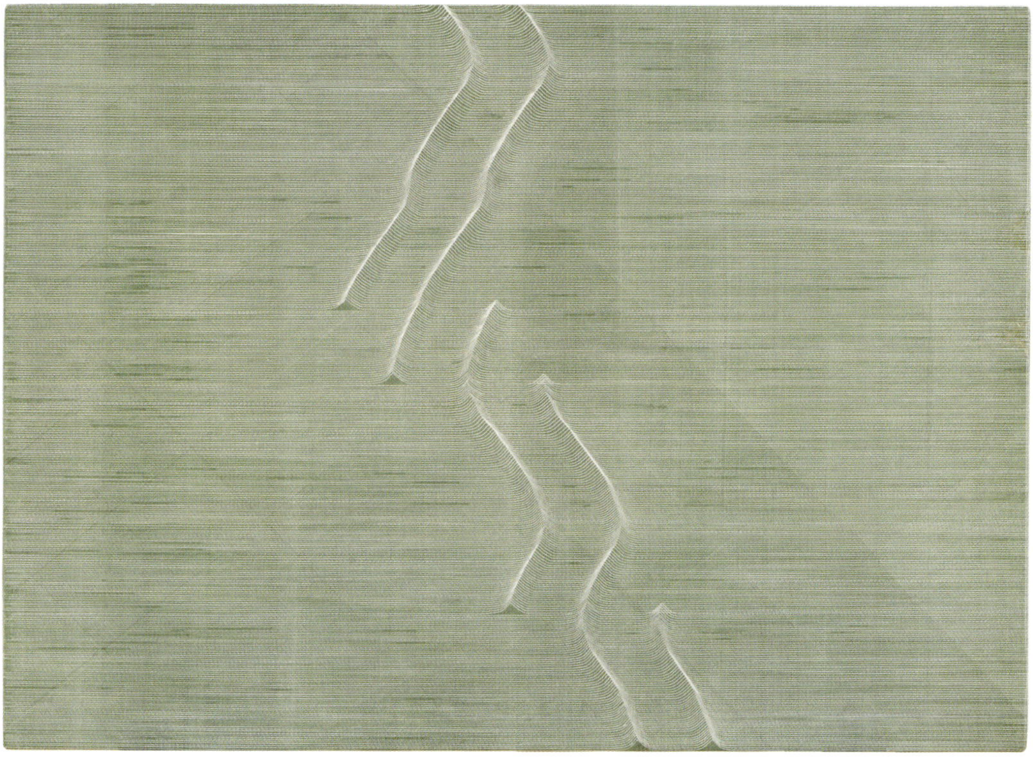

Ewan Murray

Couple

2015
Oil on board
25.5 x 20 cm

I like to think of painting as a way to notice the potential for images to provoke thought and create atmosphere, much in the way that poetry finds inspiration in the minutiae of everyday experience. A painting can negotiate a position between fiction and non-fiction, being at once a representation and a construction of reality. It is a way to balance the general appearances of the things around us with the intimacy of personal observations.

The depiction of hands is often a central element in pre-Renaissance Italian paintings. In these works, hands are used as motifs with which to imply narrative and suggest movement, yet their simplified, stylised forms belie acutely observed human gestures. *Couple* makes reference to this figurative language, while its composition points to the closely cropped photography found in contemporary fashion advertising.

Biography

Ewan Murray was born in Falkirk in 1991 and is based in Glasgow. He studied at Glasgow School of Art 2009-13 with a period at Ontario College of Art and Design 2011. Awarded DWT Cargill Fund Travel Bursary 2011. Exhibitions include *12X12X12* The Glue Factory Glasgow 2011, *The Woon Foundation Prize for Painting and Sculpture* (winner of the Cheong Kam Hee Art Prize) Gallery North Newcastle 2013, *William's Palm* McLellan Galleries Glasgow 2015, *50 Million Painters Can't Be Wrong* New Glasgow Society Glasgow 2015. His solo *Later Still* 183 Queens Drive Glasgow 2014. Undertook *Graduate Residency 2014* Hospitalfield Arbroath.

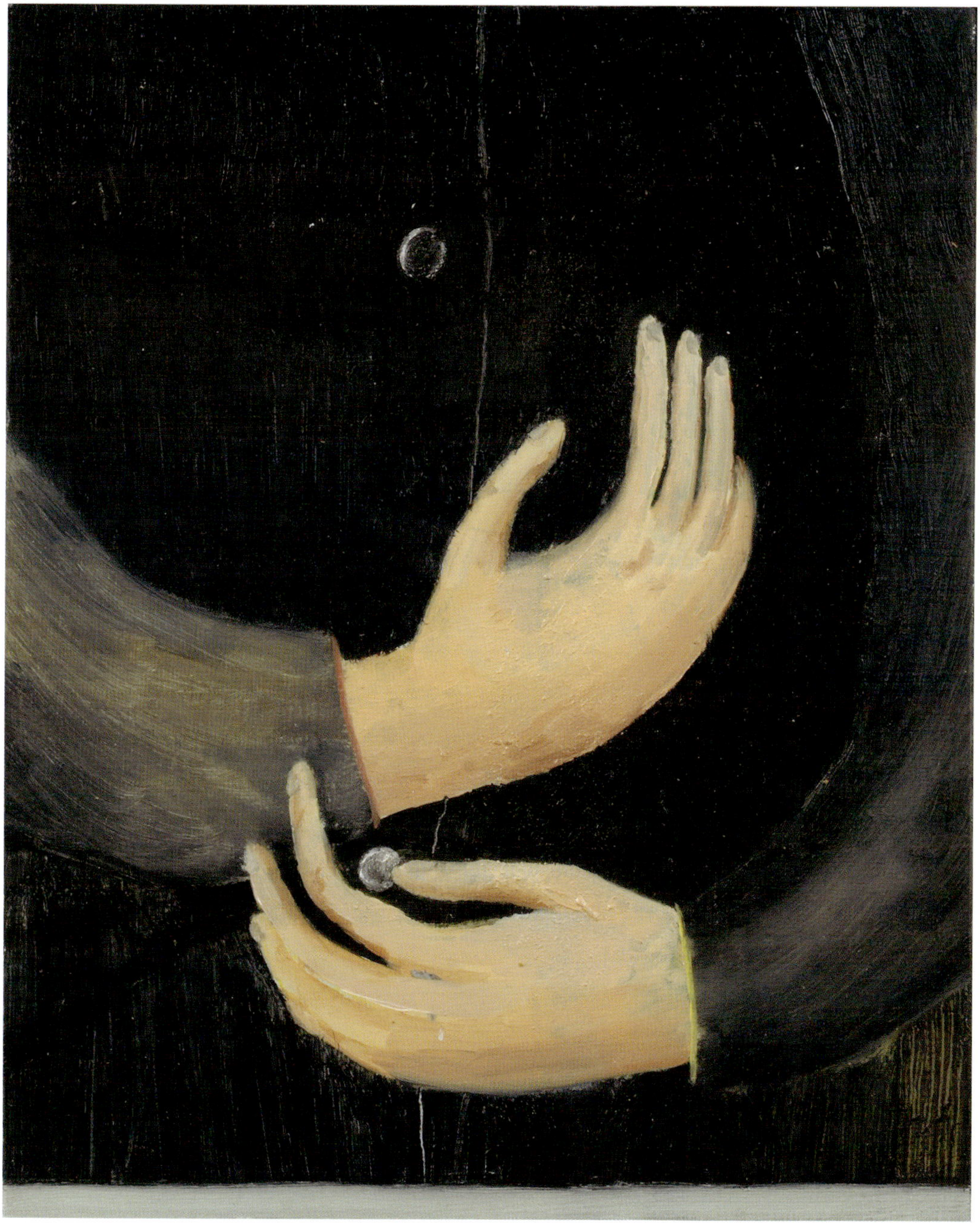

Laurence Owen

Ritual to the Westfield

2015
Oil on canvas with ceramic pins
234 x 360 cm

In *Ritual to the Westfield*, ideas and visual references gathered from past and present merge and re-form, resulting in a skewed and fractured environment. A particularly painterly aesthetic is magnified and exaggerated. The traditional technique of fixing nails to hold canvas on stretcher is employed with the use of oversized ceramic pins.

This prompts the question of whether adopted painterly aesthetics have a new function at a time when authenticity and authorship are readily shared and re-represented via digital platforms.

With these elements in place, *Ritual to the Westfield* activates our awareness of the inherited attitudes we associate with an era, its objects, images and taste, and scratches at our understanding of the hierarchical values these languages embody.

Inherent in this work are metaphors for attraction and desire, displayed through areas of playful brushwork, concealment and decoration. These visually attractive qualities act as a symbol for the seeking of pleasure in materials, and link material pleasure to consumerist goods. Here, Art becomes a product of consumerist culture, but it is in Art that the realisation of its own role in this culture can be acknowledged, acting as both a voyeur of this condition whilst also being a contender within it.

Biography

Born in Gloucester in 1984, Laurence Owen attended Stroud College of Art 2001-2, Falmouth College of Art 2002-5, Royal Academy Schools London 2012-15. Exhibitions (London unless stated) include *In The Darkest Hour There May Be Light* (Damien Hirst's Murderme Collection) Serpentine Gallery 2006, *Caustic Coastal / Rogue Studio Space* Manchester 2012, *Premiums Interim Projects* (E Vincent Harris Prize) RA Schools 2014, *Studio_Leigh* Studio_Leigh Gallery 2015, *Chimp Cracks Nut With Rock*...Kennington Residency 2015, *Suspended Fruit* C4RD 2016. Solos include *The Gold Book* 20 Hoxton Square Projects 2009, *Laurence Owen & Vivien Zhang* Rook And Raven 2015, Evelyn Yard Gallery 2016.

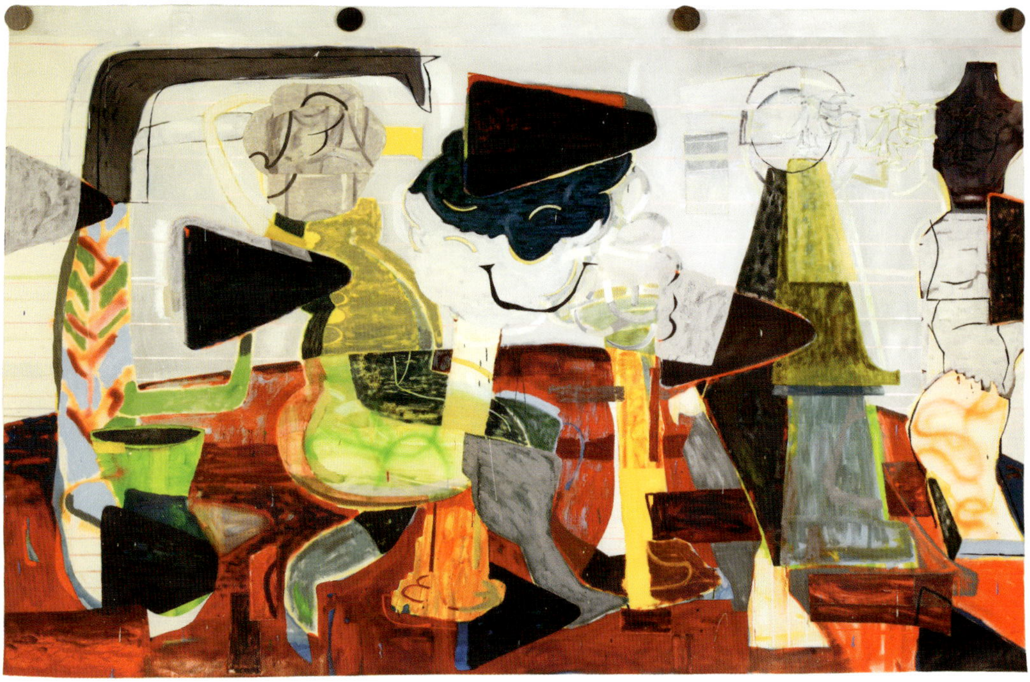

Mandy Payne

No Ball Games Here

2015
Aerosol spray and oil paint on concrete with wooden frame
33.7 x 33.9 cm

I am interested in marginal spaces, places that are often maligned or thought to be devoid of traditional aesthetic beauty. For the past four years I have been exploring Park Hill in Sheffield, the Grade II-listed council estate and one of Britain's largest examples of Brutalist architecture. The site is currently being regenerated and is in a state of flux – which makes it an interesting place to observe. Part of the estate has been transformed into shiny, luxury flats whilst half remains boarded up and derelict. I am particularly drawn to the un-refurbished parts where the memories and layers of the past are almost tangible. My intention was to create observational paintings that spoke of the displacement of the established communities and the temporality of the urban landscape.

Concrete is the unifying link throughout the estate and could be regarded as a potential palimpsest. In the refurbished sites it has been restored to exacting standards, in the old parts it is spalled, weathered and tarnished, which gives it a rawness and beauty of its own. With this in mind, I have been working with materials that are integral to the estate itself, namely concrete and aerosol spray paints.

Biography

Born in Pontypool in 1964, Sheffield-based Mandy Payne trained in Dentistry 1982-95 then Fine Art at Sheffield College 2007-10 and Nottingham University 2011-13. Recent exhibitions include *The Threadneedle Prize* Mall Galleries London 2013, *Summer Exhibition 2014, 2015* Royal Academy London, *Recording Britain Now: 2014 John Ruskin Prize Exhibition* (runner up) Millennium Galleries Sheffield, *Overlooked* (curated by S1 Artspace) Scottish Queen Sheffield 2015, *New Light Prize Exhibition* Bowes Museum Barnard Castle (touring) 2015/16. Solos *Between Places and Spaces* Tarpey Gallery 2014, *Betwixt and Between* Cupola Gallery Sheffield 2016. Elizabeth Greenshields Foundation Grant 2015. Fellow in Stone Lithography Leicester Print Workshop 2015-17. In *John Moores Painting Prize 2014* (prizewinner).

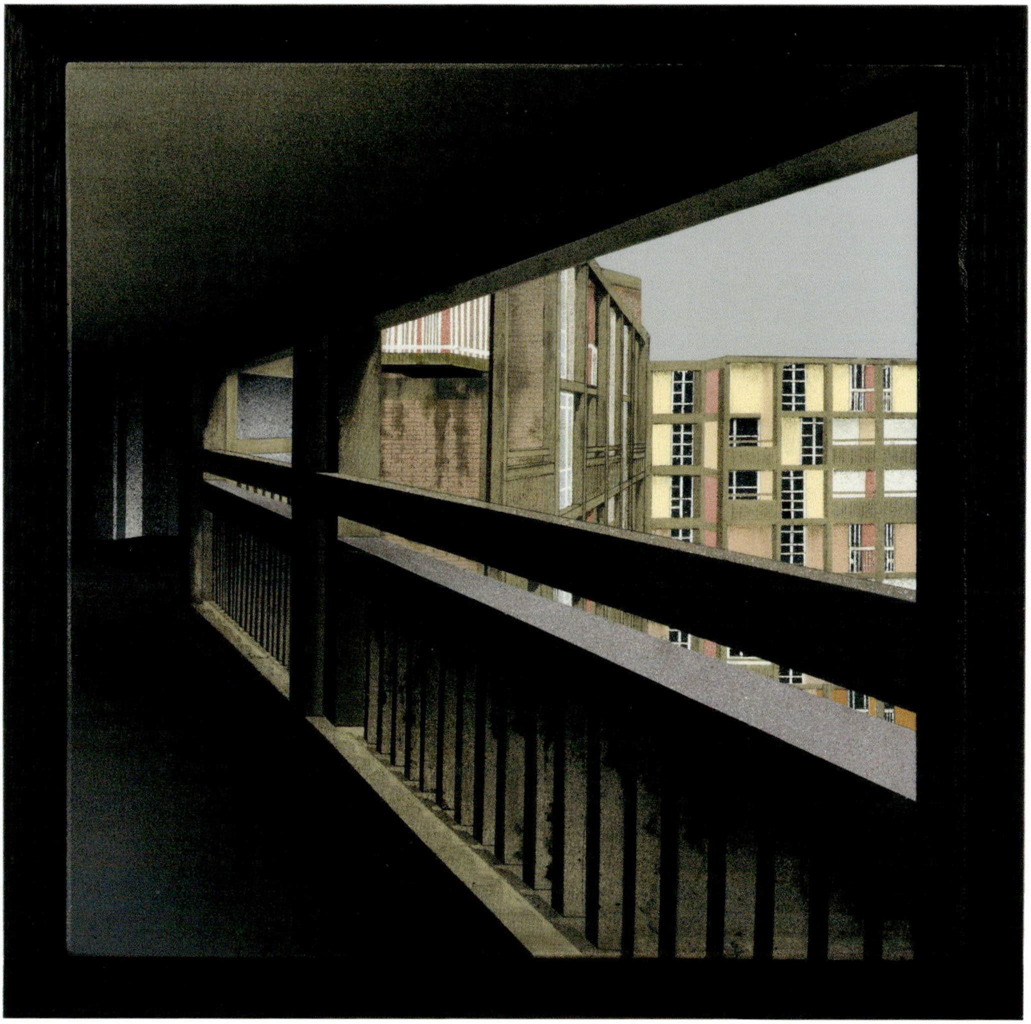

playpaint

Double Science Fiction

2015
Spray paint on canvas
127 x 127 cm

Paintings are made pragmatically. Initially each painting requires a novel or adapted technical procedure. This is either invented or modified from an alternative procedure but is necessarily limited to an approximately predictable outcome. There is a balance, or trade off, between the degree in complexity of the procedure and a plausible anticipation of the results, but this is always weighted in favour of the final outcome. A painting fails if the outcome fails, regardless of the success of the procedure. Whereas an outcome which is surprising is always allowed, so long as the outcome is a success. A procedure that fails, yet yields the anticipation of a successful outcome, can be modified or improvised. Cheating and short cuts are OK, as long as the final outcome is successful. Failed paintings can be developed as hybrids, reclaimed towards new paintings. Successful paintings can be repeated in combination with unique, reclaimed or re-enacted paintings. Any number of these variations, in any arrangement, can be combined to make new paintings. This statement is temporary.

Biography

playpaint formed in 2008, a collaboration between Michael Gittings and Damian Nelson. Michael: born Bloxwich 1962; Kent Institute of Art & Design 1989-92; Delfina Trust Award London 1994-6. Damian: born Swindon 1973; Chelsea College of Art 1992-5, Royal College of Art 1995-7. Damian left playpaint in 2015. Exhibitions (London unless stated) include *Playlist_Peeking In* (playpaint curated) New Peking Inn 2011, *Marmite Prize for Painting IV* (touring) 2012/13, *An Elixir of Photons* (curated) 63 Charlotte Street 2013, *Autocatalytic Future Games* (curated) No Format 2015, *Housework* Safehouse 1 2015. Solos *Amplifier (Part One)* 318 Old Street 2011, *Amplifier (Part Two)* New Peking Inn 2011, *Amplifier (Part Three)* Flat 3, 25 Brondesbury Road 2014.

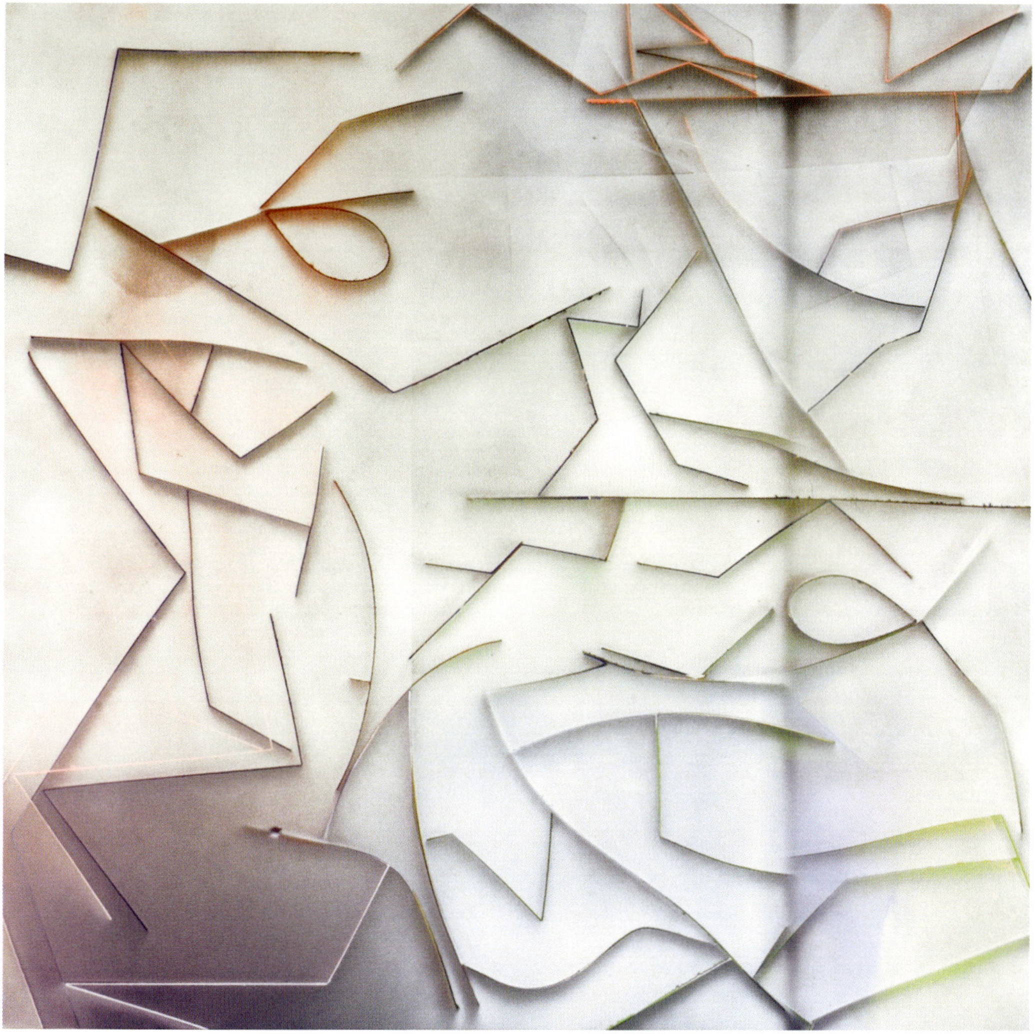

Alex Rennie

Totem

2015
Oil on linen
150.2 x 210.5 cm

Totem is one of a series of paintings exploring notions of population growth and societal shift. The compositions of earlier pieces were often determined by hard population data. More recent paintings have expanded into more conceptually abstracted areas, adapting visual metaphors of construction hoardings, beams and scaffolds to document the urban experience and to denote the boundaries of the individual.

The pared-down palette of black and luminous red is a frequent presence in my work. A field of vertical columns is formed entirely by a stark network of marks which vary in speed, intensity, weight and trajectory. The result is an abstract calligraphic language, reminiscent of cave painting, graffiti, even barcodes and digital coding. The urgency of mark making is pivotal and reflects a fast-paced environment glowing from the residual evidence of a transient population.

Biography

Alex Rennie was born in London in 1977. He attended Wimbledon School of Art London 1996-77, and Cheltenham & Gloucester CHE 1997-2000. Exhibitions include *BP Portrait Award* National Portrait Gallery London 2005, *Scope Basel* Waterhouse & Dodd Basel 2012, *Opening Exhibition* Waterhouse & Dodd London 2013, *Art Miami* Waterhouse & Dodd Miami 2013, *Pulse* Waterhouse & Dodd New York 2014, *Karen Gunderson & Alex Rennie* (two-person) Waterhouse & Dodd London 2014, *Lynn Painter-Stainers Prize* Mall Galleries London 2016. A solo *Alex Rennie: Recent Work* Waterhouse & Dodd London 2012. Included in the National Portrait Gallery publication *'500 Portraits – BP Portrait Award'* 2011.

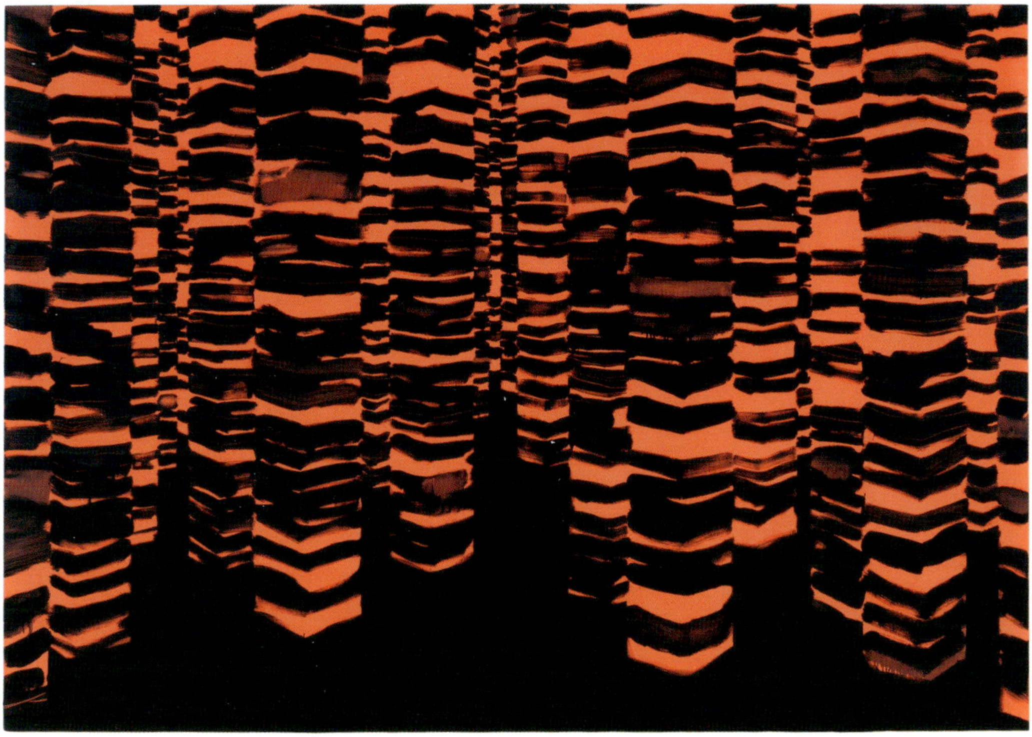

Tim Renshaw

Notebook Architecture

2015
Oil on aluminium
21 x 13 cm

Turning a page, like turning a corner, can be constructive. Likewise, by an act of rotation the structures in a picture show themselves – if you are lucky – in a better light. When I turn the page of an architecture book, the following page shows the same building pictured from a slightly different angle and the building is brought to life. In all cases, this seems to be more about the relationship and passage between two views.

The title of the ongoing series of works, *Notebook Painting*, is a metaphor for a painting that is both a surface plane made up of an infinite number of worked 'pages', and for a composition made up of 'notes' that can be potentially rearranged on subsequent pages. These notes are based on modern architecture. They aim to extend the metaphor whereby a façade or wall contains any number of previously formulated plans, and where the geometries that organise the space are contingent and open to change. Put another way, it refers to a surface that has memory, even if, as in this painting, it is only visible at the edges and may be forgotten in the turning of a page.

Biography

Tim Renshaw, born in Brighton in 1964, attended Leeds Polytechnic 1983-6 and Chelsea School of Art London 1989-90. Abbey Rome Fellow 2002 and Cocheme Fellow 2008. Group exhibitions include *Distressed Geometry* Kunstraum Baden 2014 and *Phase 1* Ruskin Gallery Cambridge 2016. He is part of the artist group Outside Architecture: recent projects include *One and One and One* CGP London 2012 and *One and One and One (part 2)* K3 Project Space Zürich 2012. Solos include *Images in the Vaguest Sense* V22 London 2008, *House in the Shape of a Stretcher* Five Years London 2011. In *John Moores Painting Prize 2004* and *2014*.

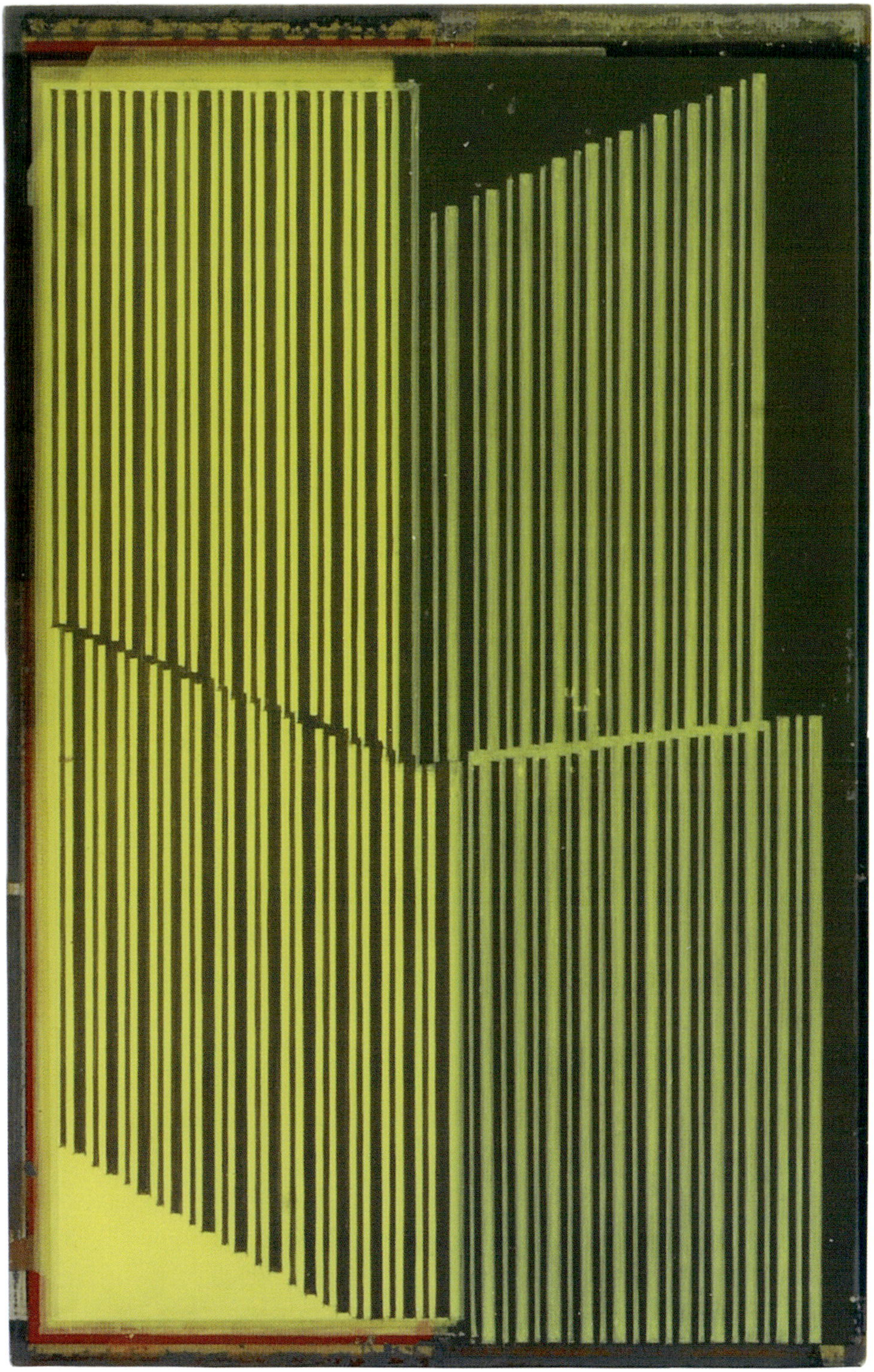

Lizi Sánchez

| | | | |

2014
Acrylic on industrial aluminium foil
214 x 270 cm

My paintings contain references derived from early 20th-century *avant-garde* movements and the emergence of abstraction in Latin America in the '50s. These combine with designs, typography and colour schemes taken from commercial sources including book covers, perfume packaging and confectionery. In *| | | | |* the panel colours match those of a brand of chocolates. My practice investigates how the language of geometric abstract painting has been adopted and transformed to commercial ends. I look at the legacy of abstract painting, and explore the intersection of modernist abstraction and its utopian ideologies with that of commercial graphic design.

I paint on industrial aluminium foil because of its material qualities and its conceptual associations. I am interested in how this foil retains traces of the making and handling but also in its association with industrial processes and, more specifically, the packaging industry. By co-opting the decorative idiom from commercial design, while pointing to its idealistic modernist heritage, I offer a reflection on the anomalies and conflicts of the artist within the commercial system. My work balances the rigour of modernism with the seductiveness and frivolities of luxury packaging, whilst acknowledging the role of the artist as a participant, however reluctant, in the commercial realm.

Statement includes passages taken from '*In a hall of mirrors*', by Sarah Kelleher, an essay accompanying Sánchez's solo show *In a world that laughs*, Domobaal, 2015.

Biography

Lizi Sánchez was born in Lima, Peru, in 1975. She studied there at Pontificia Universidad Católica del Perú 1994-9 and then Goldsmiths College London 2005-7. Group shows (all London) include *SV10: Members' Show* (selectors Jennifer Higgie, Rebecca Warren) Studio Voltaire 2010, *Material Matters* (Drawing Room offsite commission) UBM 2012/13, *Creekside Open 2013* (selector Paul Noble) A.P.T, *Drawing Biennial 2015* Drawing Room, *London Open 2015*, Whitechapel Gallery. Solos include *Beyond the Pearl* (with works by Louise Lawler) Standpoint Gallery London 2012, *Oh Locura de Diamante* (with Artists' International Development Fund) Vertice Lima 2014, *In a world that laughs* Domobaal London 2015.

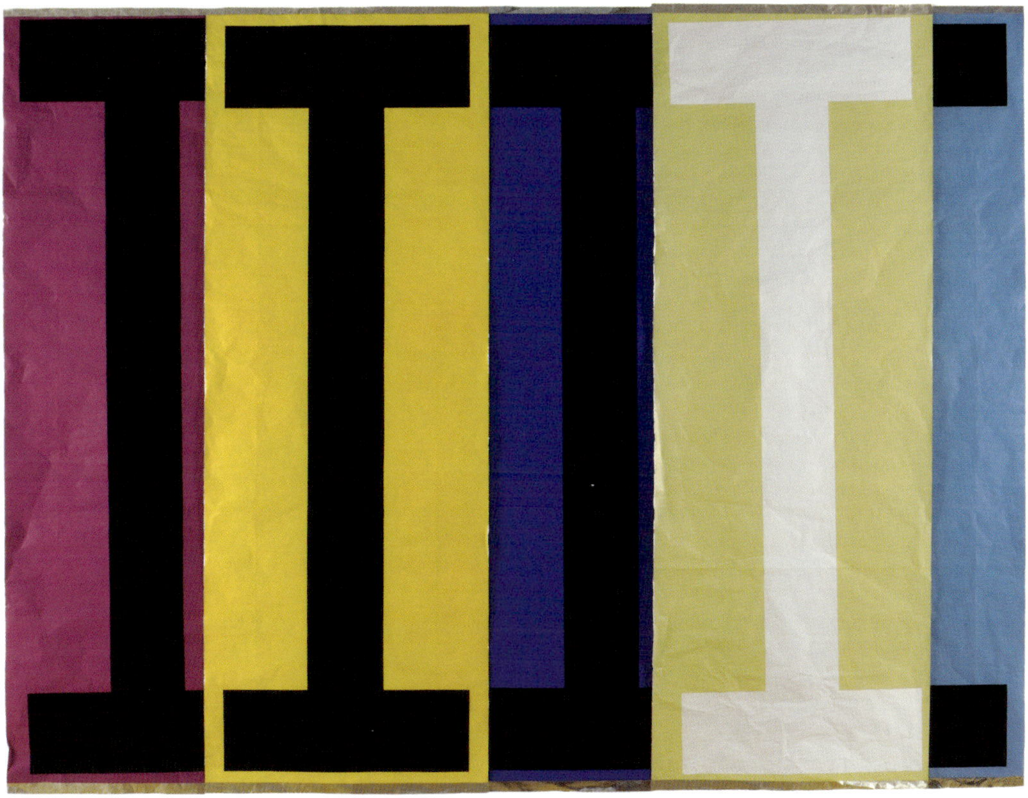

John Stark

Beasts of England II

2015
Oil on wood panel
50 x 60 cm

The painting is a midwinter's view over the free-range pig farms at Covehithe, located near the rapidly eroding coastline were I live. It is an observation that reflects my engagement with the immediate environment and its history.

The title of the work refers to the revolutionary anthem from *Animal Farm*, a book in which George Orwell tried, with full consciousness of what he was doing, *'to fuse political purpose and artistic purpose into one whole'*.

It is my intention to express the transient nature of reality whilst exploring the shadows that humans cast upon it. Together, the mist hanging on the horizon, the tyre tracks in the mud, the mirror-like puddles, the pigs, and their arks, comprise a realist landscape informed by personal and psychological reflection. The farms also remind me of concentration camps.

Biography

Born in London in 1979, John Stark is based in Suffolk. Attended University of West England Bristol 1998-2001, and Royal Academy Schools London 2001-4. Exhibitions include *Dawnbreakers* John Hansard Gallery Southampton 2010, *Modern Witchcraft* ASC London 2014, *Gute Kunst Wollen!* AEG Nuremberg 2015, *From the Almighty Incarnate. Religious motifs from the SøR Rusche Oelde Berlin collection* Museum Telgte, Telgte 2016. Solos include *Apiculture* Charlie Smith London 2011, *Field Work* Edward Cutler Gallery Milan 2013, *Witchcraft & Warfare* Charlie Smith 2014, *DoL Po* Charlie Smith London 2016. Co-curated shows include *Collateral Drawing* (with Bella Easton) UCS Waterfront Gallery Ipswich 2016.

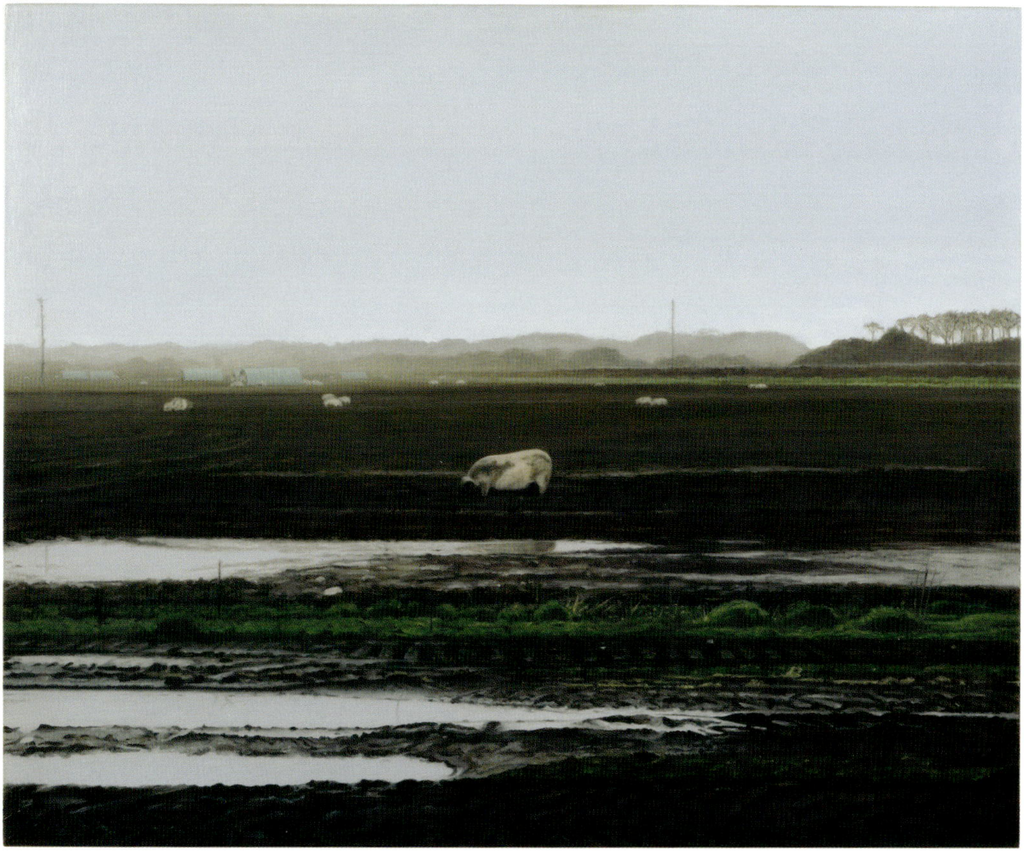

Duncan Swann

I choose the child

2015
Oil on canvas
240.2 x 190.6 cm

I choose the child is from a series of large format oil paintings called *Selected Outcomes*. Human figures are arrayed in grids or in smaller groups of three or four. They inhabit a non-space that might be the pages of a book containing infinite moments from the lives of individuals. The figures are often numbered, suggesting that they are part of a system of classification. From these multiple figures individuals are circled, underlined or crossed out according to unspecified selection criteria.

The process of making this work is often quick and contains an element of chance. Paint is poured on wet surfaces and allowed to run slowly across the surface, creating pooling and flows, depositing pigment that serves as visual information. There is an unpredictability in the process which in turn mirrors the works' content. These paintings are about life, our hopes and anxieties, and the natural and man-made processes of selection that operate beyond our control.

Biography

Duncan Swann was born in Bridport in 1969 and studied at the Royal College of Art London 2002-4. Exhibitions include *England, France, Germany* Kohn Gallery Los Angeles 2005, *Contemporary Art Society Art Futures* Bloomberg Space London 2005, *EASTinternational* Norwich Gallery Norwich 2006, *Jerwood Contemporary Painters* Jerwood Space London (touring) 2007, *EMERGENCY*[5] Aspex Portsmouth 2011, *If you look like your passport photo you're too ill to travel* Sheffield Institute of Arts 2012. Solos include *On the Other Side of the World* Alon Segev Gallery Tel Aviv 2006, *La Rosa dei Venti* Rachmaninoff's London 2007, *That Time* Neue Galerie Landshut, Landshut 2016.

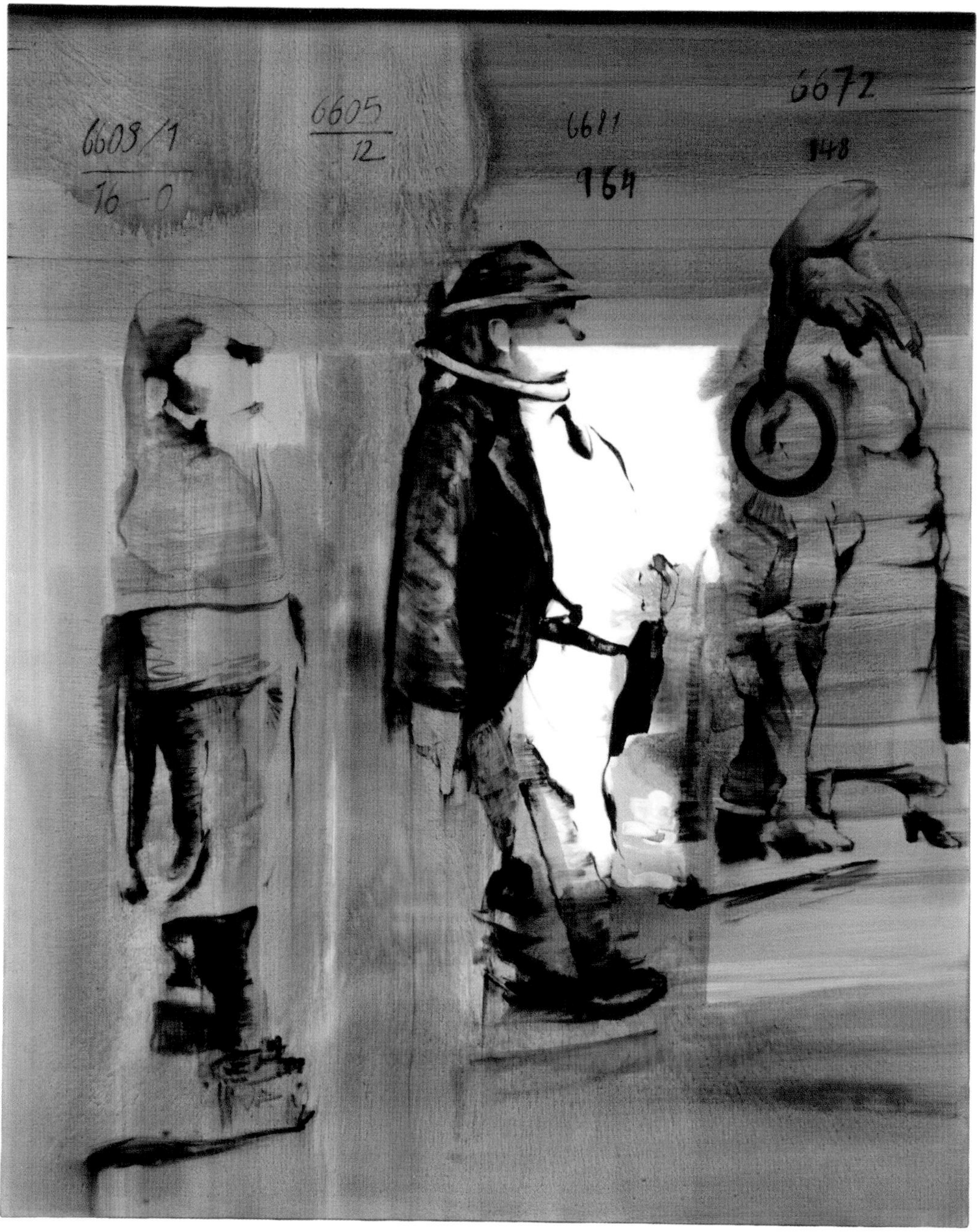
6608/1
16 0
6605
12
6681
964
6672
148

Shaan Syed

Foster

2014
Oil on canvas
230.4 x 174.3 cm

All paintings say 'here is a painting' and 'you are here'. Therefore, all paintings function as signs. The act of painting to me feels paradoxical: material is added in order to uncover. In my own work, I address these notions – that a painting may be at once a process, a reveal, and a sign. How do established systems of looking relate to how we see anew, and how do they influence the way in which we look at and make images now? In past iterations of abstract art, painting sought to expunge itself of the notion that a mark on a canvas might signify something outside of itself. Modernism, as a consequence, perfected painting in the West through its processes and its use of materials. Meanwhile, eastern art continued to place value on repetition and tradition well into the 21st century. Painting for me, however, is imperfect, variable and unpredictable. I paint in order to find a space for imperfection within these histories, with the knowledge that my own personal history is indebted to both: an area for loss, gain and negation to contend with each other, including myself, the painter.

Biography

Born in Toronto in 1975, Shaan Syed attended Ontario College of Art and Design 1998-2000, Goldsmiths College London 2004-6. Exhibitions include *ArtFutures 2008* Bloomberg Space London, *Jerwood Contemporary Painters* Jerwood Space London (touring) 2010, *Addendum* La Salles de Bains Lyon 2010, *Fifteen* S1 ArtSpace Sheffield 2010, *Fade Away* Transition Gallery London (touring) 2010, *Synesthesium* Ana Cristea New York 2013, *Emergency 6* Aspex Gallery Portsmouth 2013, *The Violet Crab* DRAF London 2015, *Shaan Syed and Sam Windett* Patrick De Brock Knokke 2016. Solos include *One Minus One* Ana Cristea 2014, *CAPITAL!* GMJ Berlin 2014, *Licking Forward Tangerine* noshowspace London 2015, *I & I* Kunsthalle Winterthur Switzerland 2015.

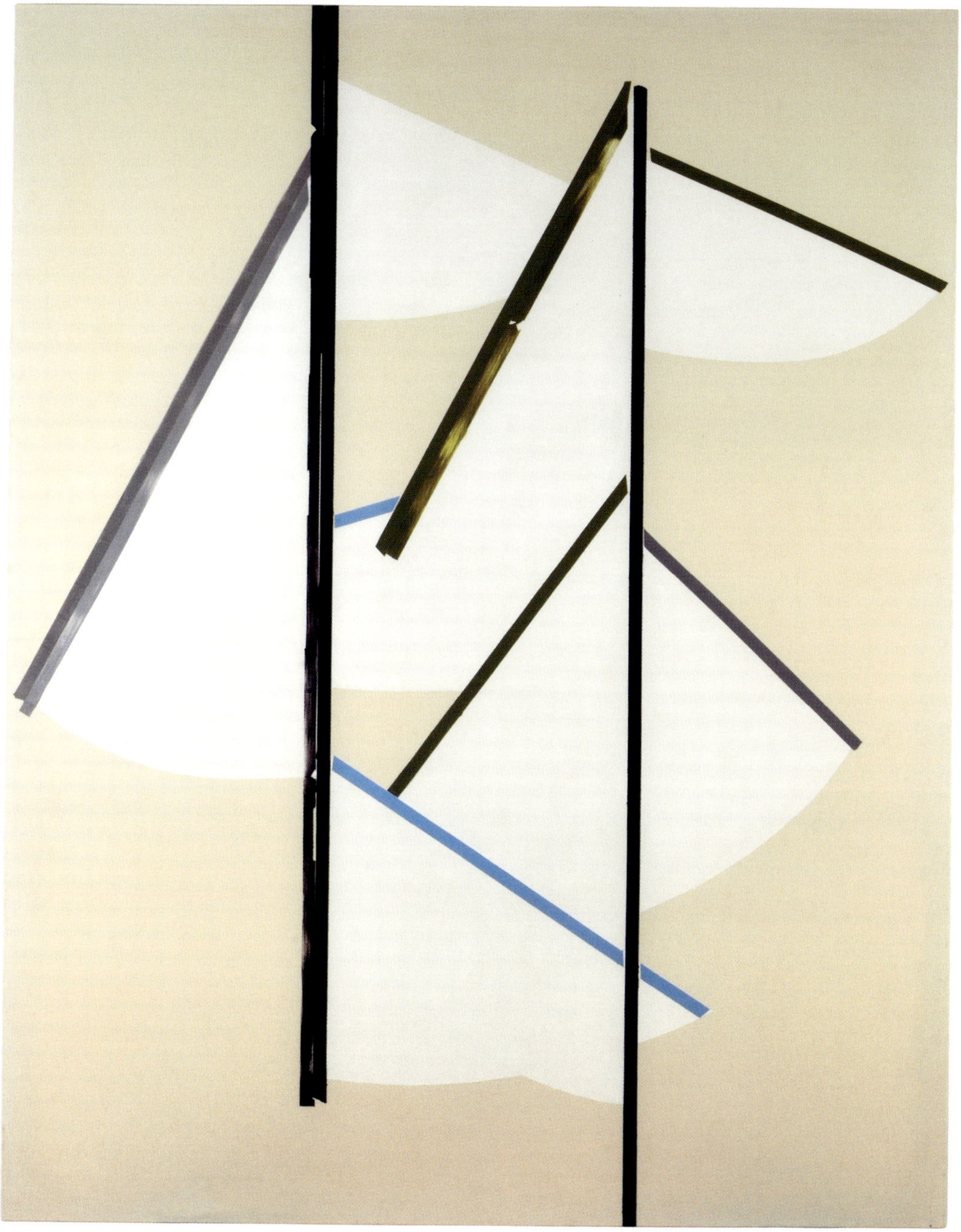

Emma Talbot

You Come To Me In A Dream

2015
Acrylic on canvas
210 x 150 cm

This painting is based on fragments of my own dreams. Shapes open out, scenes are formed and snippets of text provide an account of the non-linear narratives that occupy my unconscious thoughts. I wanted to make a pictorial space that the viewer can move through without particular direction, capturing a dream-like state.

In my work, painting allows me to crystalise and frame particular subjects out of an autobiographical stream of consciousness. I try to capture, with honesty, my thinking and personal life story. I'm interested in the way my own psychology develops, and how it organises experiences into a network of non-linear associations.

As we can't, yet, record our dreams, memories or thoughts via digital or photographic technologies, the way idiosyncratic, mental imagery is articulated offers exciting pictorial possibilities. I try to find inventive ways of translating thought images into painterly space without reliance on archetypal composition, using text and image as equal components. Working directly on to raw, sealed canvas lends immediacy, as each mark made cannot be erased. Somehow this makes painting feel daring.

Biography

Emma Talbot was born in Worcestershire in 1969 and is based in London. She attended Birmingham Institute of Art and Design 1988-91 and the Royal College of Art London 1993-5. Exhibitions include *Graphics Interchange Format* Focal Point Gallery Southend 2015, *DRKRM DAM* Gallery Berlin 2015, *William N Copley/Emma Talbot/Ina van Zyl* Galerie Onrust Amsterdam 2016, *Comic Tragics* AGWA Perth 2016. Solos include *Memories Turn to Dusk* Petra Rinck Galerie Düsseldorf 2015, *Step Inside Love* Domobaal London 2015, *Unravel These Knots* Freud Museum London 2016. In Thames and Hudson's *100 Painters of Tomorrow* and *Drawing People*, and the Saatchi and David Roberts Collections. In *John Moores Painting Prize 2012*.

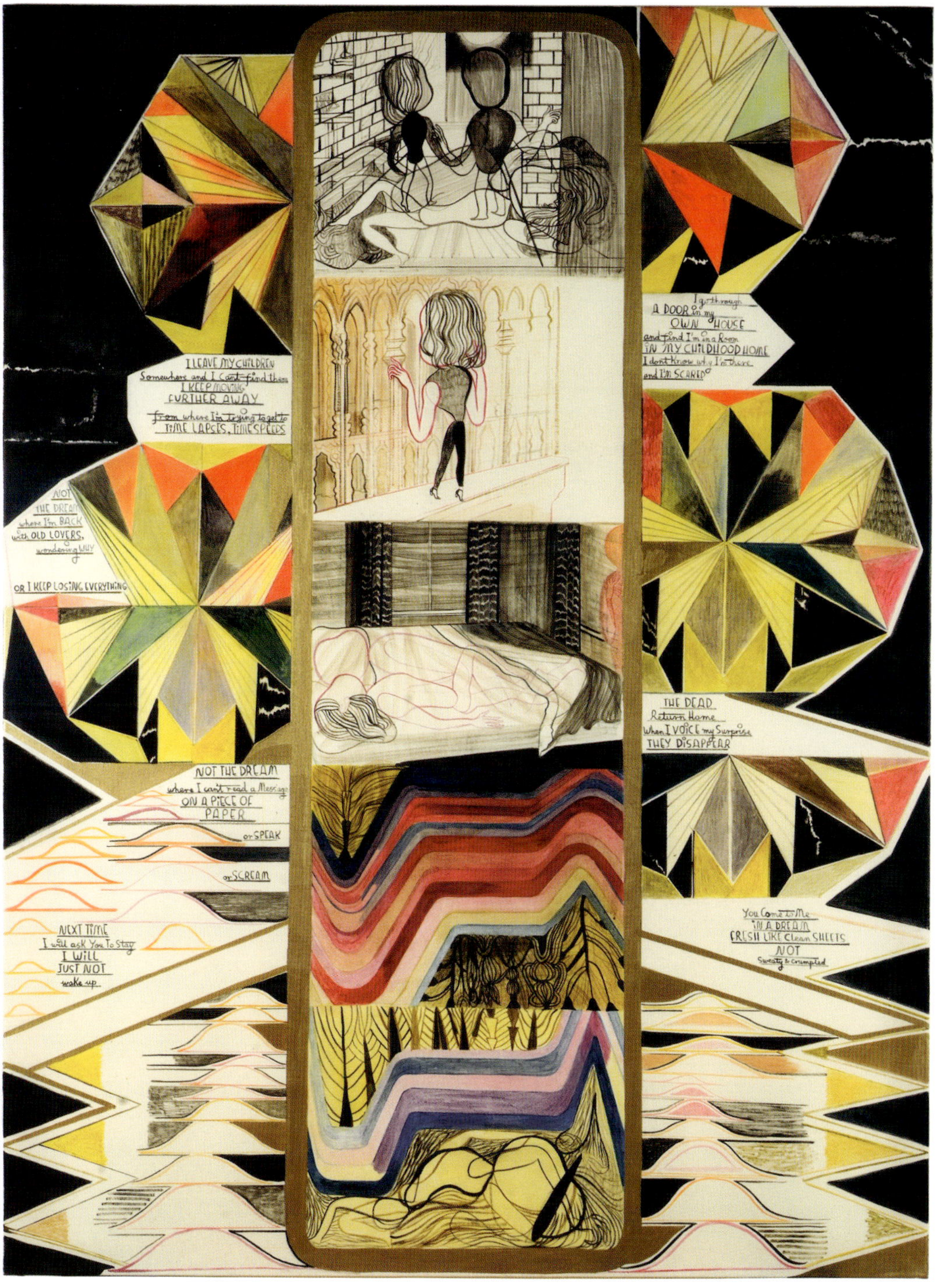
I go through
A DOOR in my
OWN HOUSE
and find I'm in a Room
IN MY CHILDHOOD HOME
I dont know why I'm there
and I'm SCARED
I LEAVE MY CHILDREN
Somewhere and I Cant find them
I KEEP MOVING
FURTHER AWAY
From where I'm trying to get to
TIME LAPSES, TIME SPEEDS
NOT
THE DREAM
where I'm BACK
with OLD LOVERS,
wondering WHY
OR I KEEP LOSING EVERYTHING
THE DEAD
Return Home
When I VOICE my Surprise
THEY DISAPPEAR
NOT THE DREAM
where I can't read a Message
ON A PIECE OF
PAPER
or SPEAK
or SCREAM
NEXT TIME
I will ask You To Stay
I WILL
JUST NOT
wake up
You Come to Me
IN A DREAM
FRESH LIKE Clean SHEETS
NOT
Sweaty & Crumpled

Julia Warr

Where do we come from? Where are we going?

2015
Acrylic and pencil on canvas
156 x 156 cm

Where do we come from? Where are we going?, an allusion to Matisse's dancing figures, makes a claim for the pleasure and freedom of movement. The figures appear like cut-outs against a sugar-coated bouquet: part joyful innocence, part subterfuge to mask the dancers' shyness as they appear on the threshold between tentative first steps and breaking out. The painting takes its name from a Paul Gauguin work and was made during my first dance residency in 2015. It is a drawing-based piece, light and improvisational, yet rooted in the shaky symmetry of a hand-drawn grid to be spilled over and erased with exuberance.

Biography

Born in San Jose in 1959, Julia Warr is based in London. Attended Goldsmiths College 1996-9 (Warden's Prize 1999). Exhibitions include *Friends and Family* Anton Kern New York 2008, *Unformed* (performer/curator) Lit Crawl London 2015, *ROOM 408* (painting/performance/curator) ASC London 2015, *The Maverick Expo* OXO Tower Wharf London 2015, *My Friend Maia* City Lights Film Festival New York 2016. Solos include *Oh the Places you'll go!* Massimo de Carlo Milan 2002, *Jo Jo* Galerie Michael Janssen Cologne 2003, *Julia Warr* Program Gallery London 2004, *Talk to her* Galeria Tomas March Valencia 2005, *Spindrift* ASC London 2014. In Goldsmiths University of London collection.

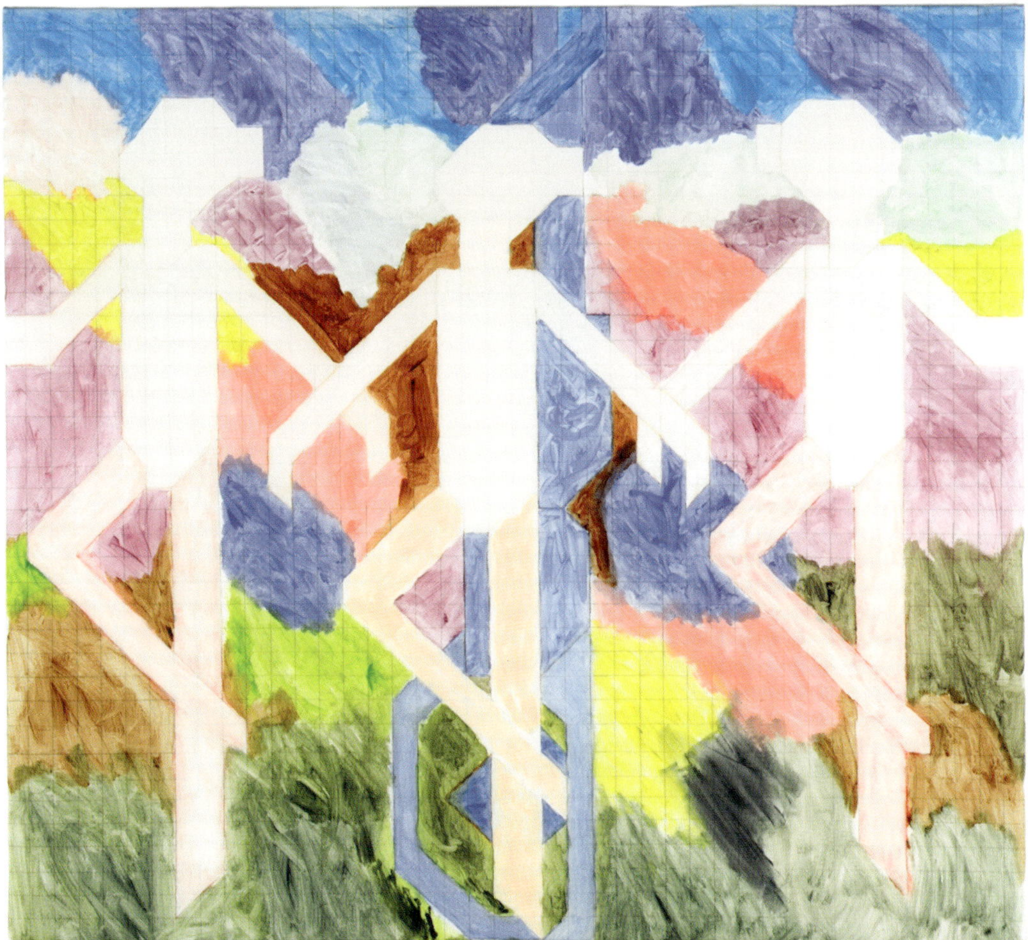

Richard Kenton Webb

The Landscape as Discourse

2014
Oil and found pigments on linen
62.2 x 65.4 cm

In 2014 I went to the other side of the world, to the copper mining town of Queenstown, buried deep in the Tasmanian rainforest. Excited to be starting a two-month residency, I was looking forward to spending each day walking through spectacular landscapes and discovering unfamiliar worlds. Despite being miles and miles away from home, I felt surprisingly close to the windswept parts of my own land – the Cotswolds, the Lakes and the Dales. A discourse began – a conversation with all I hold dear, filled with memories of paintings, poetry and music. I started to bring form to these thoughts and to the colour of the landscape around me. I dug up pigments from the earth beneath my feet, first the most incredible purple and then copper greens and oranges. I made these into paint and put them to work on canvas. This painting is my response *to* the earth *with* the earth, embodying all my feelings from that point, contained in this unobtainable moment, frozen in space and time – a split second of a thought brought to life and held, remote, waiting.

Biography

Richard Kenton Webb was born in Kent in 1959. He attended the Slade School of Fine Art London 1978-82 and Royal College of Art London 1983-86. Solo exhibitions include shows at Benjamin Rhodes Gallery London 1987, 1989, 1992, 1994, SACI Gallery Florence 1999, *Retrospective* North Light Gallery Huddersfield 2000, *Orangeness* Abbey Walk Gallery Grimsby 2011, *New Work* Celia Lendis Contemporary Moreton-in-Marsh 2014, *Thoughts in Search of a Thinker* LARQ Queenstown 2014, *Still Life with Blackbirds* Corinium Museum Cirencester 2014, *Landscape is a Conversation* LARQ 2015. Residencies include *Boise Travelling Scholarship* to Rome 1985, *SACI International* Florence 199, *LARQ Residency* Tasmania 2014/15.

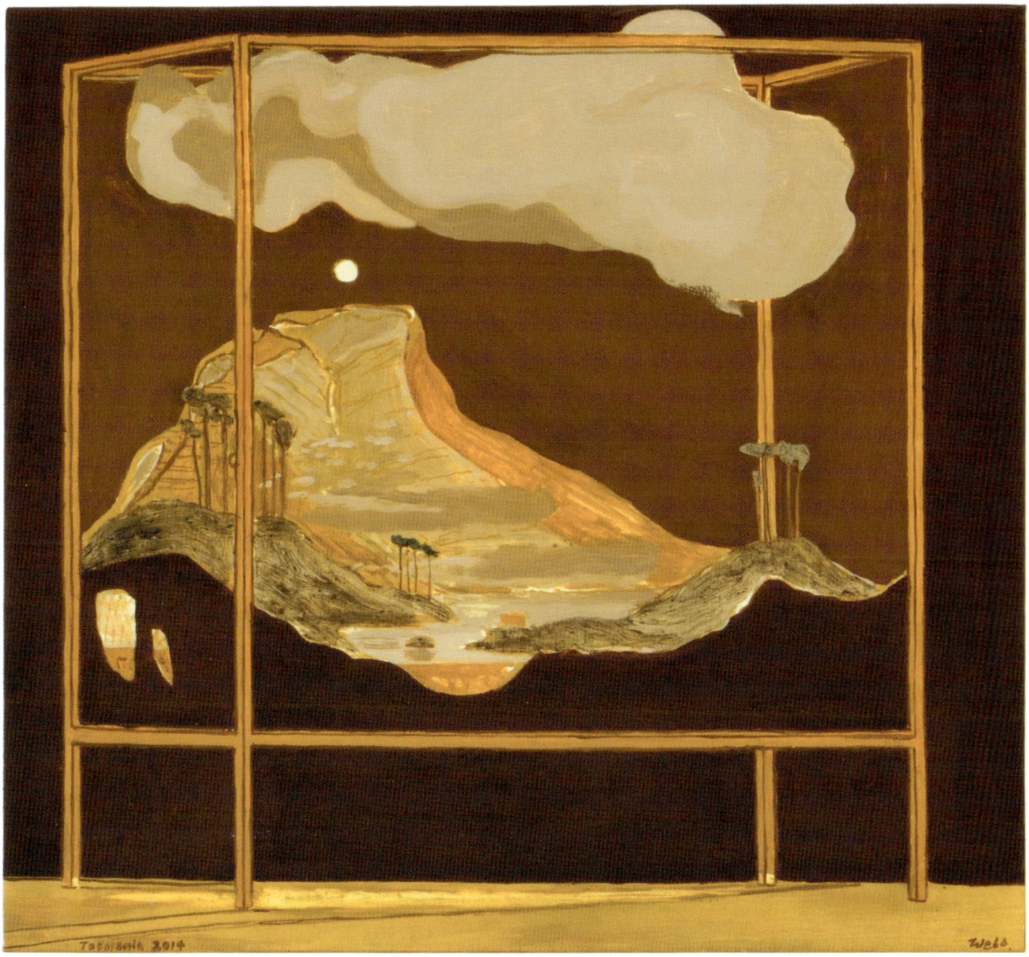
Tasmania 2014
Webb.

Simon Williams

A bout portant

2015
Alkyd oil on canvas
150 x 120 cm

My desire is to reflect something of the world we live in, a time of visual bombardment from advertising, packaging and digital technology. As an artist I'm interested in how to harness this visual stimulus to make sense of the world. Painting has become my way to develop a personal language of gestural marks, a fascination for chance alignments, for the exciting stuff that paint can do.

A 1960s poster entitled *'A bout portant'*, for a film based on Ernest Hemingway's *The Killers*, was the starting point for this painting. Something in the composition and colours really appealed. That's where my journey began, a desire to capture the energy I could see using my sense of the aesthetic, one which has been shaped by a love for vivid colours and sharp, graphic edges. I have an intuitive response to form and composition with a desire to create a dynamic between order and spontaneity.

I like to think that my paintings act as half remembered urban signs, pieces of information which, whilst intangible, may also be universal.

Biography

Born in the West Midlands in 1965, Simon Williams attended Loughborough College of Art 1984-7, Nottingham University 1989-90, and then lectured at Central School of Speech and Drama London 1993-6. He has worked as a Designer in the film industry, including with *Spitting Image, Jim Henson's Creature Shop*, and on the recent *Star Wars*. Group shows include *Bonhams Cornish Contemporary Art* Trewithin Cornwall 2005, *Limbo* Cornwall Art Biennial The Old Coffin Store Truro 2013, *Spring Salon Exhibition* Candid Arts Trust London 2015, *The Salon* ProjectSpace103 Newquay 2015. Solos include *Dynamism* Vitreous Contemporary Art Truro 2005 and *Viscosity* Vitreous Contemporary Art 2007.

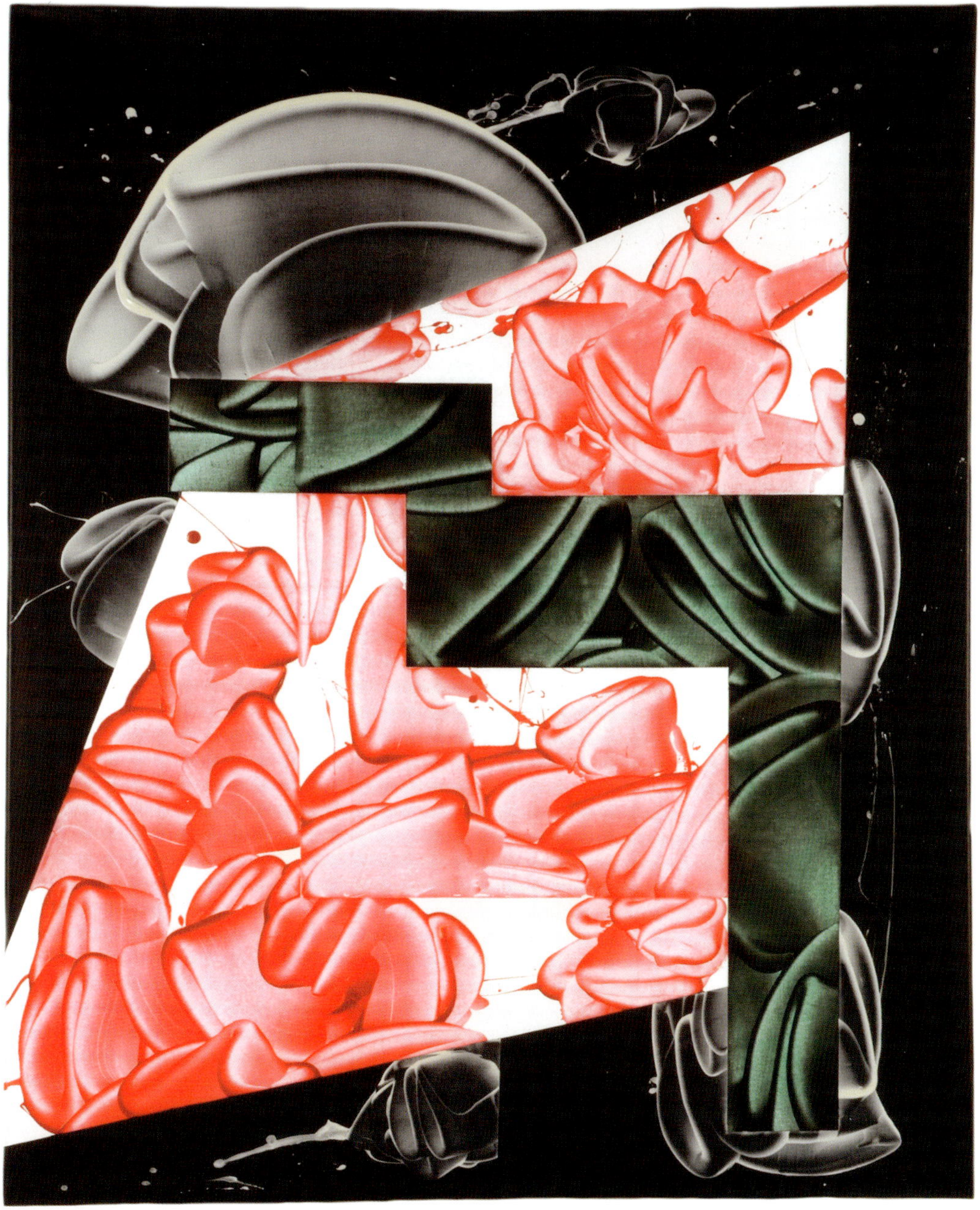

Mary Wood

Series 15 Cerulean 2

2015
Oil on canvas
126.8 x 101.6 cm

There was no pre-conceived intention here. There never is. I feel my way through. I am reminded by this painting of Hans Hofmann's suggestion: *'A picture must be finished in one sweep.'* I was able to conclude with a flurry of cerulean blue.

Biography

Born in London in 1959, Mary Wood studied at Winchester School of Art 1978-81, Manchester Polytechnic 1982-3, Goldsmiths College London 1985-6. Exhibitions (London unless stated) include *Stowells Student Exhibition* Royal Academy 1980, *MASA Associate Show* UMIST Manchester 1983, *MASA Drawing Show* Cavendish Gallery Manchester 1985, *Summer Exhibition 1986* Royal Academy, *Stephen Cooper and Mary Wood* Castlefield Gallery Manchester 1987, Warwick Arts Trust 1988, *Riverside Open* Riverside Studios 1990, *Summer Exhibition* Vanessa Devereux Gallery 1990, W3 Gallery 2015. Solos are Casson Gallery East Sussex 1988, Athawes Gallery 1988, *Mary Wood* Questors Theatre 1988, Brunel Gallery 1989, Vanessa Devereux Gallery 1991, Jersey Galleries Osterley House 2007.

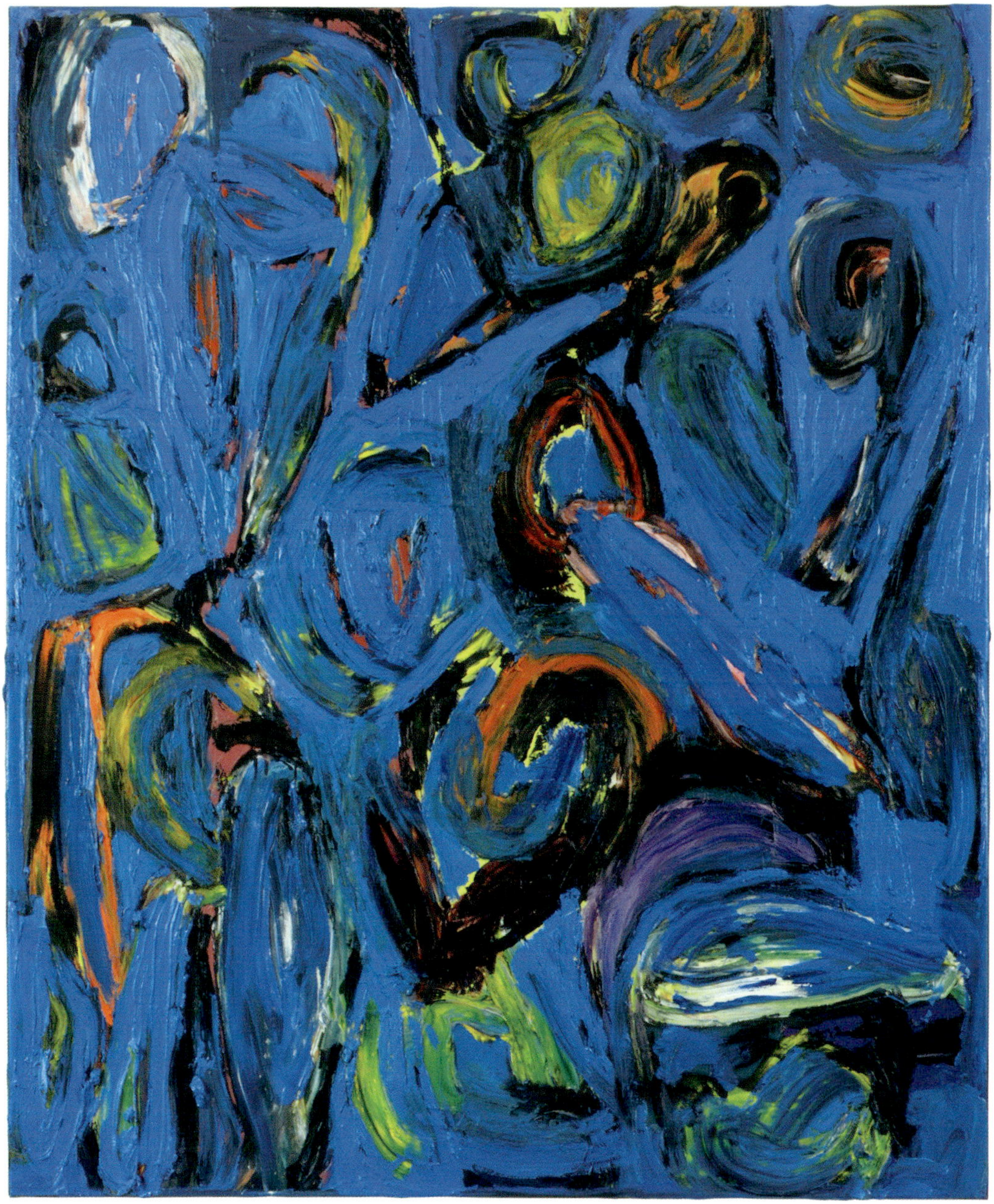

Index of artists

National Museums Liverpool cannot be held responsible for the content of external websites

Talar Aghbashian
27 Paddock Road
London
NW2 7DH
www.talaraghbashian.com
contact@talaraghbashian.com

Tristan Barlow
www.tristanbarlow.com
tristansbarlow@gmail.com

Karl Bielik
www.karlbielik.com
karlbielik@gmail.com

Gabriella Boyd
www.gabriellaboyd.co.uk
gabriella_boyd@hotmail.com

Julian Brown
41 Grantham Road
Brighton
BN1 6EF
www.julianbrownart.co.uk
julesfnbrown@gmail.com

Nici Bungey
www.nicibungey.com
nici@nicibungey.com

Bernard Charnley
www.bernardcharnley.co.uk
plainair@btinternet.com

Julie Cockburn
Flowers Gallery
82 Kingsland Road
London
E2 8DP
www.juliecockburn.com
info@flowersgallery.com

James Collins
www.collinsjames.net
jamesc.1992@live.co.uk

Gemma Cossey
www.gemmacossey.com
www.gemmacossey@hotmail.com

Ben Cove
www.bencove.com
Artist's Estate: melaniecove@googlemail.com

Graham Crowley
Greystone House
87 High Street
Wickham Market
Suffolk
IP13 0RA
www.grahamcrowley.co.uk
grahamncrowley@gmail.com

William Dick
www.williamdick.com
WILLIAMDICK@blueyonder.co.uk

Sarah Dwyer
Josh Lilley Gallery
44–46 Riding House Street
London
W1W 7EX
www.sarahdwyer.com
info@joshlilley.com

Bella Easton
www.bellaeaston.com
bella@beaston.co.uk

Róisín Fogarty
www.roisinfogarty.com
roisinfogarty@hotmail.com

Michael Ginsborg
84 Thornlaw Road
West Norwood
London
SE27 0SA
michaelginsborg@btinternet.com

Juliet Goodden
The Brook House
Pinfold Lane, Bradley
Ashbourne
Derbyshire
DE6 1PN
www.julietgoodden.org
juliet.goodden@gmail.com

Steph Goodger
www.stephgoodger.com
stephgoodger@gmail.com

Christopher Hanlon
info@domobaal.com
chris-hanlon@hotmail.co.uk

Linda Hemmersbach
www.lindahemmersbach.com
linda.hemmersbach@gmail.com

Thom Trojanowski Hobson
Meadows Farm
Church Street
Rendham
Suffolk
IP17 2AZ
www.thomhobson.com
thomisthere@msn.com

Ira Hoffecker
www.irahoffecker.com
ira.hoffecker@gmail.com

Benjamin Jamie
www.benjamie.com
ben.a.jamie@gmail.com

Benjamin Jenner
www.benjaminjenner.co.uk
benjaminthomasjenner@gmail.com

Gareth Kemp
www.garethkemp.com
mail@garethkemp.com

Nicholas Kulkarni
Studio 48
The Propeller Foundry
165 Childers Street
London
SE8 5JR
www.nicholaskulkarni.com
mail@nicholaskulkarni.com

George Lloyd-Jones
www.georgelloyd-jones.com
seven.jones@hotmail.co.uk

Enzo Marra
www.axisweb.org/p/enzomarra
enzomarra1975@gmail.com

Lee Marshall
www.lamarshall.co.uk
info@lamarshall.co.uk

Sneh Mehta
Brickfield Studios
Studio 103
Empson Street
London
E3 3LT
www.snehmehta.com
snehmehta00@gmail.com

Nicholas Middleton
139 Skeltons Lane
Leyton
London
E10 5BS
www.nicholasmiddleton.co.uk
info@nicholasmiddleton.co.uk

Nancy Milner
www.nancymilner.com
nancykatemilner@gmail.com

Frank Minoprio
www.frankminoprio.com
frankminoprio@googlemail.com

Steve Moberly
www.stevemoberly.co.uk
stevemoberly@hotmail.co.uk

Donal Moloney
www.donalmoloney.net
donaljmoloney@gmail.com

David Murphy
www.davidmurphystudio.co.uk
david@davidmurphystudio.co.uk

Ewan Murray
www.ewan-murray.com
ewanmurrayewanmurray@gmail.com

Laurence Owen
www.laurenceowenart.com
lowenstudio@gmail.com

Selma Parlour
www.selmaparlour.com
selmaparlour@hotmail.co.uk

Mandy Payne
www.mandypayneart.co.uk
mandypayne24@googlemail.com

playpaint
www.playpaint.co.uk
playpaint@live.co.uk

Alex Rennie
Studio 312
Wimbledon Art Studios
10 Riverside Yard
Riverside Road
London
SW17 0BB
www.alexrennie.co.uk
info@alexrennie.co.uk

Tim Renshaw
www.outsidearchitecture.org
t.renshaw@reading.ac.uk

Lizi Sánchez
www.lizisanchez.com
lizisanchez@gmail.com

Michael Simpson
www.michael-simpson.co.uk
michael.simpson1@virgin.net

John Stark
www.johnstarkgallery.co.uk
johnstarkisi@gmail.com

Duncan Swann
18 Hallam Grange Road
Sheffield
S10 4BJ
www.duncanswann.com
duncanswann@yahoo.co.uk

Shaan Syed
www.shaansyed.com

Emma Talbot
www.emmatalbot.org.uk
emmatalbot0@gmail.com

Julia Warr
www.juliawarr.org
myjuliawarr@gmail.com

Richard Kenton Webb
UWE Bristol
City Campus at Arnolfini
16 Narrow Quay
Bristol
BS1 4QA
www.RichardKentonWebb.com
www.rkwprints.com
Richard4.webb@uwe.ac.uk

Simon Williams
35 Dobbs Lane
Truro
Cornwall
TR1 3NB
www.simonwilliamsartist.co.uk
simonwilliams42@btinternet.com

Mary Wood
www.instagram.com/marywoodart
marywoodart@gmail.com

John Moores Painting Prize China 2016

The jury

Lewis Biggs
Non-voting Chair

Gerard Hemsworth
Artist

Tim Marlow
Director of Artistic Programmes
Royal Academy of Arts

Sarah Pickstone
Artist

Liu Wei
Artist

Yang JieCang
Artist

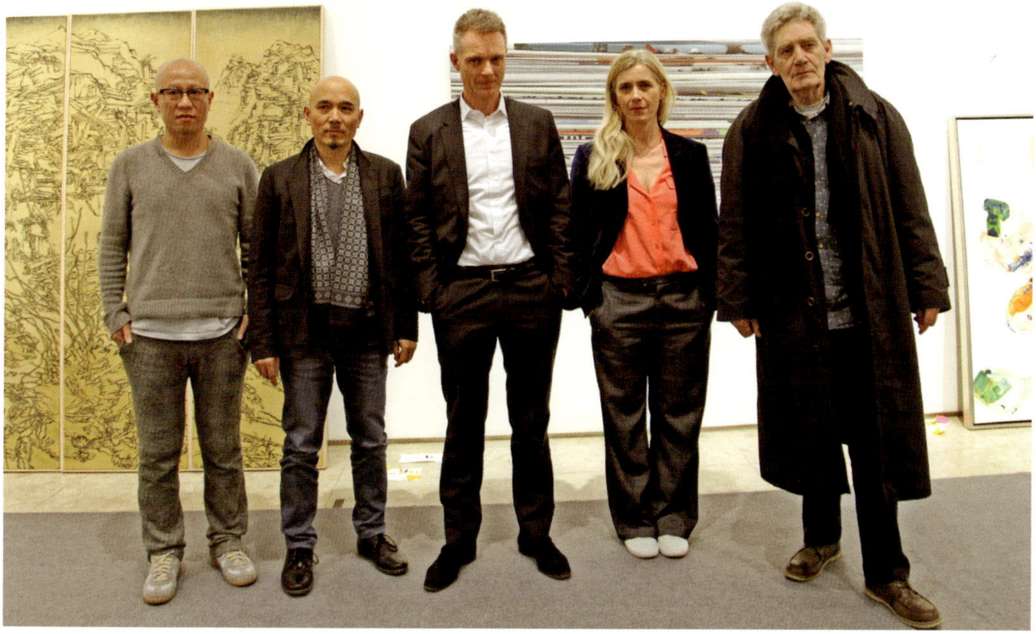

Liu Wei, Yang JieCang, Tim Marlow, Sarah Pickstone, Gerard Hemsworth

Preface

by Professor Wang DaWei
Dean, College of Fine Arts, Shanghai University
Vice Chairman, Shanghai Artists Association

The 2016 *John Moores Painting Prize China* is the fourth time the competition has been held. Its scale, and the number of artists vying for the Prize, have remained high, thanks to the efficient competition system and the professionalism of the jury.

In the past six years, since the *John Moores Painting Prize* was introduced to China, and throughout its four editions, it has served as a bridge for cultural exchanges between China and the United Kingdom, gradually building opportunities for dialogue between artists and jurors from the two countries. It is not just a high-level platform for exchanges about contemporary art, but is also a mechanism for debate.

As in the previous instalments of the competition, discussion between Chinese and British jurors has been robust, sometimes leading not to a unanimous conclusion, but rather to a kind of compromise. The objective of these compromises is that both sides should set aside their points of view and re-focus on the works themselves to examine and explore the genuine, inherent artistic value. Personal preferences have been put aside to ensure artistic value served as inspiration, as intended by the guardians of the competition, the John Moores Liverpool Exhibition Trust.

The Trustees invited a Chinese juror to serve on the judging panel for the *John Moores Painting Prize* in the UK. This type of collaboration and exchange allowed participants from the UK competition and *John Moores Painting Prize China* to gain an understanding of each other's cultural concepts, aesthetic orientation and judging practices, and contributed to the academic quality and development of the award.

After successfully holding the *John Moores Painting Prize China* on four occasions, I believe it is necessary to make the following summation and observations:

The number of entrants into the competition has risen every year and the regional provenance of the participating artists has broadened. For the inaugural exhibition in 2010, 1,100 people from 15 provinces, cities and regions registered. Over each of the following competitions the number of entrants has shown four-digit growth.

By 2014, the geographical spread of entrants had grown to include artists from cities and regions across China, as well as Taiwan, Macao and Tibet. The 2016 submission has levelled out at the same scale.

As the number of works entered into the competition has grown, the level of quality has also continuously increased, showing precisely how the international influence of the *John Moores Painting Prize* in this specialised field has been able to attract the participation of so many professional artists.

Artists entering the competition are of differing ages, and I think this boosts the diverse aesthetic appeal and richness of themes among the submitted works. It also illustrates the positive, open attitude and credibility of the Prize that comes with its transparency and integrity.

There are some distinct differences in the variety of content and expressive form of the submitted works in this year's competition. Oil painting on canvas dominates, in a representational style, with comparatively fewer submissions employing mixed media, Chinese ink painting, abstraction and conceptualism. Ink painting is representative of Chinese art, with almost half of China's painting community working in this medium. It is surprising there were so few entries from top professional ink painters working in China today. This is of concern and leads me to the following questions:

How can we attract more entries from contemporary Chinese ink painters to the Prize? How can we encourage greater representation of Chinese ink painters, imbued with the rich tradition and of a contemporary outlook, and worthy of an international stage? If high quality Chinese ink painting is not represented in the Prize, then the Prize does not fully reflect the special characteristics of Chinese culture. Likewise, the role it plays in cultural exchanges will also be limited.

This is the key issue that the *John Moores Painting Prize China* must face in the future, and is one which also has bearing upon the development of this award.

To keep the Prize moving forward, we must not stand still. The selection by the jurors and their judging methods must be optimised, while publicity and promotional activities must be thought over and improved in China.

Thinking brings the chance for change, and change brings the chance for opportunity. Opportunity brings the chance for success. Let's work together to make the *John Moores Painting Prize China* even better!

Preface two

by Lewis Biggs OBE, FLJMU
Trustee, John Moores Liverpool Exhibition Trust
Non-voting Chair of the Jurors, John Moores Painting Prize China 2016

As I write this, in April 2016, there are two '*John Moores*' exhibitions taking place simultaneously in Shanghai. At the Minsheng Art Museum, there is an exhibition of shortlisted paintings from the fourth *John Moores Painting Prize China* competition, and, at the Shanghai Minsheng 21st Century Museum, there is an exhibition of paintings by the 15 prizewinners from the first three 'China' competitions. In sporting terms, it's a 'double whammy'. It's also the clearest possible evidence of the impact the competition has had on the outlook for contemporary painting in China over the last six years. I want to reflect on its significance in four ways.

First, the success of the competition demonstrates the power of a good idea. Sir John Moores' insight nearly 60 years ago – that the Prize would achieve its own unique success if it were judged anonymously – is appealing, immediate and instinctively understood by everyone. It doesn't need repeating that, despite the mythology, famous artists often make indifferent work. It's much more exciting to remember the opposite, that 'unknown' artists can sometimes make fabulous work. The anonymous process of the jury is the guarantee that it's the quality of the painting that dictates how the artist is celebrated, not their previous reputation, or the influence of their circle or of the market. People who visit the exhibitions see exactly what the judges have seen, and they reach their own conclusions, just as the judges have done, from their knowledge of art and life.

The success of the competition also demonstrates that painting is a universal language. Globalisation has had the effect of homogenising culture around the world – the same brands are everywhere, presented in uniform ways. It's not surprising that in reaction we seek to celebrate cultural difference. But the 'technology' of painting is so flexible, so open to continual reinvention, that it can speak across cultures with unforced eloquence. The selections made by the jury are entirely credible: all we need do is open our senses and our minds and we can follow them in appreciating the qualities of these artworks. Culturally specific references may be strange to us, but they are like a sauce to the main dish of human experience, not its essence. The jurors learn from one another through discussion, and generally they arrive at an unforced consensus about the paintings with the best qualities, whether they derive from Western or Eastern traditions. Broad cultural traditions (such as ink painting and oil painting) remain paramount, while narrowly national characteristics become insignificant.

My third observation is about the future. Every new image-making technology (printmaking, film, photography, lithography, fax, photocopier, video) has been greeted as heralding the death of painting. But painting remains vigorously alive and practised worldwide, and the success of *JMPP China* suggests painting will continue to be as important in future, as a means of human expression, as in the past. That's why *JMPP China* is supported by the University of Shanghai, and why John Moores Liverpool Exhibition Trust is supported by Liverpool John Moores University (LJMU). At a time when every government acknowledges the vital role of creative thinking for the coming economy, these universities not only invest in the future, but recognise that the practice of painting is especially suited to giving talented young people the opportunity to develop creative vision and skills. The Prize captures the ambition of these two universities, and promotes their commitment to the creative future of painting.

Lastly I'm delighted that the 2016 Chinese exhibition is being shown at Shanghai's Minsheng Art Museum, whose history of programming contemporary art exhibitions is among the most illustrious in China.

Great art can only be great if it gets the audience it deserves. The purpose of *JMPP China* is to develop artists and the audiences that artists need, and after six years it is clear that this is succeeding. Likewise, Minsheng Art Museum's insistence on finding the highest quality exhibitions has been parallelled by its well-developed and coherent public events programme. Together, these have allowed it to nurture a loyal and supportive audience for many years now, which means that the visitors it receives have sharp eyes and enquiring, critical minds – the best audience that the artworks selected by the jurors in China could hope to find. The residencies offered to the Chinese prizewinners by LJMU, and the fact that their prizewinning paintings are exhibited in the context of Liverpool Biennial and the UK *John Moores Painting Prize* at the Walker Art Gallery, is both a continuation of this endeavour and a celebration of shared ambition between all of these organisations.

First prizewinner
Lang Shuilong

Prizewinners
Lei Shaowen
Bian Shaozhi
Wang Wang
Zhang Yang

郎水龙
Lang Shuilong

基本工具
Fundamental Tool

2015
Dust on linen
128 x 168 cm

This is a work from my *Fundamental Tool* series – a shovel. The shovel first appeared in the Shang dynasty as a basic farming tool, was widely used in the Han dynasty, and continues in use today. Even in contemporary urban China, such tools, with their long history, remain in use, driven by human effort. I often explore construction sites and see workmen using spades to dig, or mix cement, just as they would tend the fields. The turned dust flies around on the wind until the moment the workmen lay down their tools, then it slowly settles on the ground. I seize this opportunity to lay a canvas flat on the construction site and place a shovel on top. Using the scattering dust as ink, I employ the unpredictable wind to help me trace an outline in accordance with how the dust naturally settles on the canvas. At the same time I use a paint brush to wipe the dust off the canvas – hoping that art will be able to outdo nature, and creating a painting that sits between control and chance. Usually this will take a number of days and nights – time passes quickly. I share the elapsing time with a canvas, farm tools, wind and dust, savouring time from the settling dust, savouring history.

Biography

Lang Shuilong was born in 1965 and graduated with a Master's degree from the Department of Art and Design Theories, School of Design, at the China Academy of Art, Hangzhou, in 2009. Currently teaching in the Department of Photography, School of Media and Animation, China Academy of Art. He exhibited in *The 12th National Exhibition of Fine Arts* China Artists' Association Beijing 2014 and *The 1st National Biennial of Paintings with Mixed Media* China Artists' Association Ningbo 2015.

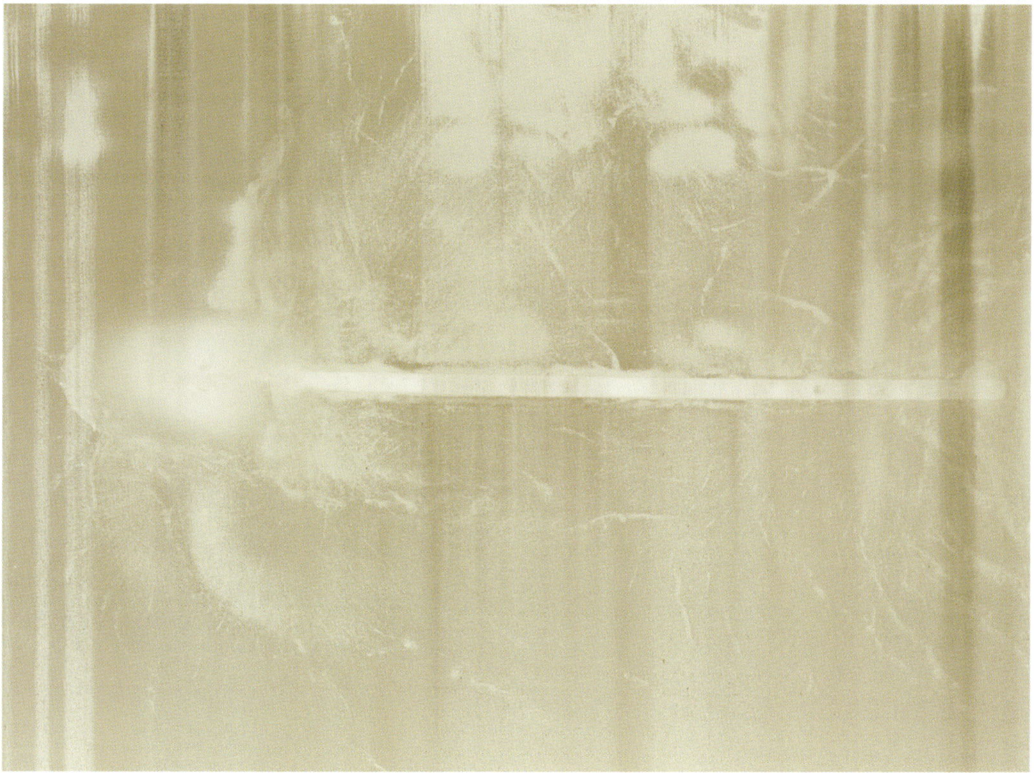

雷绍文
Lei Shaowen

废墟图
Wasteland

2013
Chinese ink on silk scroll and linen
251 x 175 cm

I have used Chinese ink painting techniques to depict the trash left behind at a site of ruined buildings, featuring broken pieces of steel, concrete and bricks. My aim was to reproduce the ruins through this traditional medium of ink wash painting on silk.

Biography

Lei Shaowen was born in 1981. He graduated from the Chinese Painting Department of Guangzhou Academy of Fine Arts with a Bachelor's degree in 2006. His solo exhibition *Black and Blue and Flowery* was at Hooray Laboratory Guangzhou in 2009. Group exhibitions include *Vision is Economy* Gongnong Road Art District Shunde and *Macao - Xiaozhou Art in Life Festival* Xiaozhou Art District Guangzhou 2009, *Frozen Conversation* Babu Gallery Beijing 2011, and *Hello, Star Island* hosted by the Zigen Foundation Singapore 2012.

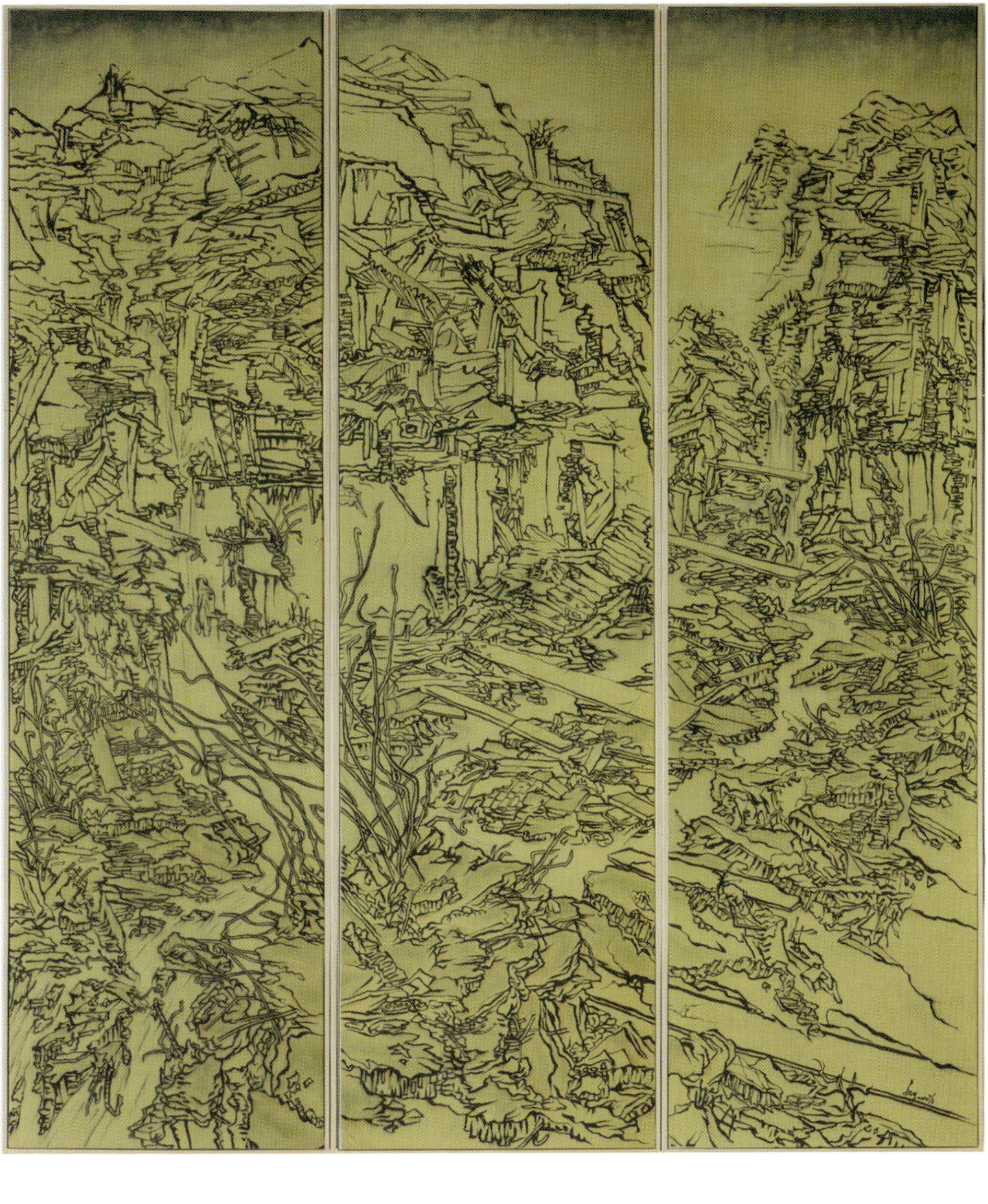

卞少之
Bian Shaozhi

显影
Visualization

2015
Oil and tempera on canvas
150 x 150 cm

Illumination by an X-ray machine reflects strongly the special personal information about a living individual, presenting a textural transparency of what they contain. This type of 'transparency' offers a new method and experience of viewing still life, penetrating the image itself. It also enables us to make conscious connections about what may be dispensable in the life of that person. We have no choice but to acknowledge the existence of this transparent force. In an era in which we are inundated with transient images, this type of transparency, to the contrary, profoundly reinforces reality. From this, people also often have a partially distorted view of their partner. Sometimes this distortion is unavoidable, especially when there are many layers of interest, holding deep significance.

Biography

Bian Shaozhi was born in 1984. He graduated from the Oil Painting Department of Nanjing Normal University with a Bachelor's degree in 2007, gaining a Master's degree there in the Western Oil Painting Department in 2010. His solo exhibition *Bian Shaozhi's 6 Years' Undergraduate and Postgraduate Works Exhibition* was at the university in 2009. Group exhibitions include Phoenix *Chinese Young Artists Plan 2012-2013 Invitational Exhibition* Phoenix Art Palace Wuxi 2013, *The 1st Nanjing International Art Festival* Nanjing International Expo Center 2014, *Choir•Harmonious* Shanghai, Nanjing, Changsha and *The 2nd Nanjing International Art Festival* Nanjing International Expo Center, both 2015.

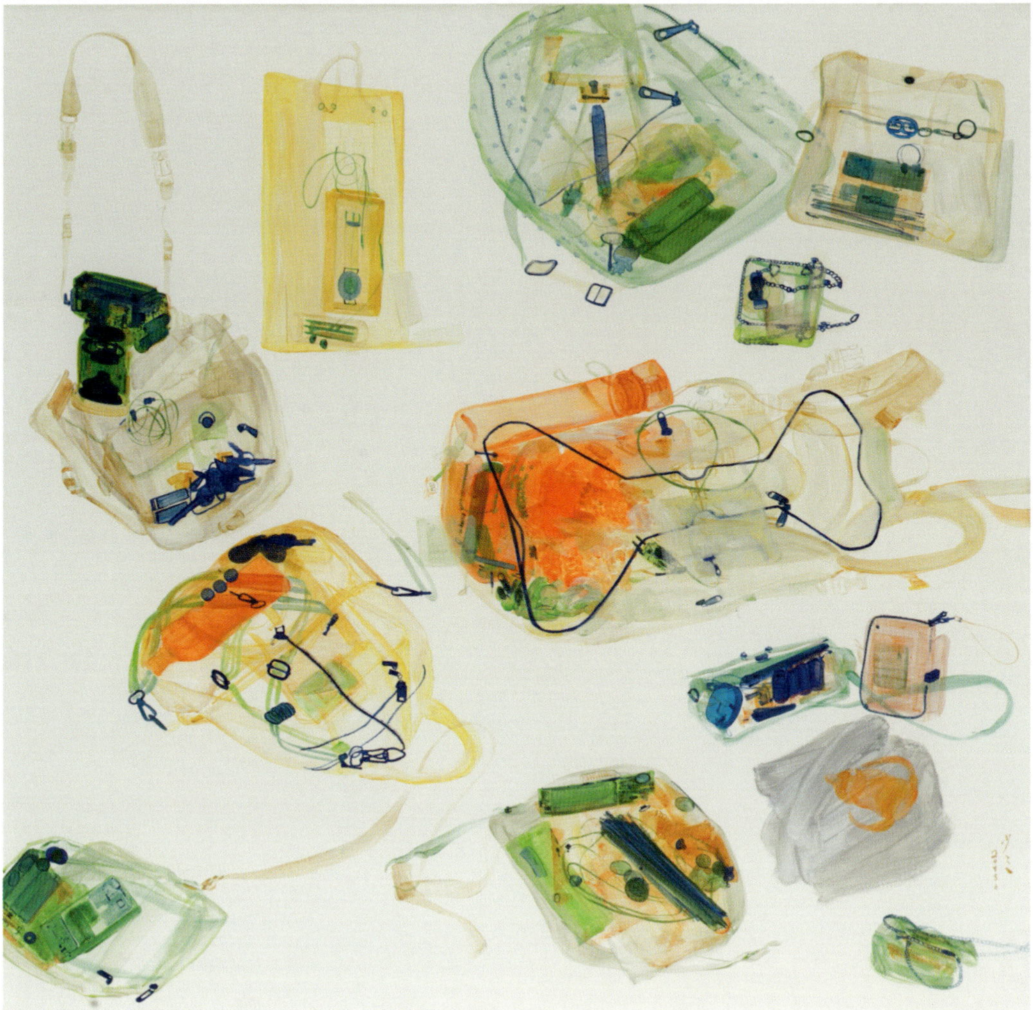

王旺
Wang Wang

蚀地
Corrupted Land

2015
Oil on canvas
100 x 200 cm

I used a single colour of oil paint to create this work, which depicts the damage industrial pollution has caused to the natural environment. I have reorganised some of the scenery in the landscape, combining the figurative and the expressive in order to convey my concern about how people's awareness of industrial pollution has weakened over the course of industrialisation.

Biography

Wang Wang was born in 1984 and graduated from the Oil Painting Department of Sichuan Fine Arts Institute with a Bachelor's degree in 2012. He obtained a Master's degree there in 2014. His group exhibitions include *The 11th Exhibition of Postgraduate Art* Sichuan Fine Arts Institute Chongqing 2014, and in 2015 *Original Creative Art 2015 by the Academics* CAFA Art Museum Beijing, *Porsche Empowering the Future Art Contest* Chongqing Art Gallery Chongqing, *The 6th New Star Art Festival* Xi'an Art Museum and *The 12th Art Exhibition of Postgraduate Art* Sichuan Fine Arts Institute.

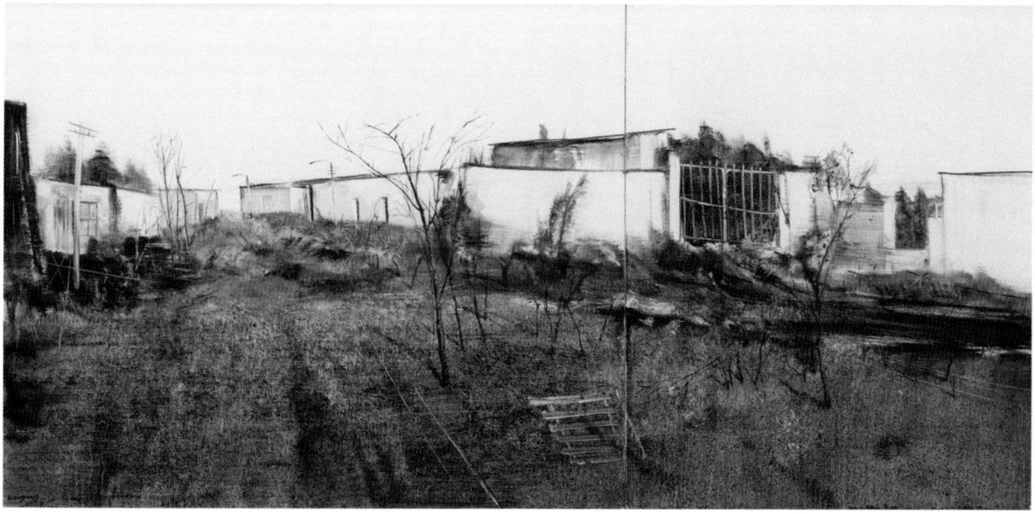

张杨
Zhang Yang
OLD NEWS

2015
Oil on canvas
101 x 200 cm

I drew material from common, outdated printed information, extracting the narrative and other related information from the articles. I artificially obscured the text on the printed material, turning it into an unrecognisable abstract symbol. At the same time, the expressive technique I used during the creative process was an attempt to use a purely mechanical painting method in order to restrain the potential of my restoring the printed matter to its original form. Consequently, it produced associations and contradictions between the out of date information and these newly reproduced products. Creating unusual presentations from the most commonplace of objects also brought visual strangeness. The rapid development of modern information technology is creating an era in which people's virtual perception is becoming more and more numb. This may inspire among viewers greater space and potential for thought.

Biography

Zhang Yang was born in 1992. She graduated from the Printmaking Department of Sichuan Fine Arts Institute in 2015 with a Bachelor's degree.

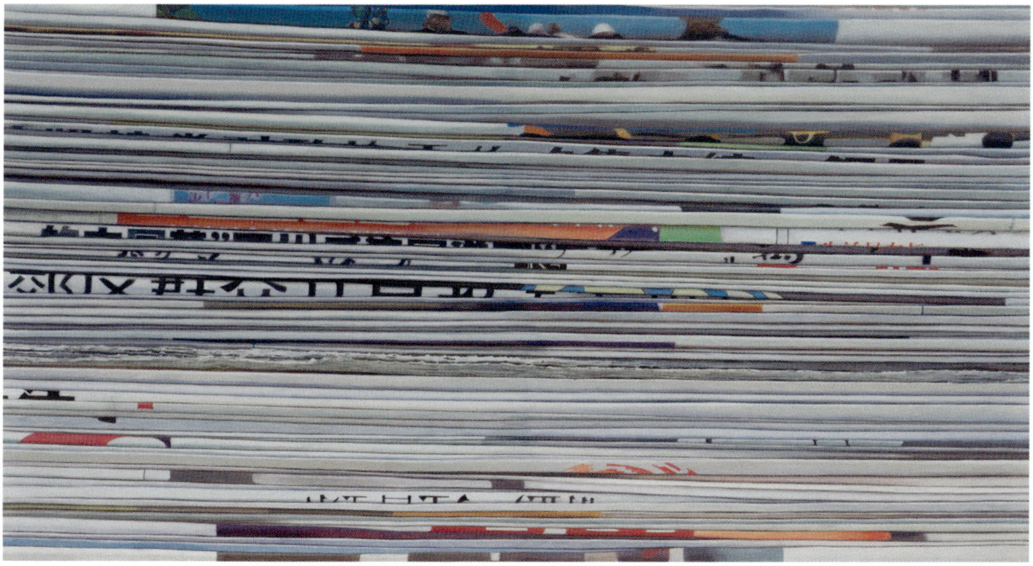

约翰·莫尔绘画奖(中国)

John Moores Painting Prize (China)

29 March – 15 May 2016

Hosts

JOHN MOORES
LIVERPOOL
EXHIBITION TRUST

上海大学美術學院
COLLEGE OF FINE ARTS SHANGHAI UNIVERSITY

民生美术馆
MINSHENG ART MUSEUM
SHANGHAI
上海

Co-organisers

LIVERPOOL
JOHN MOORES
UNIVERSITY

BRITISH
COUNCIL

英国文化教育协会
英国总领事馆文化教育处

Sponsors

中国民生银行
CHINA MINSHENG BANK

Sheraton
SHANGHAI HONGKOU HOTEL
上海虹口三至喜来登酒店

John Moores Painting Prize previous first prizewinners

1957
Jack Smith
Creation and Crucifixion

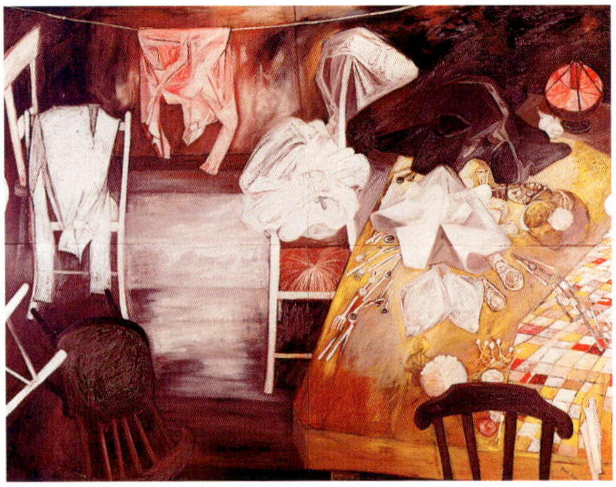

1961
Henry Mundy
Cluster
Bristol Museum & Art Gallery

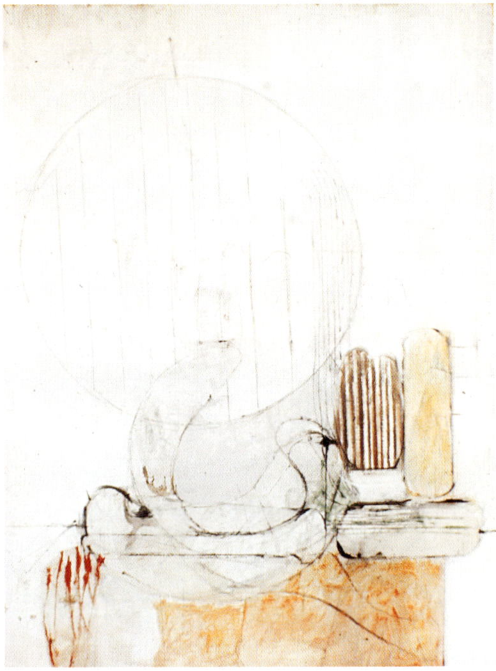

1959
Patrick Heron
Black Painting – Red, Brown, Olive: July 1959
Private Collection, courtesy of Offer Waterman & Co

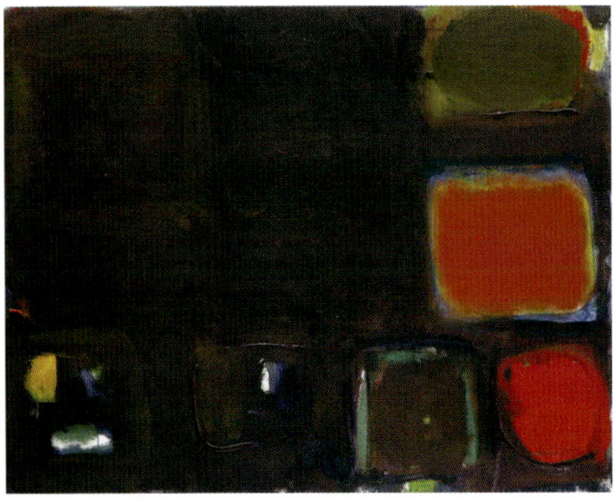

1963
Roger Hilton
March 1963

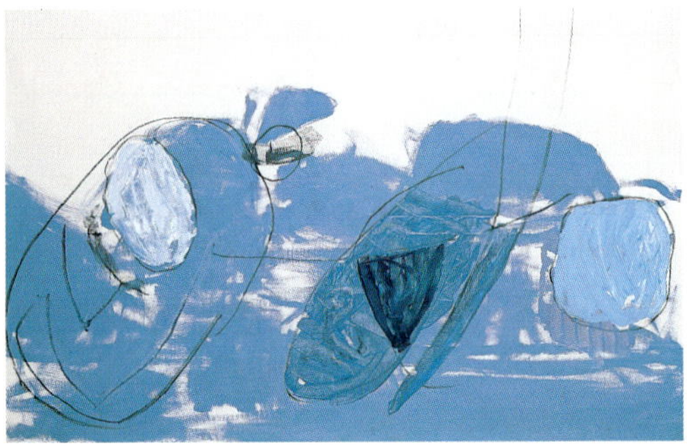

Unless otherwise stated, these artworks are now part of the Walker Art Gallery's collection.

1965
Michael Tyzack
Alesso B

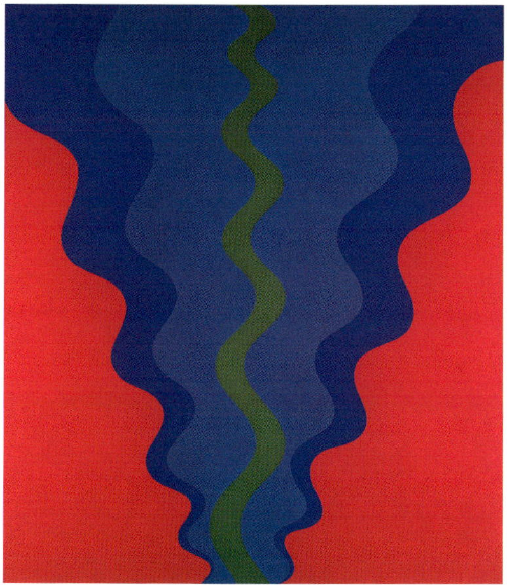

1969 (joint winner)
Mary Martin
Cross

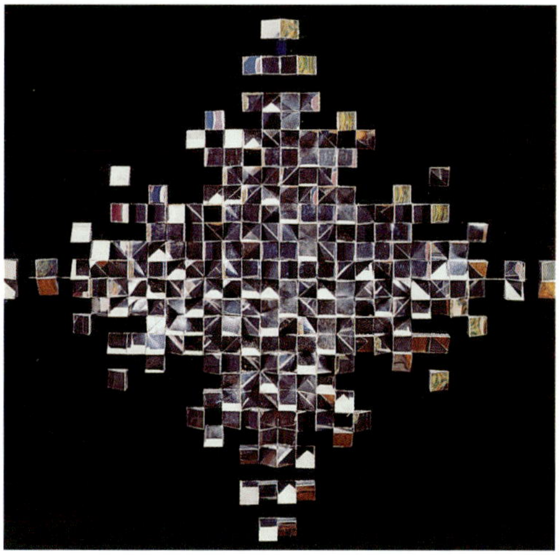

1967
David Hockney
Peter Getting Out of Nick's Pool

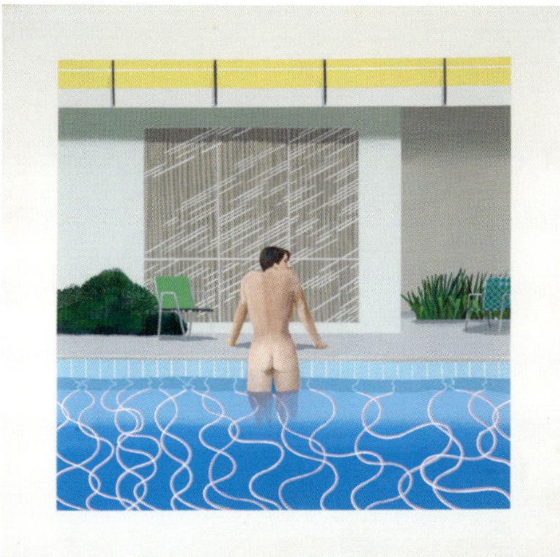

1969 (joint winner)
Richard Hamilton
Toaster
Private collection

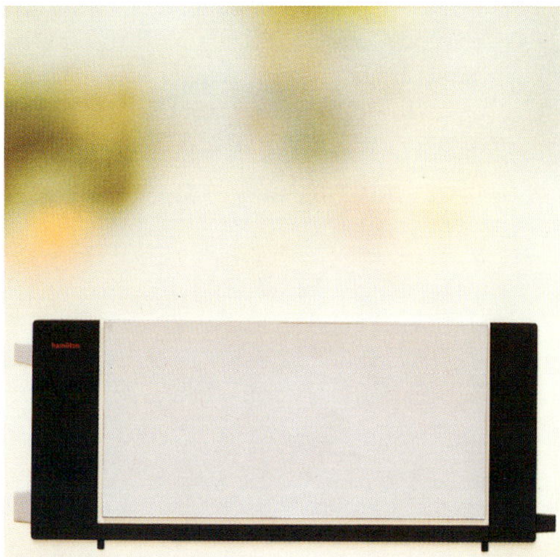

1972
Euan Uglow
Nude, 12 regular vertical positions from the eye
University of Liverpool Victoria Gallery and Museum Collection

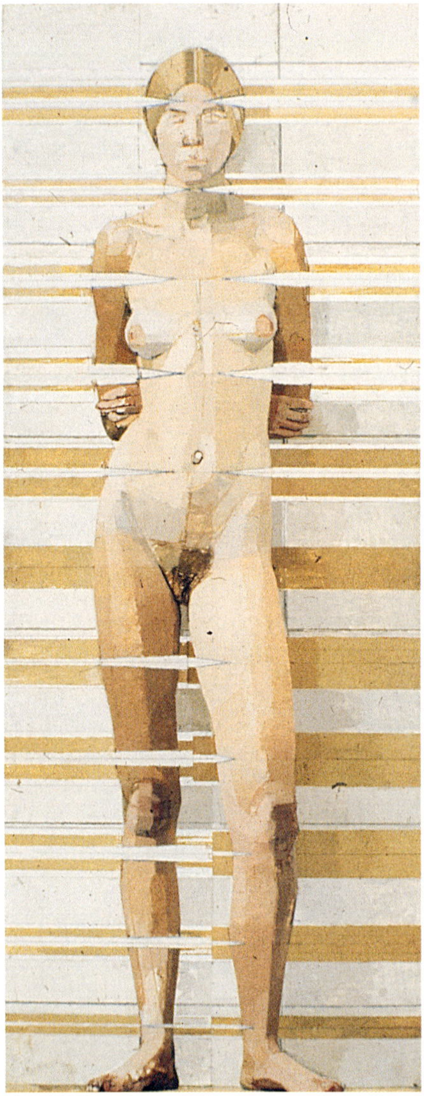

1974
Myles Murphy
Figure Against a Yellow Foreground
Tate

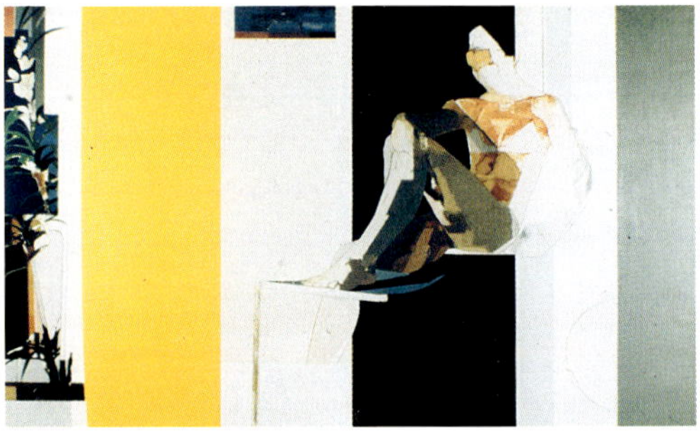

1976
John Walker
"Juggernaut with Plume - for P. Neruda"
Collection of the artist

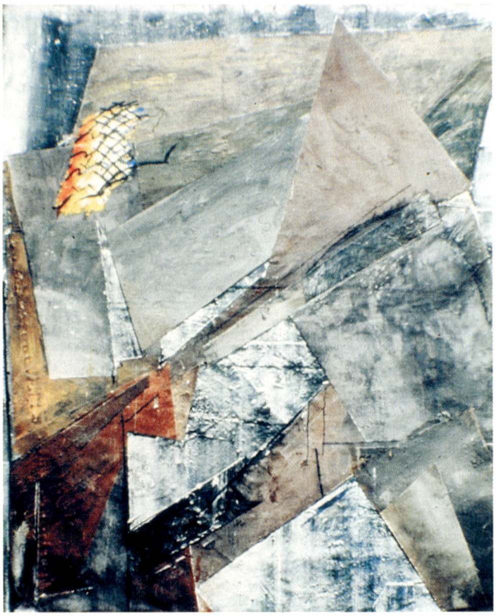

1978
Noel Forster
A Painting in Six Stages with a Blue Triangle

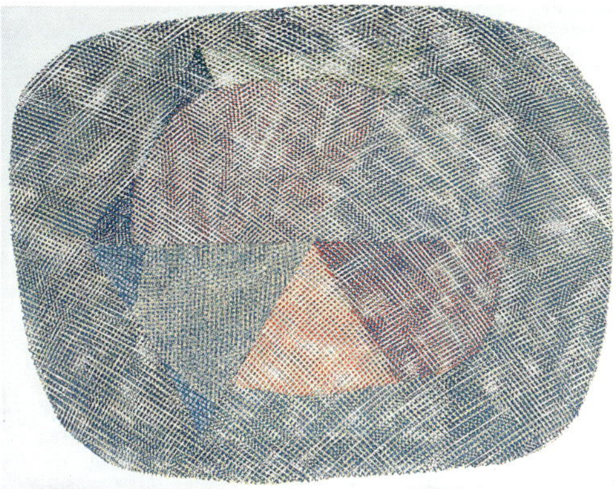

1980
Mick Moon
Box Room

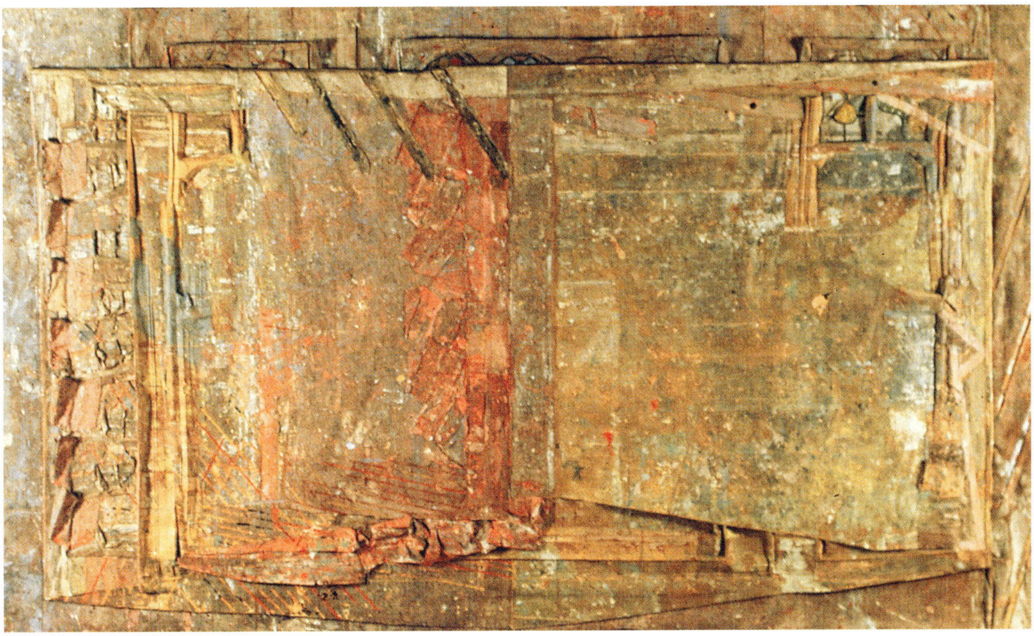

1982
John Hoyland
Broken Bride

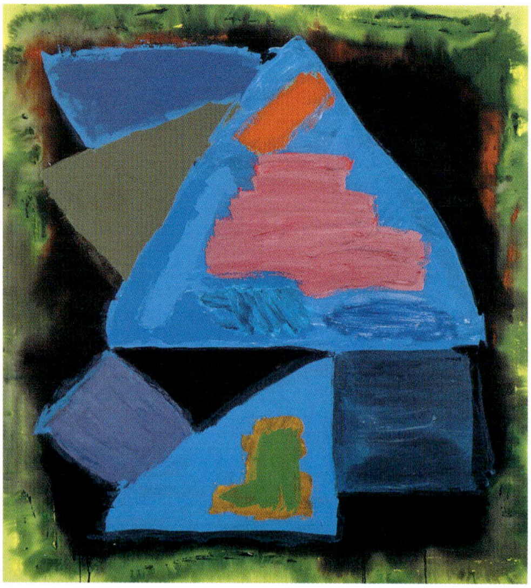

1987
Tim Head
Cow Mutations

1985
Bruce McLean
Oriental Garden, Kyoto

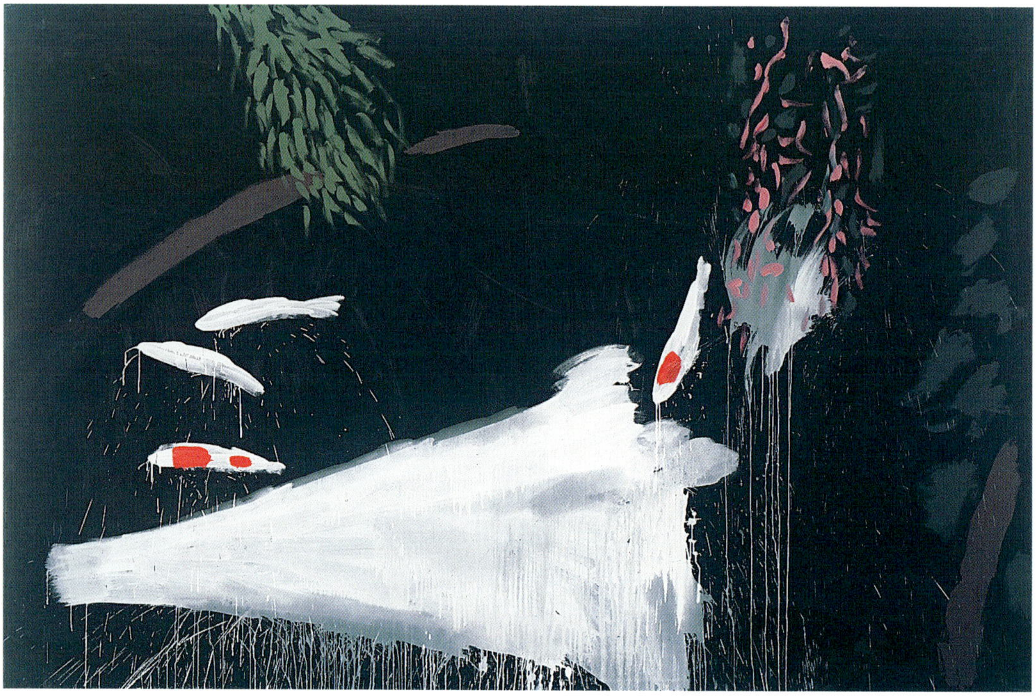

1989
Lisa Milroy
Handles

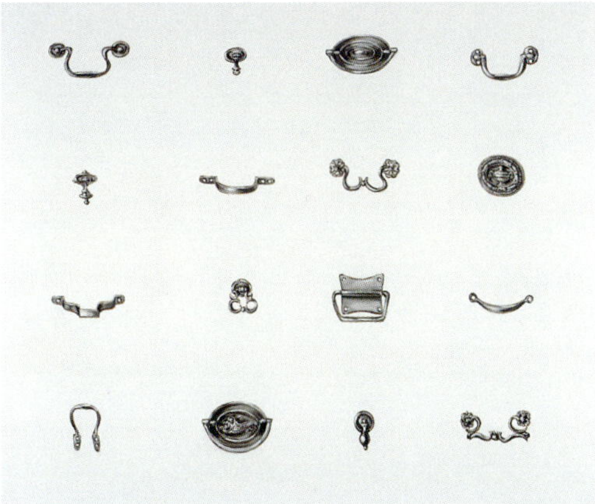

1993
Peter Doig
Blotter

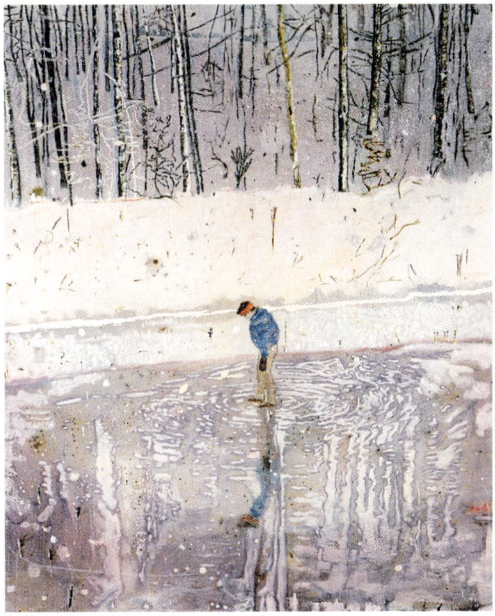

1991
Andrzej Jackowski
Beekeeper's Son

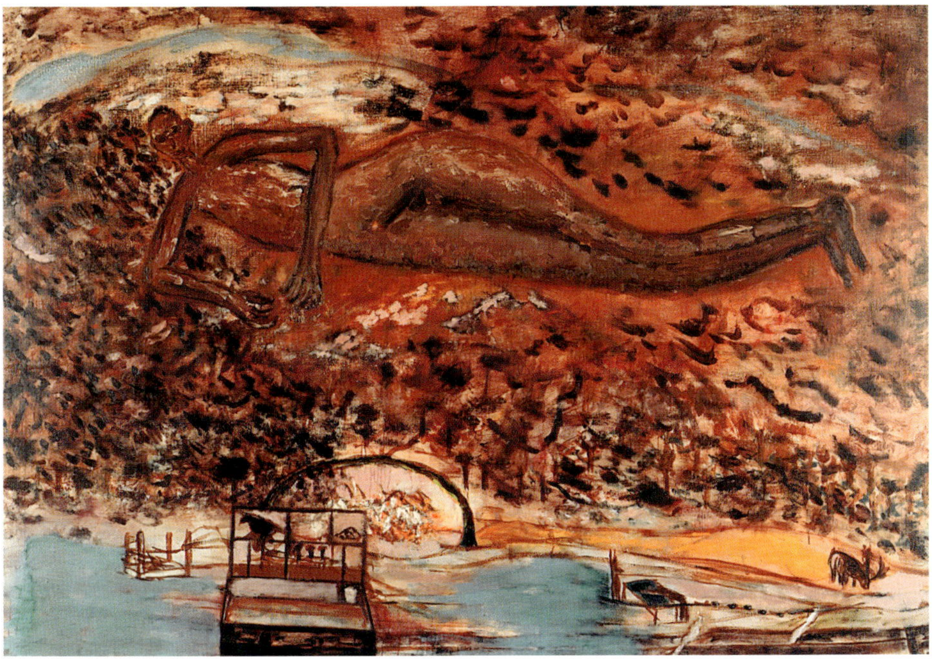

1995
David Leapman
Double Tongued Knowability

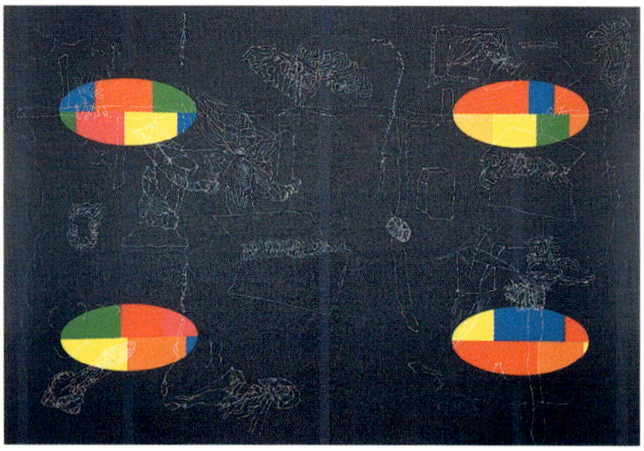

© David Leapman

1997
Dan Hays
Harmony in Green

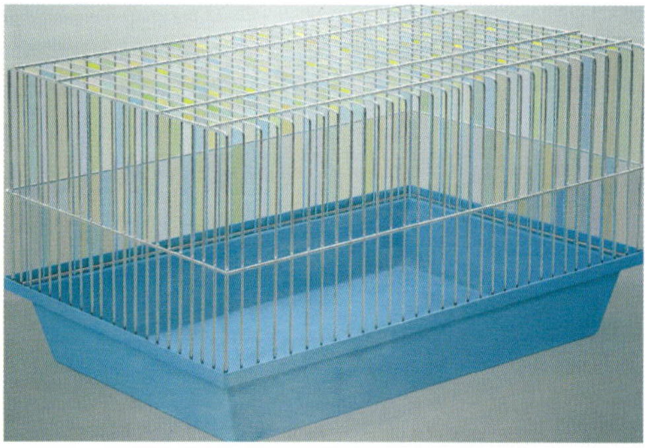

© Dan Hays

2002
Peter Davies
Super Star Fucker

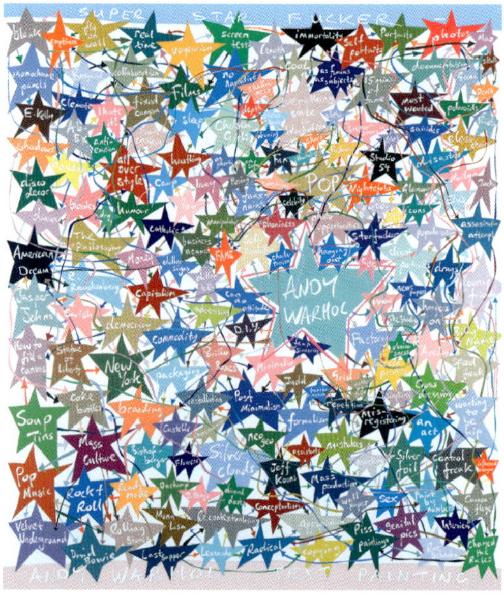

© Peter Davies

1999
Michael Raedecker
Mirage

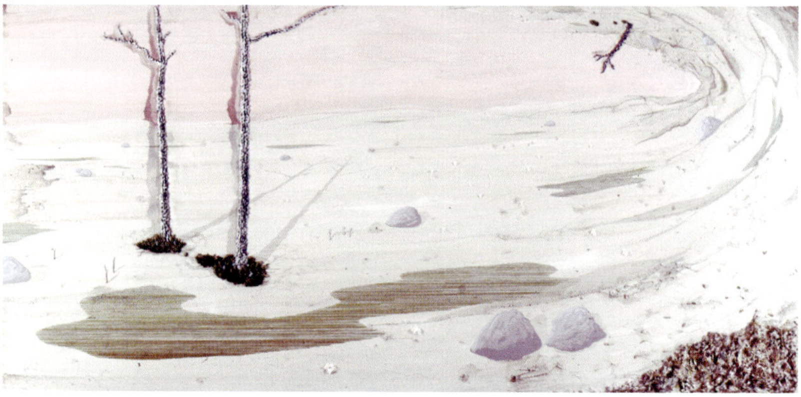

Courtesy of the artist and Hauser & Wirth

2004
Alexis Harding
Slump/Fear (orange/black)

Courtesy of the artist and Mummery & Schnelle Gallery

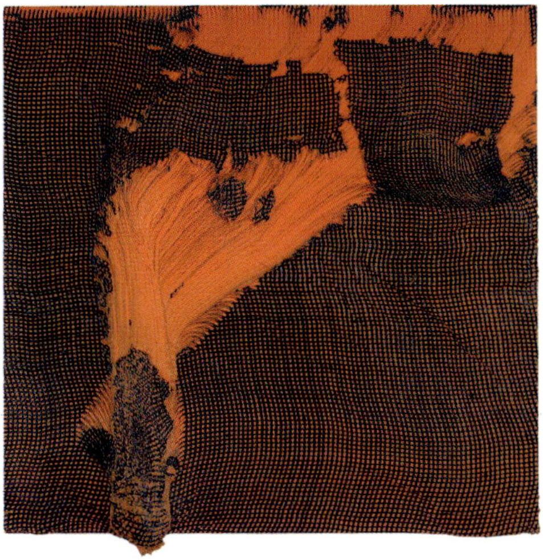

2006
Martin Greenland
Before Vermeer's Clouds

© Martin Greenland

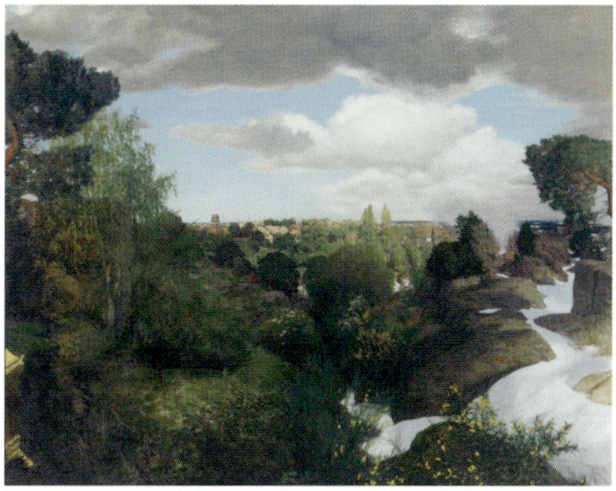

2008
Peter McDonald
Fontana

Courtesy of the artist and Kate MacGarry

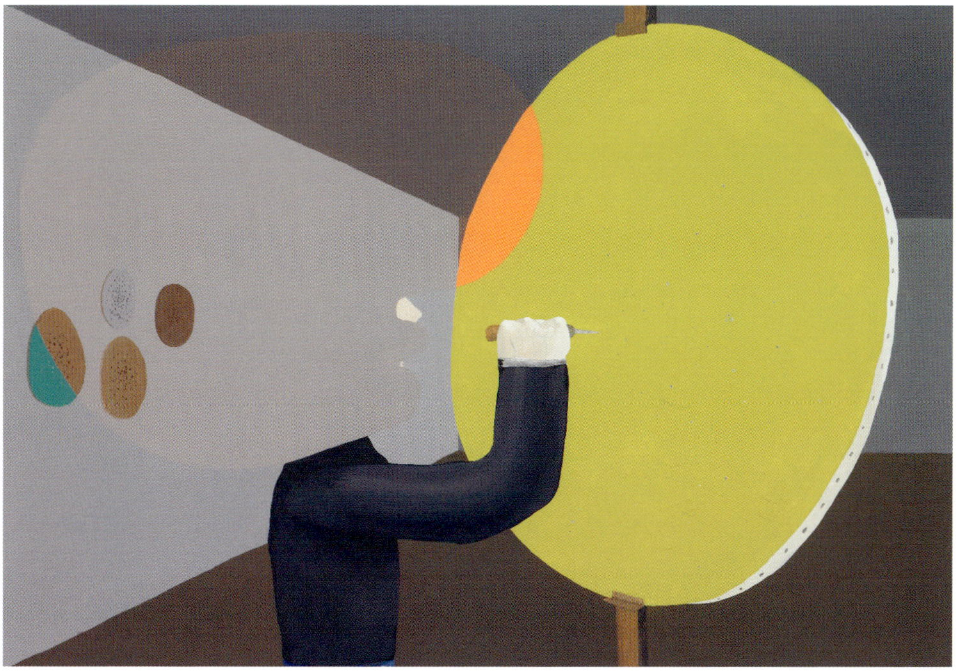

2010

Keith Coventry

Spectrum Jesus, 2009

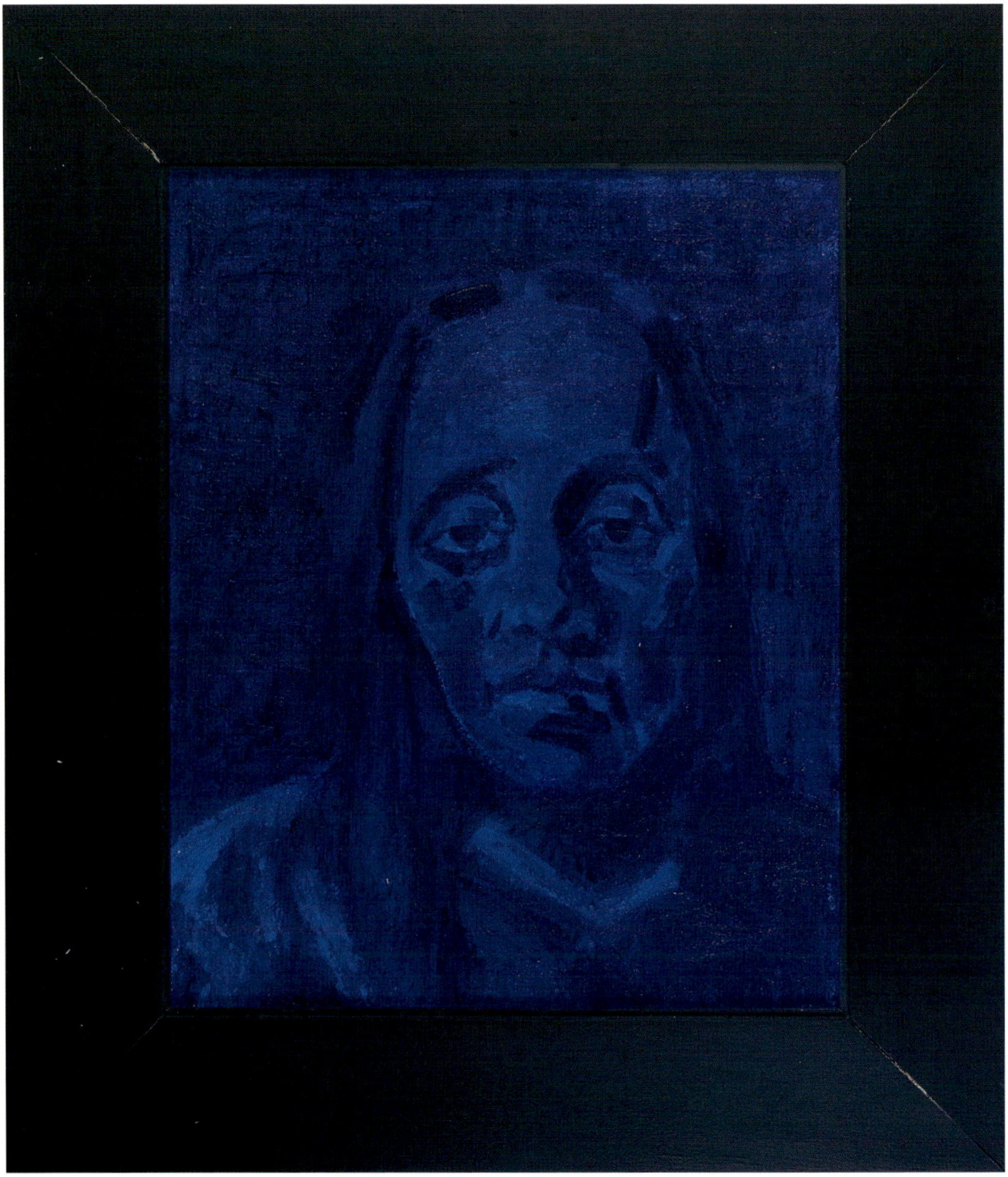

2012
Sarah Pickstone
Stevie Smith and the Willow

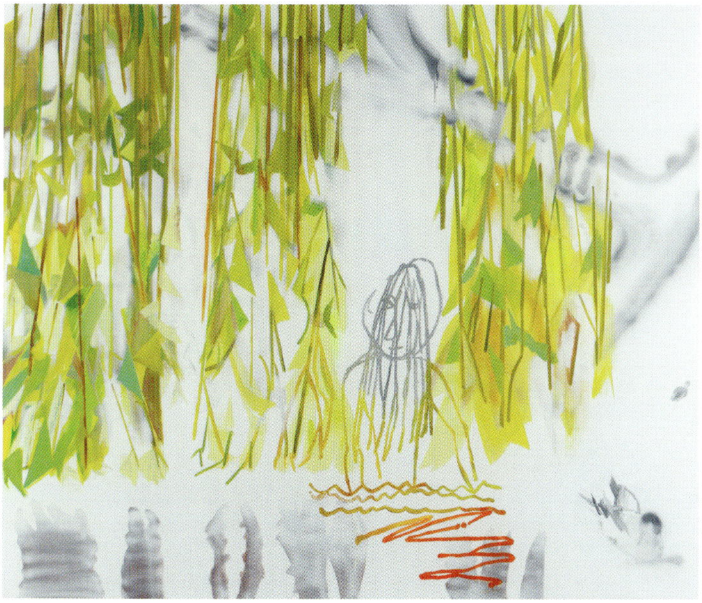

© Sarah Pickstone

2014
Rose Wylie
PV Windows and Floorboards

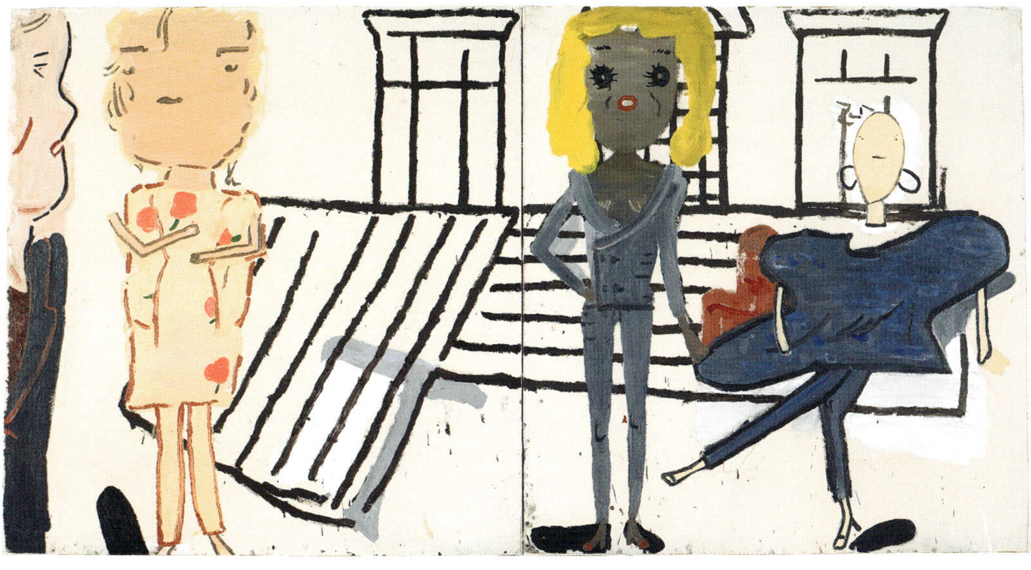

© Rose Wylie

We dedicate this catalogue to Sir Peter Moores.

This catalogue accompanies the
John Moores Painting Prize 2016
9 July-27 November 2016
Walker Art Gallery
William Brown Street
Liverpool L3 8EL

www.liverpoolmuseums.org.uk/johnmoores

Photography: Clare Bates
Design: Mark Johnson
Compiler/Editor: Ann Bukantas
Exhibition Officer (John Moores Painting Prize 2016): Nicola Cunningham
Publications Manager: Lisa Middleton
National Museums Liverpool 2016

Catalogue in publication data available
ISBN: 978-1-902700-55-7

A PARTNERSHIP BETWEEN NATIONAL MUSEUMS LIVERPOOL AND THE JOHN MOORES LIVERPOOL EXHIBITION TRUST

Weightmans

Liverpool
Biennial
2016